Contents

Getting Started

Maybe you can't wait to bang the first nail. Or you may be just as happy leaving town until the windows are cleaned. The extent of your involvement with the construction phase is up to you. Your time, interests, and abilities can help you decide how to get the project from lines on paper to reality. But building a house requires more than putting pieces together. Whoever is in charge of the process must competently manage people as well as supplies, materials, and construction. He or she will have to

- Make a project schedule to plan the orderly progress of the work. This can be a bar chart that shows the time period of activity by each trade.
- Establish a budget for each category of work, such as foundation, framing, and finish carpentry.
- Arrange for a source of construction financing.
- Get a building permit and post it conspicuously at the construction site.
- Line up supply sources and order materials.
- Find subcontractors and negotiate their contracts.
- Coordinate the work so that it progresses smoothly with the fewest conflicts.
- Notify inspectors at the appropriate milestones.
- Make payments to suppliers and subcontractors.

You as the Builder

You'll have to take care of every logistical detail yourself if you decide to act as your own builder or general contractor. But along with the responsibilities of managing the project, you gain the flexibility to do as much of your own work as you want and subcontract out the rest. Before taking this path, however, be sure you have the time and capabilities. Do you also have the

time and ability to schedule the work, hire and coordinate subs, order materials, and keep ahead of the accounting required to manage the project successfully? If you do, you stand to save the amount that a general contractor would charge to take on these responsibilities, normally 15 to 30 percent of the construction cost. If you take this responsibility on but mismanage the project, the potential savings will erode and may even cost you more than if you had hired a builder in the first place. A subcontractor might charge extra for hav-

Acting as the builder, above, requires the ability to hire and manage subcontractors.

Building a home, opposite, includes the need to schedule building inspections at the appropriate milestones.

ing to return to the site to complete work that was originally scheduled for an earlier date. Or perhaps because you didn't order the windows at the beginning, you now have to pay for a recent cost increase. (If you had hired a builder in the first place he or she would absorb the increase.)

order direct: 1-800-523-6789

Hiring a Builder to Handle Construction

A builder or general contractor will manage every aspect of the construction process. Your role after signing the construction contract will be to make regular progress payments and ensure that the work for which you are paying has been completed. You will also consult with the builder and agree to any changes that may have to be made along the way.

Leads for finding builders might come from friends or neighbors who have had contractors build, remodel, or add to their homes. Real-estate agents and bankers may have some names handy but are more likely familiar with the builder's ability to complete projects on time and budget than the quality of the work itself.

The next step is to narrow your list of candidates to three or four who you think can do a quality job and work harmoniously with you. Phone each builder to see whether he or she is interested in being considered for your project. If so, invite the builder to an interview at your home. The meeting will serve two purposes. You'll be able to ask the candidate about his or her experience, and you'll be able to see whether or not your personalities are compatible. Go over the plans with the builder to make certain that he or she understands the scope of the project. Ask if they have constructed similar houses. Get references, and check the builder's standing with the Better Business Bureau. Develop a short list of builders, say three, and ask them to submit bids for the project.

Contracts

Lump-Sum Contracts

A lump-sum, or fixed-fee, contract lets you know from the beginning just what the project will cost, barring any changes made because of your requests or unforeseen conditions. This form works well for projects that promise few surprises and are well defined from the outset by a complete set of contract documents. You can enter into a fixed-price contract by negotiating with a single builder on your short list or by obtaining bids from three or four builders. If you go the latter route, give each bidder a set of documents and allow at least two weeks for them to submit their bids. When you get the bids, decide who you want and call the others to thank them for their efforts. You don't have to accept the lowest bid, but it probably makes sense to do so since you have already honed the list to builders you trust. Inform this builder of your intentions to finalize a contract.

Cost-Plus-Fee Contracts

Under a cost-plus-fee contract, you agree to pay the builder for the costs of labor and materials, as verified by receipts, plus a fee that represents the builder's overhead and profit. This arrangement is sometimes referred to as "time and materials." The fee can range between 15 and 30 percent of the incurred costs. Because you ultimately pick up the tab—whatever the costs—the contractor is never at risk, as he is with a lump-sum contract. You won't know the final total cost of a cost-plus-fee contract until the project is built and paid for. If you can live with that uncertainty, there are offsetting advantages. First, this form allows you to accommodate unknown conditions much more easily than does a lump-sum contract. And rather than being tied down by the project documents, you will be free to make changes at any point along the way. This can be a trap, though. Watching the project take shape will spark the desire to add something or do something differently. Each change costs more, and the accumulation can easily exceed your budget. Because of the uncertainty of the final tab and the built-in advantage to the contractor, you should think twice before entering into this form of contract.

Contract Content

The conditions of your agreement should be spelled out thoroughly in writing and signed by both parties, whatever contractual arrangement you make with your builder. Your contract should include provisions for the following:

- The names and addresses of the owner and builder.
- A description of the work to be included ("As described in the plans and specifications dated . . .").
- The date that the work will be completed if time is of the essence.
- The contract price for lump-sum contracts and the builder's allowed profit and overhead costs for changes.
- The builder's fee for cost-plus-fee contracts and the method of accounting and requesting payment.
- The criteria for progress payments (monthly, by project milestones) and the conditions of final payment.
- A list of each drawing and specification section that is to be included as part of the contract.
- Requirements for guarantees. (One year is the standard period for which contractors guarantee the entire project, but you may require specific guarantees on

When submitting bids, all of the builders should base their estimates on the same specifications. Once the work begins, communicate with your builder to keep the work proceeding smoothly.

Inspect your newly built home, if possible, before the builder closes it up and finishes it.

certain parts of the project, such as a 20-year guarantee on the roofing.)

- Provisions for insurance.
- A description of how changes in the work orders will be handled.

The builder may have a standard contract that you can tailor to the specifics of your project. These contain complete specific conditions with blanks that you can fill in to fit your project and a set of "general conditions" that cover a host of issues from insurance to termination provisions. It's always a good idea to have an attorney review the draft of your completed contract before signing it.

Working with Your Builder

The construction phase officially begins when you have a signed copy of the contract and copies of any insurance required from the builder. It's not unheard of for a builder to request an initial payment of 10 to 20 percent of the total cost to cover mobilization costs, those costs associated with obtaining permits and getting set up to begin the actual construction. If you agree to this, keep a careful eye on the progress of the work to ensure that the total paid out at any one time doesn't get too far out of sync with the actual work completed.

What about changes? From here on, it's up to you and your builder to proceed in good faith and to keep the channels of communication open. Even so, changes of one sort or another beset every project, and they usually add to its cost.

Light at the End of the Tunnel.

The builder's request for a final inspection marks the end of the construction phase— almost. At the final inspection meeting, you and the builder will inspect the work, noting any defects or incomplete items on a "punch list." When the builder tidies up the punch list items, you should reinspect. Sometimes, builders go on to another job and take forever to clean up the last few details, so only after all items on the list have been completed satisfactorily should you release the final payment, which often accounts for the builder's profit.

Some Final Words

Having a positive attitude is important when undertaking a project as large as building a home. A positive attitude can help you ride out the rigors and stress of the construction process.

Stay Flexible. Expect problems, because they certainly will occur. Weather can upset the schedule you have established for subcontractors. A supplier may get behind on deliveries, which also affects the schedule. An unexpected pipe may surprise you during excavation. Just as certain, every problem that comes along has a solution if you are open to it.

Be Patient. The extra days it may take to resolve a construction problem will be forgotten once the project is completed.

Express Yourself. If what you see isn't exactly what you thought you were getting, don't be afraid to look into changing it. Or you may spot an unforeseen opportunity for an improvement. Changes usually cost more money, though, so don't make frivolous decisions.

Finally, watching your home go up is exciting, so stay upbeat. Get away from your project from time to time. Dine out. Take time to relax. A positive attitude will make for smoother relations with your builder. An optimistic outlook will yield better-quality work if you are doing your own construction. And though the project might seem endless while it is under way, keep in mind that all the planning and construction will fade to a faint memory at some time in the future, and you will be getting a lifetime of pleasure from a home that is just right for you.

Plan #161035

Dimensions: 75' W x 64'11" D
Levels: 2
Square Footage: 3,688
Main Level Sq. Ft.: 2,702
Upper Level Sq. Ft.: 986
Bedrooms: 4
Bathrooms: 3½
Foundation: Basement
Materials List Available: No
Price Category: H

CAD FILE AVAILABLE

You'll appreciate the style of the stone, brick, and cedar shake exterior of this contemporary home.

Features:

- Hearth Room: Positioned for an easy flow for guests and family, this hearth room features a bank of windows that integrate it with the yard.

- Breakfast Room: Move through the sliding doors here to the rear porch on sunny days.

- Kitchen: Outfitted for a gourmet cook, this kitchen is also ideal for friends and family who can perch at the island or serve themselves at the bar.

- Master Suite: A stepped ceiling, crown moldings, and boxed window make the bedroom easy to decorate, while the two walk-in closets, lavish dressing area, and whirlpool tub in the bath make this area comfortable and luxurious.

Main Level Floor Plan

Upper Level Floor Plan

Left Elevation

Right Elevation

Kitchen

Dining Room

SMARTtip

How to Arrange Seating Around Your Fireplace

When the TV is near or on the same wall as the fireplace, you can arrange seating that places you at the best advantage to enjoy both. Position sofas and chairs in front of the fire, and remember that the distance between you and the TV should be at least three times the size of the screen.

Living Room

Master Bathroom

Plan #131031

Dimensions: 69'8" W x 48'4" D
Levels: 2
Square Footage: 4,027
Main Level Sq. Ft.: 2,198
Upper Level Sq. Ft.: 1,829
Bedrooms: 5
Bathrooms: 4½
Foundation: Crawl space, slab, or basement
Materials List Available: Yes
Price Category: I

Images provided by designer/architect.

If you love dramatic lines and contemporary design, you'll be thrilled by this lovely home.

Features:

- Foyer: A gorgeous vaulted ceiling sets the stage for a curved staircase flanked by a formal living room and dining room.

- Living Room: The foyer ceiling continues in this room, giving it an unusual presence.

- Family Room: This sunken family room features a fireplace and a wall of windows that look out to the backyard. It's open to the living room, making it an ideal spot for entertaining.

- Kitchen: With a large island, this kitchen flows into the breakfast room.

- Master Suite: The luxurious bedroom has a dramatic tray ceiling and includes two-walk-in closets. The dressing room is fitted with a sink, and the spa bath is sumptuous.

Main Level Floor Plan

Copyright by designer/architect.

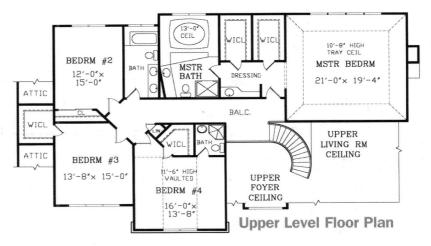

Upper Level Floor Plan

Plan #151020

Dimensions: 96'10" W x 75'10" D
Levels: 2
Square Footage: 4,532
Main Level Sq. Ft.: 3,732
Upper Level Sq. Ft.: 800
Bedrooms: 3
Bathrooms: 3½
Foundation: Crawl space or slab; basement available for fee
CompleteCost List Available: Yes
Price Category: I

Images provided by designer/architect.

From the arched entry to the lanai and exercise and game rooms, this elegant home is a delight.

CAD FILE AVAILABLE

Features:

• Foyer: This spacious foyer with 12-ft. ceilings sets an open-air feeling for this home.

• Hearth Room: This cozy hearth room shares a 3-sided fireplace with the breakfast room. French doors open to the rear lanai.

• Dining Room: Entertain in this majestic dining room, with its arched entry and 12-ft. ceilings.

• Master Suite: This stunning suite includes a sitting room and access to the lanai. The bath features two walk-in closets, a step-up whirlpool tub with 8-in. columns, and glass-block shower.

• Upper Level: You'll find an exercise room, a game room, and attic storage space upstairs.

Rear View

Main Level Floor Plan

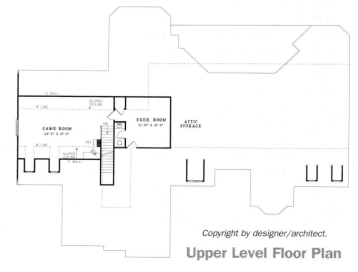

Copyright by designer/architect.

Upper Level Floor Plan

Living Room

Plan #111004

Dimensions: 76' W x 85' D

Levels: 1

Square Footage: 2,968

Bedrooms: 4

Full Bathrooms: 3½

Foundation: Slab; crawl space available for fee

Materials List Available: No

Price Category: F

If you've been looking for a home that includes a special master suite, this one could be the answer to your dreams.

Features:

- **Living Room:** Make a sitting area around the fireplace here so that the whole family can enjoy the warmth on chilly days and winter evenings. A door from this room leads to the rear covered porch, making this room the heart of your home.

- **Kitchen:** An island with a cooktop makes cooking a pleasure in this well-designed kitchen, and the breakfast bar invites visitors at all times of day.

- **Utility Room:** A sink and a built-in ironing board make this room totally practical.

- **Master Suite:** A private fireplace in the corner sets a romantic tone for this bedroom, and the door to the covered porch allows you to sit outside on warm summer nights. The bath has two vanities, a divided walk-in closet, a standing shower, and a deluxe corner bathtub.

Bonus Area

Gameroom 13'5"x17'

Wood Deck

Covered Porch

Master Bedroom 16'9"x21'5"

Master Bath

WIC

Breakfast 14'x12'1"

Living 24'8"x19'3"

Bedroom 12'4"x12'1"

Kitchen 18'4"x14'10"

Dining 13'1"x14'7"

Foyer

Bedroom 13'x12'

Bedroom 12'1"x13'

Utility

Porch

Garage 21'2"x27'2"

Plan #121064

Dimensions: 44' W x 40' D

Levels: 2

Square Footage: 1,846

Main Level Sq. Ft.: 919

Upper Level Sq. Ft.: 927

Bedrooms: 4

Bathrooms: 2½

Foundation: Basement

Materials List Available: Yes

Price Category: D

Images provided by designer/architect.

You'll love the features and design in this compact but amenity-filled home.

Features:

• Entry: A balcony overlooks this two-story entry, where a plant shelf tops the coat closet.

• Great Room: A trio of tall windows points up the large dimensions of this room, which is sure to be the hub of your home. Arrange the

furniture to create a cozy space around the fireplace, or leave it open to the room.

• Kitchen: You'll love to work in this well-designed kitchen area.

• Master Suite: On the second floor, this master suite features a tiered ceiling and two walk-in closets. In the bath, you'll find a double vanity, whirlpool tub, and separate shower.

Main Level Floor Plan

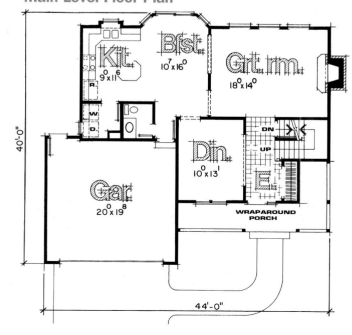

Upper Level Floor Plan

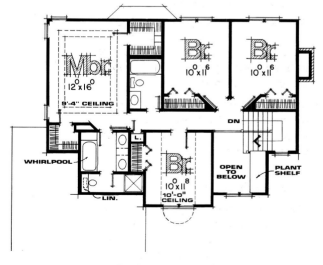

Copyright by designer/architect.

Plan #121062

Dimensions: 70' W x 62' D
Levels: 2
Square Footage: 3,448
Main Level Sq. Ft.: 2,375
Upper Level Sq. Ft.: 1,073
Bedrooms: 4
Bathrooms: 3½
Foundation: Basement
Materials List Available: Yes
Price Category: G

Images provided by designer/architect.

You'll love this design if you're looking for a comfortable home with dimensions and details that create a sense of grandeur.

Features:

- Entry: A soaring ceiling, curved staircase, and balcony that overlooks a tall plant shelf combine to create your first impression of grandeur in this home.

- Great Room: A transom-topped bowed window highlights this room, with its 11-ft., beamed ceiling, built-in wet bar, and see-through fireplace.

- Kitchen: Designed for the gourmet cook, this kitchen has every amenity you could desire.

- Breakfast Room: Adjacent to the great room and the kitchen, this gazebo-shaped breakfast area lights both the kitchen and hearth room.

Main Level Floor Plan

Upper Level Floor Plan

Copyright by designer/architect.

Plan #131005

Dimensions: 70' W x 37'4" D
Levels: 1
Square Footage: 1,595
Bedrooms: 3
Bathrooms: 2
Foundation: Crawl space, slab, or basement
Materials List Available: Yes
Price Category: C

SMARTtip

Create a Courtyard

Create a private walled-garden retreat with fences covered by climbing vines. Add height with trellises, and divide spaces with clipped boxwood hedges. Include an (almost) instant patio by digging away an area of sod and then covering it with a layer of sand and landscaping mesh to discourage weeds. Then cover it with pea gravel, and add a garden bench, statuary, and perhaps an antique or two. The result? European ambiance for even the most nondescript suburban yard.

With the finest features of an open design in the main living areas, this home gives privacy where you need it. Best of all, it's wheelchair accessible.

Features:

• Foyer: A high ceiling gives this area real presence and serves to blend it seamlessly with the great room and the dining room.

• Great Room: The open design allows you to use this room as an extension of the dining room or, if you wish, furnish it to create a private reading nook or visually separate media center.

• Breakfast Room: Both this room and the adjacent well-appointed kitchen flow into the rest of the living area. However, access to the rear porch, where you can sit out and enjoy the weather while you eat, distinguishes this room.

• Master Suite: Located in the same wing as the other bedrooms, this suite has a separate entrance and features a vaulted ceiling, three closets, and a compartmented bath.

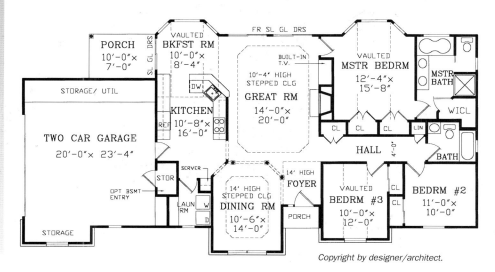

Copyright by designer/architect.

Plan #151031

Dimensions: 60'2" W x 60'2" D
Levels: 2
Square Footage: 3,130
Main Level Sq. Ft.: 1,600
Upper Level Sq. Ft.: 1,530
Bedrooms: 3
Bathrooms: 3½
Foundation: Crawl space, slab
CompleteCost List Available: Yes
Price Category: G

Images provided by designer/architect.

If you love traditional Southern plantation homes, you'll want this house with its wraparound porches that are graced with boxed columns.

Features:

- Great Room: Use the gas fireplace for warmth in this comfortable room, which is open to the kitchen.

- Living Room: 8-in. columns add formality as you enter this living and dining room.

- Kitchen: You'll love the island bar with a sink. An elevator here can take you to the other floors.

- Master Suite: A gas fireplace warms this area, and the bath is luxurious.

- Bedrooms: Each has a private bath and built-in bookshelves for easy organizing.

- Optional Features: Choose a 2,559-sq.-ft. basement and add a kitchen to it, or finish the 1,744-sq.-ft. bonus room and add a spiral staircase and a bath.

Main Level Floor Plan

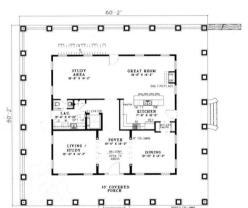

Upper Level Floor Plan

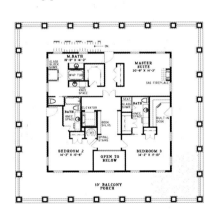

Basement Level Floor Plan

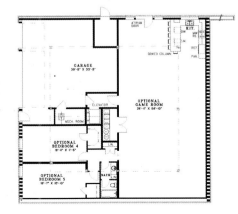

Optional Upper Level Floor Plan

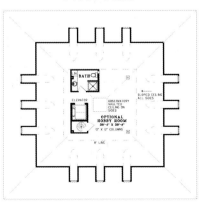

Plan #161002

Dimensions: 64'2" W x 44'2" D
Levels: 1
Square Footage: 1,860
Bedrooms: 3
Bathrooms: 2
Foundation: Basement
Materials List Available: Yes
Price Category: D

CAD FILE AVAILABLE · CAD ·

The brick, stone, and cedar shake facade provides color and texture to the exterior, while the unique nooks and angles inside this delightful one-level home give it character.

Features:

- Great Room/Dining Room: This spacious great room is furnished with a wood-burning fireplace, a high ceiling, and French doors. Wide entrances to the breakfast room and dining room expand its space to comfortably hold large gatherings.

- Kitchen: The breakfast bar offers additional seating. The covered porch lets you enjoy a view of the landscape and is conveniently located for outdoor meals off this kitchen and breakfast area.

- Master Bedroom: The master bedroom is a private retreat. An alcove creates a comfortable sitting area, and an angled entry leads to the bath with whirlpool and a double-bowl vanity.

Great Room/Foyer

Rear Elevation

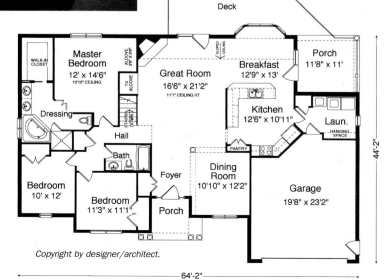

Copyright by designer/architect.

Plan #131022

Dimensions: 54'8" W x 43' D
Levels: 2
Square Footage: 2,092
Main Level Sq. Ft.: 1,152
Upper Level Sq. Ft.: 940
Bedrooms: 4
Bathrooms: 2½
Foundation: Crawl space, slab, or basement
Materials List Available: Yes
Price Category: E

Images provided by designer/architect.

This home, as shown in the photograph, may differ from the actual blueprints. For more detailed information, please check the floor plans carefully.

Copyright by designer/architect.

Main Level Floor Plan

Upper Level Floor Plan

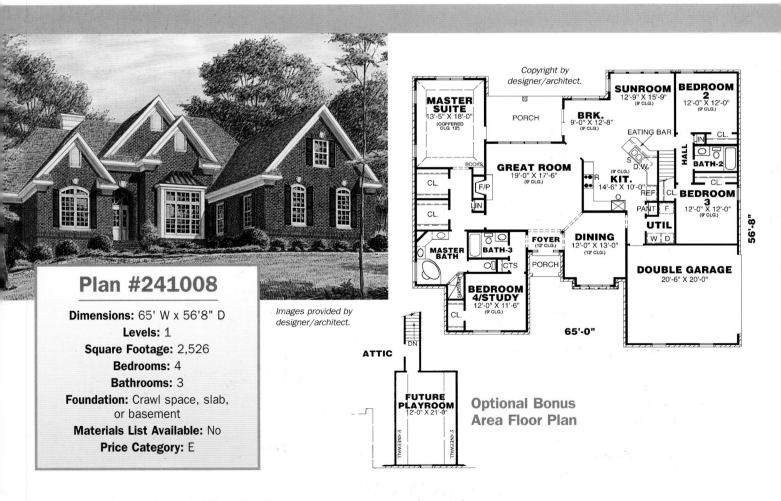

Plan #241008

Dimensions: 65' W x 56'8" D
Levels: 1
Square Footage: 2,526
Bedrooms: 4
Bathrooms: 3
Foundation: Crawl space, slab, or basement
Materials List Available: No
Price Category: E

Images provided by designer/architect.

Copyright by designer/architect.

Optional Bonus Area Floor Plan

Plan #101004

Dimensions: 55'8" W x 56'6" D

Levels: 1

Square Footage: 1,787

Bedrooms: 3

Bathrooms: 2

Foundation: Crawl space, slab, or basement

Materials List Available: Yes

Price Category: C

Images provided by designer/architect.

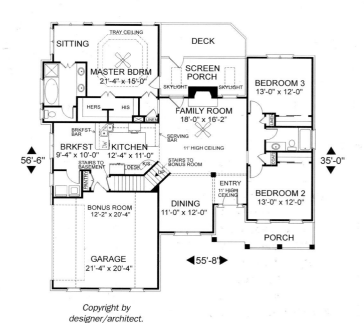

Copyright by designer/architect.

Plan #101011

Dimensions: 71'2" W x 58'1" D

Levels: 1

Square Footage: 2,184

Bedrooms: 3

Bathrooms: 3

Foundation: Crawl space, slab, basement, or walkout

Materials List Available: Yes

Price Category: D

Images provided by designer/architect.

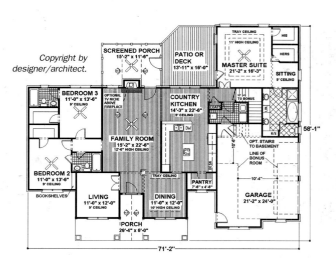

Copyright by designer/architect.

Kitchen

Plan #441031

Dimensions: 78'2" W x 68' D
Levels: 2
Square Footage: 4,150
Main Level Sq. Ft.: 2,572
Upper Level Sq. Ft.: 1,578
Bedrooms: 4
Bathrooms: 4½
Foundation: Crawl space;
slab or basement available for fee
Materials List Available: No
Price Category: I

Features:

- **Great Room:** The main level offers this commodious room, with its beamed ceiling, alcove, fireplace, and built-ins.
- **Kitchen:** Go up a few steps to the dining nook and this kitchen, and you'll find a baking center, walk-in pantry, and access to a covered side porch.
- **Formal Dining Room:** This formal room lies a few steps up from the foyer and sports a bay window and hutch space.
- **Guest Suite:** This suite, which is located at the end of the hall, features a private bathroom and walk-in closet.
- **Master Suite:** A fireplace flanked by built-ins warms this suite. Its bath contains a spa tub, compartmented toilet, and huge shower.

Graceful and gracious, this superb shingle design delights with handsome exterior elements. A whimsical turret, covered entry, upper-level balcony, and bay window all bring their charm to the facade.

CAD FILE AVAILABLE

Main Level Floor Plan

Upper Level Floor Plan

Copyright by designer/architect.

Kitchen

Dining Room

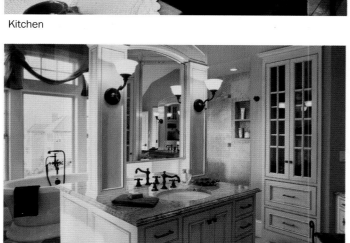

Master Bath

Foyer

Master Bedroom

Great Room

Rear View

DECK
31'-8" x 11'-8"

DINING
15'-10" x 11'-

LINEN
PLANT SHELF

STEP

10' HIGH CEILING

SITTING
12' HIGH CEILING

HEARTH
ROOM
16'-7" x 13'-0"
TV NICHE

K/S

HER CLOSET
8'-4" x 6'-3"

TRAY CEILING

HIS CLOSET
8'-4" x 6'-3"

MASTER BDRM
19'-0" x 18'-4"

FAMILY
18'-0" x 22'-4"
14' HIGH CEILING

KITCHEN
16'-0" x 13'-0"

BREAKFAST
10'-0" x 10'-6"

PANTRY
4'-7" x 7'-5"

STAIRS TO
BONUS ROOM

LINEN

BEDROOM 2
11'-0" x 14'-0"

BEDROOM
11'-0" x 14'-0"

ENTRY
12' HIGH CEILING

UP

DN

STAIRS TO
BASEMENT

SHLVS

PORCH
12' HIGH CEILING

VLT

VLT

66'

GARAGE
21'-0" x 25'-6"

BONUS ROOM ABOVE

◄ 72' ►

Plan #101013

Dimensions: 72' W x 66' D

Levels: 1

Square Footage: 2,564

Bedrooms: 3

Bathrooms: 2½

Foundation: Crawl space, slab, basement, or walkout

Materials List Available: Yes

Price Category: E

Images provided by designer/architect.

Master
Bedroom

84'-0"

DECK

GRILLING
PORCH
18'-0" x 12'-0"

BEDROOM 2
12'-2" x 12'-2"

DINING /
HEARTH ROOM
18'-0" x 19'-0"

ATRIUM
DOORS

LAU.
13'-8" x 6'-8"

BATH

KITCHEN
14'-6" x 18'-0"

PAN

REF

DW

M. BATH
13'-8" x 7'-4"

CLARERT

GARAGE
23'-8" x 21'-4"

55'-6"

BEDROOM 3
12'-2" x 12'-2"

LIVING RM.
21'-0" x 19'-0"

MASTER
SUITE
13'-8" x 13'-0"

MEDIA
CENTER

8' COVERED PORCH

4' WALL

6'8" LINE

8' LINE

ATTIC
STORAGE

GAME ROOM
37'-4" x 18'-8"

8' LINE

BATH

6'8" LINE

VAULTED

4' WALL

Plan #151089

Dimensions: 84' W x 55'6" D

Levels: 1

Square Footage: 1,921

Bedrooms: 3

Bathrooms: 3

Foundation: Crawl space, slab, or basement

CompleteCost List Available: Yes

Price Category: D

Images provided by designer/architect.

**Bonus Area
Floor Plan**

Plan #131014

Dimensions: 48' W x 43'4" D

Levels: 1

Square Footage: 1,380

Bedrooms: 3

Bathrooms: 2

Foundation: Crawl space, slab, or basement

Materials List Available: Yes

Price Category: C

Illustration provided by designer/architect.

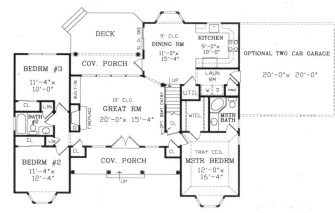

Copyright by designer/architect.

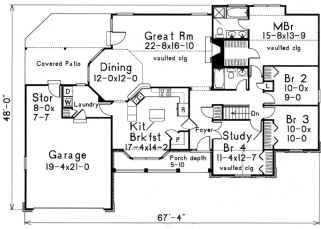

Rear Elevation

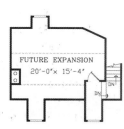

FUTURE EXPANSION
20'-0"x 15'-4"

Bonus Room

Plan #321003

Dimensions: 67'4" W x 48' D

Levels: 1

Square Footage: 1,791

Bedrooms: 4

Bathrooms: 2

Foundation: Basement

Materials List Available: Yes

Price Category: C

Images provided by designer/architect.

Copyright by designer/architect.

Plan #131003

Dimensions: 60' W x 39'10" D
Levels: 1
Square Footage: 1,466
Bedrooms: 3
Bathrooms: 2
Foundation: Crawl space, slab, or basement
Materials List Available: Yes
Price Category: C

Victorian styling adds elegance to this compact and easy-to-maintain ranch design.

Features:

- Ceiling Height: 8 ft.

- Foyer: Bridging between the front door and the great room, this foyer is a surprise feature.

- Great Room: A 10-ft. ceiling adds to the spacious feeling of this room, while the corner fireplace gives it an intimate feeling. Sliding glass doors at the rear of the room open to the backyard.

- Dining Room: This formal room adjoins the great room, allowing guests and family to flow between the rooms.

- Breakfast Room: Turrets add a Victorian feeling to this room that's just off the kitchen and overlooks the front porch.

- Master Suite: Privacy is assured in this suite, which is separated from the main part of the house. A compartmented bath and large walk-in closet add convenience to its beauty.

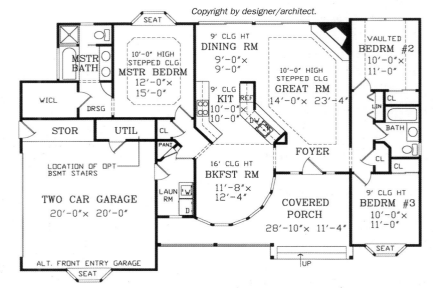

Breakfast Room

Plan #121001

Dimensions: 56' W x 58' D

Levels: 1

Square Footage: 1,911

Bedrooms: 3

Bathrooms: 2

Foundation: Basement

Materials List Available: Yes

Price Category: D

Images provided by designer/architect.

Detailed, soaring ceilings and top-notch amenities set this distinctive home apart.

Features:

- Ceiling Height: 8 ft. except as noted.

- Great Room: A soaring ceiling and six tall transom-topped windows make this a light and airy spot for entertaining.

- Formal Dining Room: The entry enjoys a pleasing view of this dining room's detailed 12-ft. ceiling and picture window.

- Great Room: At the back of the home, a see-through fireplace in this great room is joined by a built-in entertainment center.

- Hearth Room: This bayed room shares the see-through fireplace with the great room.

- Master Suite: Enjoy the stars and the sun in the private bath's whirlpool and separate shower. The bath features the same decorative ceiling as the dining room.

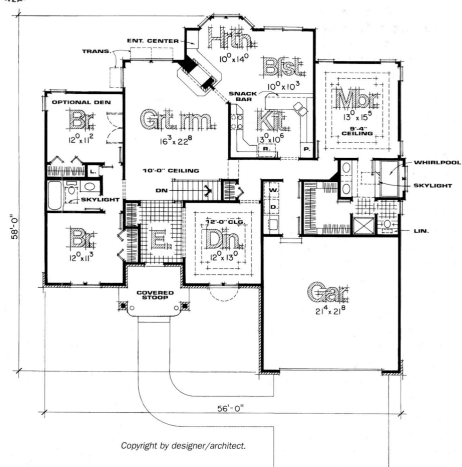

Copyright by designer/architect.

Plan #241013

Dimensions: 68' W x 46' D
Levels: 2
Square Footage: 3,033
Main Level Sq. Ft.: 1,918
Upper Level Sq. Ft.: 1,115
Bedrooms: 4
Bathrooms: 3½
Foundation: Crawl space, slab, or walkout
Materials List Available: No
Price Category: G

The generous front porch and balcony of this home signal its beauty and comfortable design.

Features:

- Great Room: A large fireplace is the focal point of this spacious room, which opens from the foyer.

- Kitchen: Open to the dining room and breakfast room, the kitchen is designed for convenience.

- Sunroom: A fireplace and tray ceiling highlight this room that's just off the breakfast room.

- Study: Positioned for privacy, the study is ideal for quiet time alone.

- Master Suite: You'll love the decorative drop ceiling, huge walk-in closet, and bath with two vanities, a tub, and separate shower.

- Playroom: This enormous space gives ample room for play on rainy afternoons. Set up a media center here when the children have outgrown the need for a playroom.

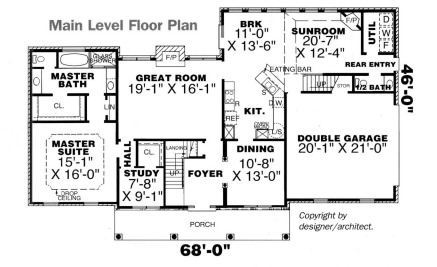

Main Level Floor Plan

BRK 11'-0" X 13'-6"
SUNROOM 20'-7" X 12'-4"
UTIL
F/P
D W F
MASTER BATH
GLASS SHOWER
CL. LIN
F/P
GREAT ROOM 19'-1" X 16'-1"
EATING BAR
REAR ENTRY
UP STOR ½ BATH
46'-0"
MASTER SUITE 15'-1" X 16'-0"
HALL
CL. LANDING
KIT.
REF OVEN MICRO L/S D.W.
DINING 10'-8" X 13'-0"
DOUBLE GARAGE 20'-1" X 21'-0"
STUDY 7'-8" X 9'-1"
UP FOYER
DROP CEILING
PORCH
Copyright by designer/architect.
68'-0"

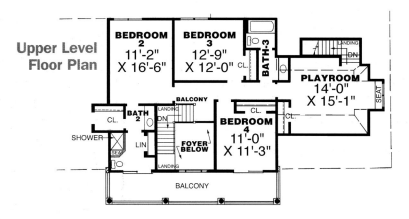

Upper Level Floor Plan

BEDROOM 2 11'-2" X 16'-6"
BEDROOM 3 12'-9" X 12'-0"
BATH-3
CL.
LANDING
DN
PLAYROOM 14'-0" X 15'-1"
SEAT
BALCONY
BATH 2
CL.
SHOWER
LIN
LANDING DN
CL.
CL.
SEAT
FOYER BELOW
BEDROOM 4 11'-0" X 11'-3"
LANDING
BALCONY

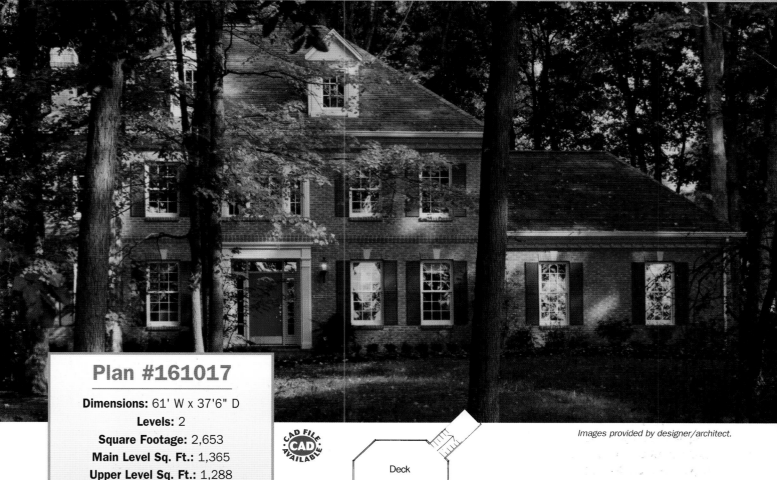

Plan #161017

Dimensions: 61' W x 37'6" D
Levels: 2
Square Footage: 2,653
Main Level Sq. Ft.: 1,365
Upper Level Sq. Ft.: 1,288
Bedrooms: 4
Bathrooms: 2½
Foundation: Basement
Materials List Available: Yes
Price Category: F

If a traditional look makes you feel comfortable, you'll love this spacious, family-friendly home.

Features:

• Family Room: Accessorize with cozy cushions to make the most of this sunken room. Windows flank the fireplace, adding warm, natural light. Doors leading to the rear deck make this room a family "headquarters."

• Living and Dining Rooms: These formal rooms open to each other, so you'll love hosting gatherings in this home.

• Kitchen: A handy pantry fits well with the traditional feeling of this home, and an island adds contemporary convenience.

• Master Suite: Relax in the whirlpool tub in your bath and enjoy the storage space in the two walk-in closets in the bedroom.

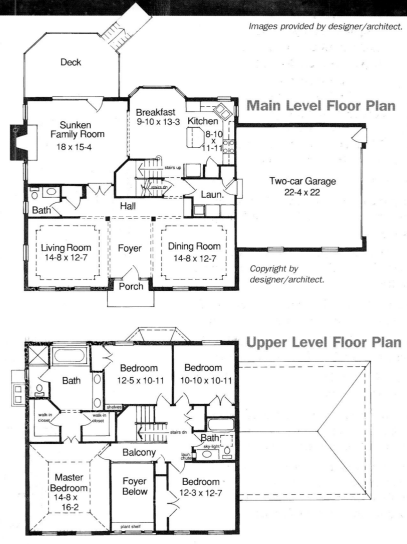

Images provided by designer/architect.

Main Level Floor Plan

Upper Level Floor Plan

Copyright by designer/architect.

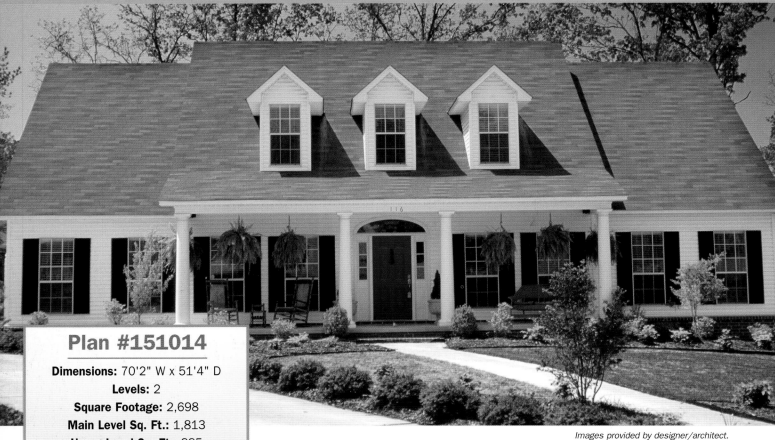

Plan #151014

Dimensions: 70'2" W x 51'4" D

Levels: 2

Square Footage: 2,698

Main Level Sq. Ft.: 1,813

Upper Level Sq. Ft.: 885

Bedrooms: 5

Bathrooms: 3

Foundation: Crawl space, slab, optional basement for fee

CompleteCost List Available: Yes

Price Category: F

Images provided by designer/architect.

A comfortable front porch welcomes you into this home that features a balcony over the great room, a study, and a kitchen designed for gourmet cooks.

CAD FILE AVAILABLE

Features:

- Ceiling Height: 9 ft.
- Front Porch: Stately 12-in.-wide pillars form the entryway.
- Foyer: Open to upper story.
- Great Room: A fireplace, vaulted 9-ft. ceiling, and balcony from the second floor add character to this lovely room.
- Dining Room: Open to the kitchen for convenience.
- Kitchen: A large walk-in pantry, well-designed work areas, and eat-in bar make this room a treasure.
- Breakfast Room: Enjoy this spot that opens to both the kitchen and a large covered porch at the rear of the house.
- Study: This quiet room has French doors leading to the yard.
- Master Suite: This spacious area has cozy window seats as well as his and her walk-in closets. The master bathroom is fitted with a whirlpool tub, a glass shower, and his and her sinks.

Upper Level Floor Plan

Main Level Floor Plan

Copyright by designer/architect.

Plan #131028

Dimensions: 69'2" W x 50'2" D
Levels: 2
Square Footage: 2,696
Main Level Sq. Ft.: 1,960
Upper Level Sq. Ft.: 736
Bedrooms: 4
Bathrooms: 3
Foundation: Crawl space, slab, or basement
Materials List Available: Yes
Price Category: F

Images provided by designer/architect.

Imagine owning a home with Victorian styling and a dramatic, contemporary interior design.

Features:

- **Foyer:** Enter from the curved covered porch into this foyer with its 17-ft. ceiling.
- **Great Room:** A vaulted ceiling sets the tone for this large room, where friends and family are sure to congregate.

- **Dining Room:** A 14-ft. ceiling here accentuates the rounded shape of this room.
- **Kitchen:** From the angled corner sink to the angled island with a snack bar, this room has character. A pantry adds convenience.
- **Master Suite:** A 13-ft. tray ceiling exudes elegance, and the bath features a spa tub and designer shower.
- **Upper Level:** The balcony hall leads to a turreted recreation room, two bedrooms, and a full bath.

Main Level Floor Plan

Upper Level Floor Plan

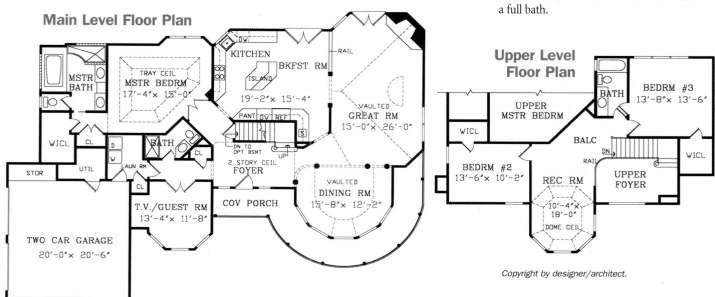

Copyright by designer/architect.

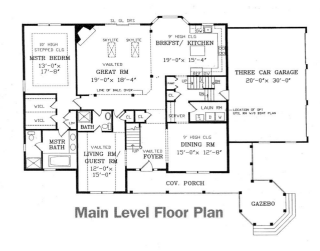

Copyright by designer/architect.

Plan #321007

Dimensions: 76' W x 55'2" D
Levels: 1
Square Footage: 2,695
Bedrooms: 3
Bathrooms: 2½
Foundation: Basement
Materials List Available: Yes
Price Category: F

Images provided by designer/architect.

Main Level Floor Plan

Upper Level Floor Plan

Copyright by designer/architect.

Plan #131050

Dimensions: 72'8" W x 47' D
Levels: 2
Square Footage: 2,874
Main Level Sq. Ft.: 2,146
Upper Level Sq. Ft.: 728
Bedrooms: 4
Bathrooms: 3
Foundation: Crawl space, slab, or basement
Materials List Available: Yes
Price Category: G

Images provided by designer/architect.

Plan #141011

Dimensions: 54' W x 60'6" D

Levels: 1

Square Footage: 1,869

Bedrooms: 3

Bathrooms: 2

Foundation: Crawl space, slab, or basement

Materials List Available: Yes

Price Category: D

The blending of brick and stone on this plan gives the home an old-world appeal.

Features:

• Ceiling Height: 8 ft. unless otherwise noted.

• Tall Ceilings: The main living areas feature dramatic 12-ft. ceilings.

• Open Plan: This home's open floor plan maximizes the use of space and makes it flexible. This main living area has plenty of room for large gatherings.

• Kitchen: The kitchen is integrated into the main living area. It features a breakfast room that is ideal for informal family meals.

• Master Suite: You'll enjoy unwinding at the end of the day in this luxurious space. It's located away from the rest of the house for maximum privacy.

• Secondary Bedrooms: You have the option of adding extra style to the secondary bedrooms by including volume ceilings.

This home, as shown in the photograph, may differ from the actual blueprints. For more detailed information, please check the floor plans carefully.

Images provided by designer/architect.

Copyright by designer/architect.

Plan #161018

Dimensions: 74'4" W x 69'11" D
Levels: 2
Square Footage: 2,816
+ 325 Sq. Ft. bonus room
Main Level Sq. Ft.: 2,231
Upper Level Sq. Ft.: 624
Bedrooms: 3
Bathrooms: 3 full, 2 half
Foundation: Basement
Materials List Available: No
Price Category: F

If you love classic European designs, look closely at this home with its multiple gables and countless conveniences and luxuries.

Images provided by designer/architect.

Features:

- Foyer: Open to the great room, the 2-story foyer offers a view all the way to the rear windows.

- Great Room: A fireplace makes this room cozy in any kind of weather.

- Kitchen: This large room features an island with a sink, and an angled wall with French doors to the back yard.

- Dining Room: The furniture alcove and raised ceiling make this room both formal and practical.

- Master Suite: You'll love the quiet in the bedroom and the luxuries—a whirlpool tub, separate shower, and double vanities—in the bath.

- Basement: The door from the basement to the side yard adds convenience to outdoor work.

Rear View

Main Level Floor Plan

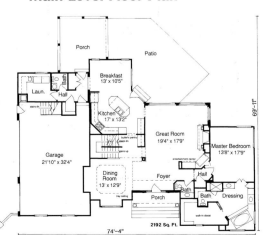

Upper Level Floor Plan

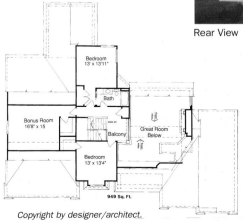

Copyright by designer/architect.

Foyer/Dining Room

Plan #161025

Dimensions: 63'4" W x 48' D

Levels: 2

Square Footage: 2,738

Main Level Sq. Ft.: 1,915

Upper Level Sq. Ft.: 823

Bedrooms: 4

Bathrooms: 3½

Foundation: Basement

Materials List Available: No

Price Category: F

This home, as shown in the photograph, may differ from the actual blueprints. For more detailed information, please check the floor plans carefully.

One look at the octagonal tower, boxed window, and wood-and-stone trim, and you'll know how much your family will love this home.

Features:

• Foyer: View the high windows across the rear wall, a fireplace, and open stairs as you come in.

• Great Room: Gather in this two-story-high area.

• Hearth Room: Open to the breakfast room, it's close to both the kitchen and dining room.

• Kitchen: A snack bar and an island make the kitchen ideal for family living.

• Master Suite: You'll love the 9-ft. ceiling in the bedroom and 11-ft. ceiling in the sitting area. The bath has a whirlpool tub, double-bowl vanity, and walk-in closet.

• Upper Level: A balcony leads to a bedroom with a private bath and 2 other rooms with private access to a shared bath.

Main Level Floor Plan

Upper Level Floor Plan

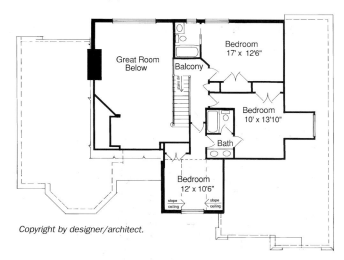

Copyright by designer/architect.

Plan #151034

Dimensions: 58'6" W x 64'6" D
Levels: 1
Square Footage: 2,133
Bedrooms: 3
Bathrooms: 2
Foundation: Crawl space, slab, or basement
CompleteCost List Available: Yes
Price Category: D

You'll love the high ceilings, open floor plan, and contemporary design features in this home.

Features:

• Great Room: A pass-through tiled fireplace between this lovely large room and the adjacent hearth room allows you to notice the mirror effect created by the 10-ft. boxed ceilings in both rooms.

• Dining Room: An 11-ft. ceiling and 8-in. boxed column give formality to this lovely room, where you're certain to entertain.

• Kitchen: If you're a cook, this room may become your favorite spot in the house, thanks to its great design, which includes plenty of work and storage space, and a very practical layout.

• Master Suite: A 10-ft. boxed ceiling gives elegance to this room. A pocket door opens to the private bath, with its huge walk-in closet, glass-blocked whirlpool tub, separate glass shower, and private toilet room.

This home, as shown in the photograph, may differ from the actual blueprints. For more detailed information, please check the floor plans carefully.

Images provided by designer/architect.

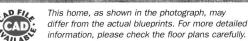

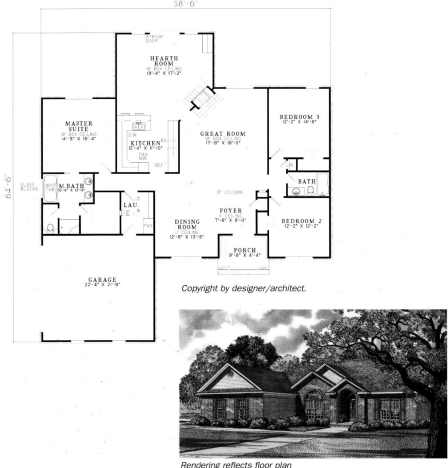

Copyright by designer/architect.

Rendering reflects floor plan

Plan #131023

Dimensions: 78'8" W x 36'2" D
Levels: 2
Square Footage: 2,460
Main Level Sq. Ft.: 1,377
Upper Level Sq. Ft.: 1,083
Bedrooms: 4
Bathrooms: 3½
Foundation: Crawl space, slab, or basement
Materials List Available: Yes
Price Category: F

Images provided by designer/architect.

You'll love the modern floor plan inside this traditional two-story home, with its attractive facade.

Features:

- Ceiling Height: 8 ft.

- Living Room: The windows on three sides of this room make it bright and sunny. Choose the optional fireplace for cozy winter days and the wet bar for elegant entertaining.

- Family Room: Overlooking the rear deck, this spacious family room features a fireplace and a skylight.

- Dining Room: The convenient placement of this large room lets guests flow into it from the living room and allows easy to access from the kitchen.

- Kitchen: The island cooktop and built-in desk make this space both modern and practical.

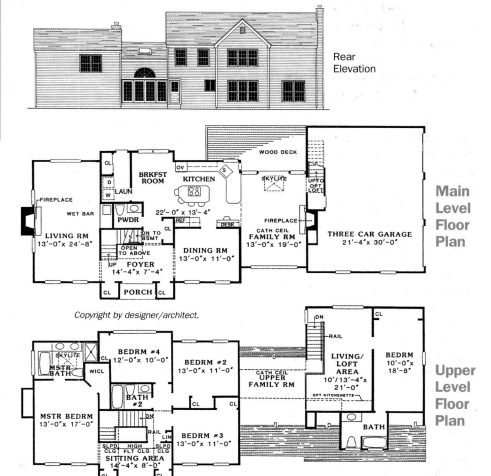

Rear Elevation

Main Level Floor Plan

Copyright by designer/architect.

Upper Level Floor Plan

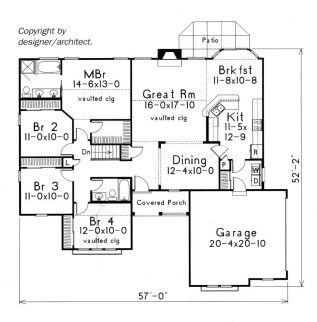

Copyright by designer/architect.

Images provided by designer/architect.

Plan #321008

Dimensions: 57' W x 52'2" D
Levels: 1
Square Footage: 1,761
Bedrooms: 4
Bathrooms: 2
Foundation: Basement
Materials List Available: Yes
Price Category: C

Copyright by designer/architect.

Rear Elevation

Images provided by designer/architect.

Plan #161007

Dimensions: 66'4" W x 43'10" D
Levels: 1
Square Footage: 1,611
Bedrooms: 3
Bathrooms: 2
Foundation: Basement; crawl space option for fee
Materials List Available: Yes
Price Category: C

Plan #121049

Dimensions: 82' W x 60'8" D
Levels: 2
Square Footage: 3,335
Main Level Sq. Ft.: 2,054
Upper Level Sq. Ft.: 1,281
Bedrooms: 4
Bathrooms: 3½
Foundation: Slab; basement for fee
Materials List Available: Yes
Price Category: G

Images provided by designer/architect.

This charming Craftsman-style home creates a welcoming environment with its covered porch, two-story foyer, and attractive accommodations.

CAD FILE AVAILABLE

Features:

- Great Room: Bask in the quiet glow of abundant natural light; cozy up to the smoldering fireplace; or gather with the family in this large, relaxing area.

- Kitchen: This design creates a great balance between workspace and play space. The kitchen surrounds the household chef with workspace without feeling closed-in.

A breakfast bar opens into the large breakfast area, making life a little simpler in the mornings.

- Master Bedroom: This spacious room is yours for the styling, a private space that features a walk-in closet and full bath, which includes his and her sinks, a standing shower, and a large tub.

- Second Floor: "Go to your room" sounds much better when that room is separated by a story. Identically sized bedrooms with ample closet space save you from family squabbles. The second floor has everything you need, with a compartmentalized full bathroom and computer loft.

Upper Level Floor Plan

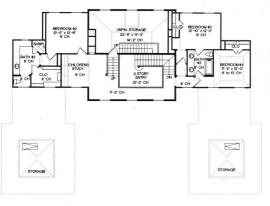

Third Floor Bedroom Floor Plan

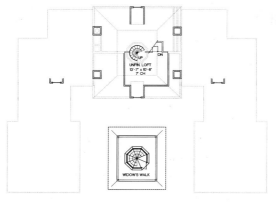

Copyright by designer/architect.

Main Level Floor Plan

Plan #351008

Dimensions: 64'6" W x 61'4" D
Levels: 1
Square Footage: 2,002
Bedrooms: 3
Bathrooms: 2
Foundation: Crawl space or basement
Materials List Available: Yes
Price Category: E

This home has the charming appeal of a quaint cottage that you might find in an old village in the English countryside. It's a unique design that maximizes every inch of its usable space.

Features:

• Great Room: This room has a vaulted ceiling and built-in units on each side of the fireplace.

• Kitchen: This kitchen boasts a raised bar open to the breakfast area; the room is also open to the dining room.

• Master Bedroom: This bedroom retreat features a raised ceiling and a walk-in closet.

• Master Bath: This bathroom has a double vanity, large walk-in closet, and soaking tub.

• Bedrooms: Two bedrooms share a common bathroom and have large closets.

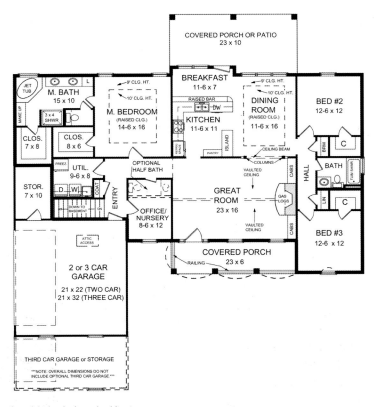

Plan #321006

Dimensions: 76' W x 45' D
Levels: 1, optional lower
Square Footage: 1,977
Optional Basement Level
Sq. Ft.: 1,416
Bedrooms: 4
Bathrooms: 2½
Foundation: Basement
Materials List Available: Yes
Price Category: D

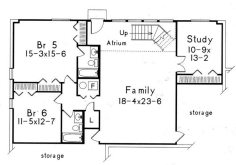

Images provided by designer/architect.

Optional Basement Level Floor Plan

Copyright by designer/architect.

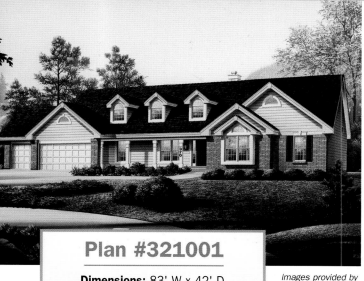

Plan #321001

Dimensions: 83' W x 42' D
Levels: 1
Square Footage: 1,721
Bedrooms: 3
Bathrooms: 2
Foundation: Crawl space, slab, or basement
Materials List Available: Yes
Price Category: C

Images provided by designer/architect.

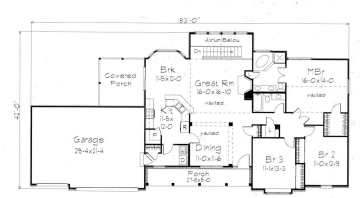

Copyright by designer/architect.

Rear View

Plan #131007

Dimensions: 59'10" W x 47'8" D
Levels: 1
Square Footage: 1,595
Bedrooms: 3
Bathrooms: 2
Foundation: Crawl space, slab, basement, or walkout
Materials List Available: Yes
Price Category: D

Imagine living in this home, with its traditional country comfort and individual brand of charm.

Features:

- Exterior elements: The mixture of a front porch with a cameo front door, decorative posts, bay windows, and dormers will delight you.

- Great Room: A tray ceiling gives distinction to this large room, and a wet bar eases entertaining.

- Screened Porch: At dusk and dawn, this porch is sure to be your favorite outdoor spot.

- Kitchen: Eat any meal in this large kitchen for a touch of homey charm.

- Dining Room: Perfect for hosting a formal dinner, this bayed dining room can increase your enjoyment of simple family meals.

- Master Bedroom: For the sake of privacy, this room is somewhat secluded. Decorate to emphasize the elegant tray ceiling.

Images provided by designer/architect.

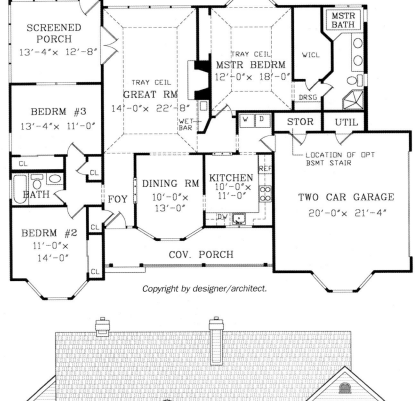

Copyright by designer/architect.

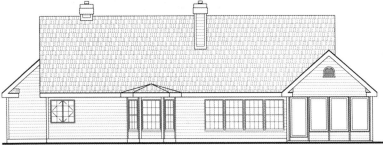

Rear Elevation

Plan #121028

Dimensions: 54'8" W x 42' D

Levels: 2

Square Footage: 2,644

Main Level Sq. Ft.: 1,366

Upper Level Sq. Ft.: 1,278

Bedrooms: 4

Bathrooms: 2½

Foundation: Basement

Materials List Available: Yes

Price Category: F

Images provided by designer/architect.

This home is filled with special touches and amenities that add up to gracious living.

Features:

- Ceiling Height: 8 ft.

- Formal Living Room: This large, inviting room is the perfect place to entertain guests.

- Family Room: This cozy, comfortable room is accessed through elegant French doors in the living room. It is sure to be the favorite family gathering place with its bay window, see-through fireplace, and bay window.

- Breakfast Area: This area is large enough for the whole family to enjoy a casual meal as they are warmed by the other side of the see-through fireplace. The area features a bay window and built-in bookcase.

- Master Bedroom: Upstairs, enjoy the gracious and practical master bedroom with its boxed ceiling and two walk-in closets.

- Master Bath: Luxuriate in the whirlpool bath as you gaze through the skylight framed by ceiling accents.

Main Level Floor Plan

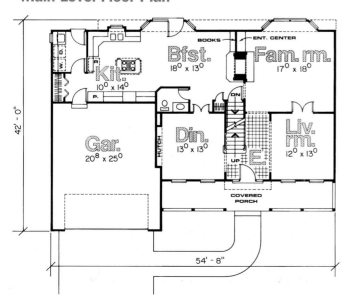

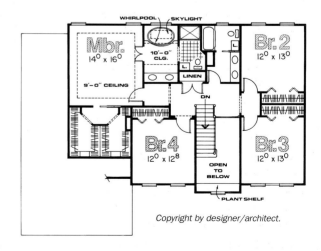

Copyright by designer/architect.

Upper Level Floor Plan

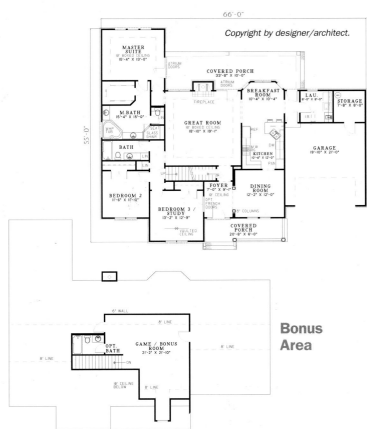

Copyright by designer/architect.

Images provided by designer/architect.

Plan #151117

Dimensions: 66' W x 55' D
Levels: 1
Square Footage: 1,957
Bedrooms: 3
Bathrooms: 3
Foundation: Crawl space, slab, or basement
CompleteCost List Available: Yes
Price Category: D

Bonus Area

Rear Elevation

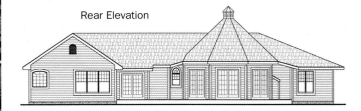

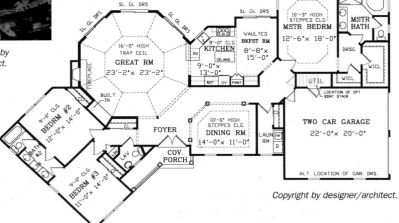

Plan #131019

Dimensions: 83'6" W x 53'4" D
Levels: 1
Square Footage: 2,243
Bedrooms: 3
Bathrooms: 2½
Foundation: Crawl space, slab, or basement
Materials List Available: Yes
Price Category: F

Images provided by designer/architect.

Copyright by designer/architect.

Plan #101009

Dimensions: 70'2" W x 59' D
Levels: 1
Square Footage: 2,097
Bedrooms: 3
Bathrooms: 3
Foundation: Crawl space, slab, or basement
Materials List Available: Yes
Price Category: D

Images provided by designer/architect.

Round columns enhance this country porch design, which will nestle into any neighborhood.

Features:

- Ceiling Height: 9 ft. unless otherwise noted.

- Family Room: This large family room seems even more spacious, thanks to the vaulted ceiling. It's the perfect spot for all kinds of family activities.

- Dining Room: This elegant dining room is adorned with a decorative round column and a tray ceiling.

- Kitchen: You'll love the convenience of this enormous 14-ft.-3-in. x 22-ft.-6-in. country kitchen, which is open to the living room.

- Screened Porch: A French door leads to this breezy porch, with its vaulted ceiling.

- Master Suite: This sumptuous suite includes a double tray ceiling, a sitting area, a large walk-in closet, and a luxurious bath.

- Patio or Deck: This area is accessible from both the screened porch and master bedroom.

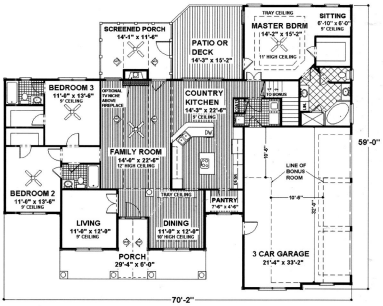

Copyright by designer/architect.

SMARTtip

Single-Level Decks

A single-level deck can use a strong vertical element, such as a pergola or a gazebo, to make it interesting. A simple and less-expensive option is a potted conical shrub or a clematis growing on a trellis.

Plan #121030

Dimensions: 58' W x 45' D

Levels: 2

Square Footage: 2,613

Main Level Sq. Ft.: 1,333

Upper Level Sq. Ft.: 1,280

Bedrooms: 4

Bathrooms: 2½

Foundation: Basement

Materials List Available: Yes

Price Category: F

Images provided by designer/architect.

This home is packed with all the amenities you need for a gracious and comfortable lifestyle.

Features:

• Ceiling Height: 8 ft. unless otherwise noted.

• Foyer: The elegant entry opens into the living room and formal dining room.

• Adaptable Space: An area linking the formal living room and the family room would make a great area for the family computer. Alternately, it can become a wet bar with window seat.

• Breakfast Area: The family will enjoy informal meals in this sun-bathed area.

• Snack Bar: Perfect for a quick bite, this angled area joins the kitchen to the breakfast area.

• Master Suite: Two walk-in closets make this suite convenient as well as luxurious. The bayed whirlpool tub under a cathedral ceiling invites you to unwind and relax.

• Bonus Room: The second level includes a large room that could become an extra bedroom, a guest room, or a home office.

Main Level Floor Plan

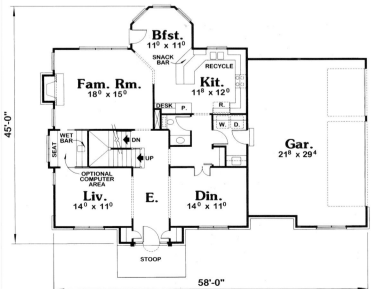

Upper Level Floor Plan

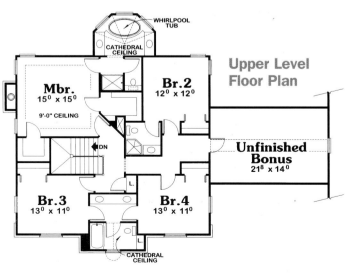

Copyright by designer/architect.

Plan #211077

Dimensions: 94' W x 68' D

Levels: 2

Square Footage: 5,560

Main Level Sq. Ft.: 4,208

Upper Level Sq. Ft.: 1,352

Bedrooms: 4

Bathrooms: 4 full, 2 half

Foundation: Crawl space or slab

Materials List Available: Yes

Price Category: J

This palatial home has a two-story veranda and offers room and amenities for a large family.

Features:

- Ceiling Height: 10 ft.

- Library: Teach your children the importance of quiet reflection in this library, which boasts a full wall of built-in bookshelves.

- Master Suite: Escape the pressures of a busy day in this truly royal master suite. Curl up in front of your own fireplace. Or take a long, soothing soak in the private bath, with his and her sinks and closets.

- Kitchen: This room offers many modern comforts and amenities, and free-flowing traffic patterns.

Images provided by designer/architect.

Copyright by designer/architect.

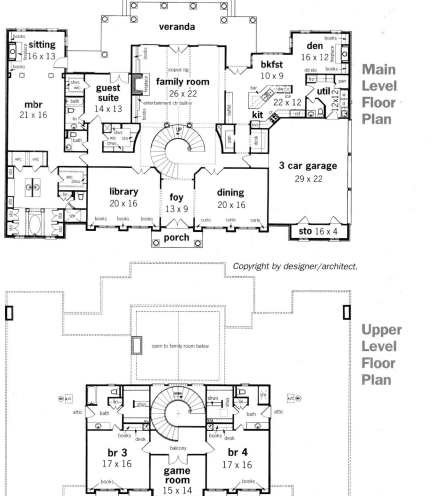

Plan #121090

Dimensions: 60' W x 58' D
Levels: 2
Square Footage: 2,645
Main Level Sq. Ft.: 1,972
Upper Level Sq. Ft.: 673
Bedrooms: 4
Bathrooms: 2½
Foundation: Basement
Materials List Available: Yes
Price Category: F

Images provided by designer/architect.

You'll be amazed at the amenities that have been designed into this lovely home.

Features:

• Den: French doors just off the entry lead to this lovely room, with its bowed window and spider-beamed ceiling.

• Great Room: A trio of graceful arched windows highlights the volume ceiling in this room. You might want to curl up to read next to the see-through fireplace into the hearth room.

• Kitchen: Enjoy the good design in this room.

• Hearth Room: The shared fireplace with the great room makes this a cozy spot in cool weather.

• Master Suite: French doors lead to this well-lit area, with its roomy walk-in closet, sunlit whirlpool tub, separate shower, and two vanities.

Main Level Floor Plan

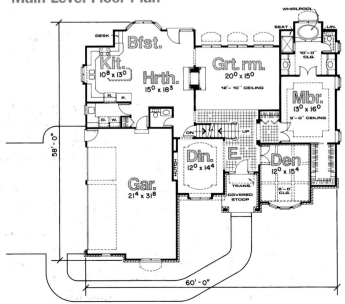

Upper Level Floor Plan

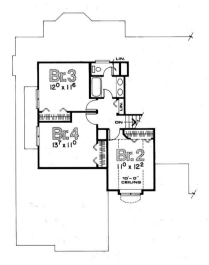

Copyright by designer/architect.

Plan #211003

Dimensions: 62' W x 64' D
Levels: 1
Square Footage: 1,865
Bedrooms: 3
Bathrooms: 2
Foundation: Crawl space or slab
Materials List Available: Yes
Price Category: D

SMARTtip
Fire Extinguishers

The word PASS is an easy way to remember the proper way to use a fire extinguisher.

Pull the pin at the top of the extinguisher that keeps the handle from being accidentally pressed.

Aim the nozzle of the extinguisher toward the base of the fire.

Squeeze the handle to discharge the extinguisher. Stand approximately 8 feet away from the fire.

Sweep the nozzle back and forth at the base of the fire. After the fire appears to be out, watch it carefully because it may reignite!

The traditional style of this home is blended with all the amenities required for today's lifestyle.

Features:

• Ceiling Height: 8 ft. unless otherwise noted.

• Front Porch: Guests will feel welcome arriving at the front door under this sheltering front porch.

• Dining Room: This large room will accommodate dinner parties of all sizes, from large formal gatherings to more intimate family get-togethers.

• Living Room: Guests and family alike will feel right at home in this inviting room. Sunlight streaming through the skylights in the 12-ft. ceiling, combined with the handsome fireplace, makes the space both airy and warm.

Images provided by designer/architect.

• Back Patio: When warm weather comes around, step out the sliding glass doors in the living room to enjoy entertaining or just relaxing on this patio.

• Kitchen: A cathedral ceiling soars over this efficient modern kitchen. It includes an eating area that is perfect for informal family meals.

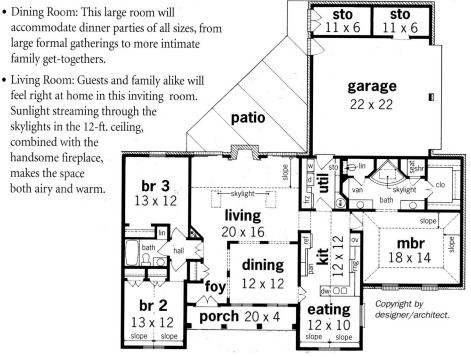

Copyright by designer/architect.

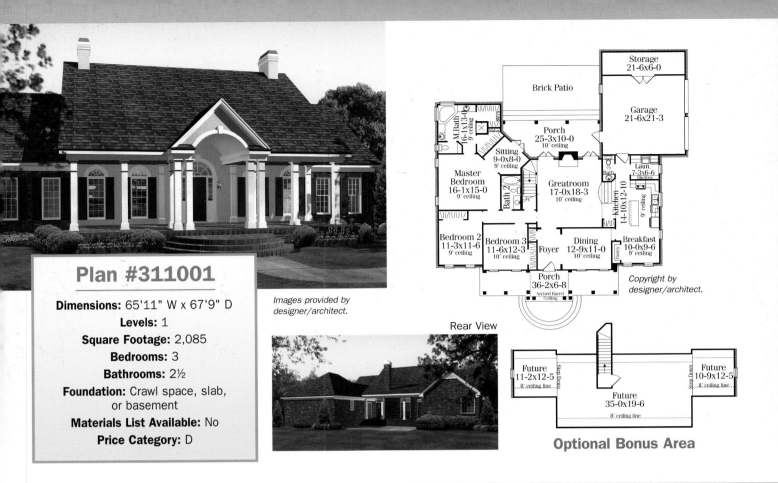

Images provided by designer/architect.

Copyright by designer/architect.

Rear View

Optional Bonus Area

Plan #311001

Dimensions: 65'11" W x 67'9" D

Levels: 1

Square Footage: 2,085

Bedrooms: 3

Bathrooms: 2½

Foundation: Crawl space, slab, or basement

Materials List Available: No

Price Category: D

Plan #321005

Dimensions: 69' W x 53'8" D

Levels: 1

Square Footage: 2,483

Bedrooms: 3

Bathrooms: 2

Foundation: Basement

Materials List Available: Yes

Price Category: E

Images provided by designer/architect.

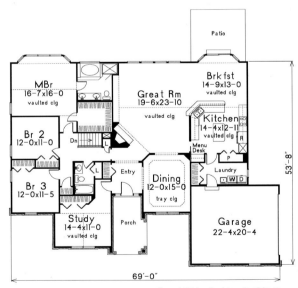

Copyright by designer/architect.

SMARTtip

Art in Pools

The tiled walls and floor of a pool make great canvases for art, so incorporate a serious or whimsical design. Also, make the stairs wide and shallow to form a wading area for kids.

Plan #151009

Dimensions: 44' W x 86'2" D
Levels: 1
Square Footage: 1,601
Bedrooms: 3
Bathrooms: 2
Foundation: Crawl space, slab
CompleteCost List Available: Yes
Price Category: C

Images provided by designer/architect.

This can be the perfect home for a site with views you can enjoy in all seasons and at all times.

Features:

- Porches: Enjoy the front porch with its 10-ft. ceiling and the more private back porch where you can set up a grill or just get away from it all.

- Foyer: With a 10-ft. ceiling, this foyer opens to the great room for a warm welcome.

- Great Room: Your family will love the media center and the easy access to the rear porch.

- Kitchen: This well-designed kitchen is open to the dining room and the breakfast nook, which also opens to the rear porch.

- Master Suite: The bedroom has a 10-ft. boxed ceiling and a door to the rear. The bath includes a corner whirlpool tub with glass block windows.

- Bedrooms: Bedroom 2 has a vaulted ceiling, while bedroom 3 features a built-in desk.

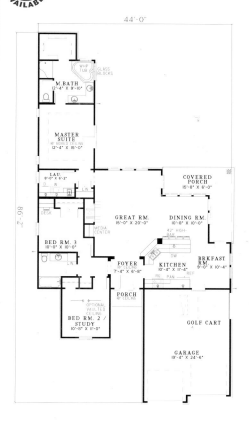

Copyright by designer/architect.

SMARTtip
Fertilizing Your Grass

Fertilizers contain nutrients balanced for different kinds of growth. The ratio of nutrients is indicated on the package by three numbers (for example, 10-10-10). The first specifies nitrogen content; the second, phosphorus; and the third, potash.

Nitrogen helps grass blades to grow and improves the quality and thickness of the turf. Fertilizers contain up to 30 percent nitrogen.

Phosphorus helps grass to develop a healthy root system. It also speeds up the maturation process of the plant.

Potash helps grass stay healthy by providing amino acids and proteins to the plants.

Plan #161034

Dimensions: 56' W x 53' D
Levels: 2
Square Footage: 2,156
Main Level Sq. Ft.: 1,605
Upper Level Sq. Ft.: 551
Bedrooms: 3
Bathrooms: 2½
Foundation: Basement
Materials List Available: No
Price Category: D

Images provided by designer/architect.

Multiple gables, a covered porch, and circle-topped windows combine to enhance the attractiveness of this exciting home.

Features:

• Great Room: A raised foyer introduces this open combined great room and dining room. Enjoy the efficiency of a dual-sided fireplace that warms both the great room and kitchen.

• Kitchen: The kitchen, designed for easy traffic patterns, offers an abundance of counter space and features a cooktop island.

• Master Suite: This first-floor master suite, separated for privacy, includes twin vanities and a walk-in closet. A deluxe corner bath and walk-in shower complete its luxurious detail.

• Additional Rooms: Two additional bedrooms lead to the second-floor balcony, which overlooks the great room. You can use the optional bonus room as a den or office.

Copyright by designer/architect.

Main Level Floor Plan

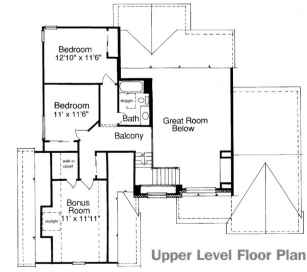

Upper Level Floor Plan

Plan #271081

Dimensions: 86' W x 54' D
Levels: 1
Square Footage: 2,539
Bedrooms: 3
Bathrooms: 2
Foundation: Slab
Materials List Available: No
Price Category: E

This traditional home is sure to impress your guests and even your neighbors.

Features:

- Living Room: This quiet space off the foyer is perfect for pleasant conversation.

- Family Room: A perfect gathering spot, this room is nicely enhanced by a fireplace.

- Kitchen: This room easily serves the bayed morning room and the formal dining room.

- Master Suite: The master bedroom overlooks a side patio, and boasts a private bath with a skylight and a whirlpool tub.

- Library: This cozy room is perfect for curling up with a good novel. It would also make a great extra bedroom.

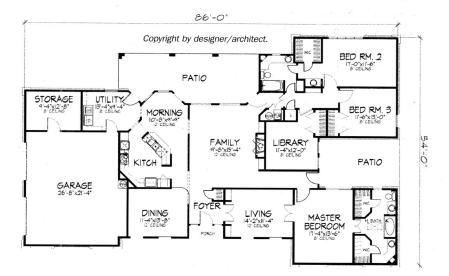

SMARTtip

Determining Curtain Length

Follow length guidelines for foolproof results, but remember that they're not rules. Go ahead and play with curtain and drapery lengths. Instead of shortening long panels at the hem, for instance, take up excess material by blousing them over tiebacks for a pleasing effect.

Plan #271077

Dimensions: 69'6" W x 53' D
Levels: 1
Square Footage: 1,786
Bedrooms: 1
Bathrooms: 1½
Foundation: Basement or daylight basement
Materials List Available: No
Price Category: C

Images provided by designer/architect.

This wonderful home has an optional finished basement plan to add three more bedrooms—ideal for a growing family.

Features:

• Great Room: This large gathering room has a fireplace with built-in cabinets on either side.

• Kitchen: This island kitchen, with dinette area, is open to the great room.

• Master Bedroom: This luxurious room provides a view of the backyard.

• Master Bath: This private bathroom has a walk-in closet and double vanities.

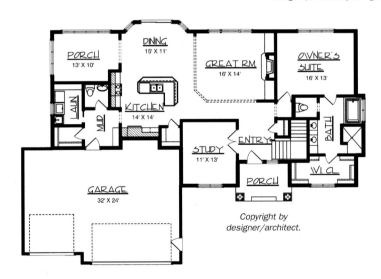

Copyright by designer/architect.

Optional Basement Level Floor Plan

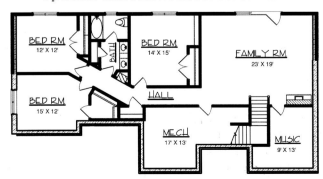

Plan #241005

Dimensions: 53' W x 55'9" D

Levels: 1

Square Footage: 1,670

Bedrooms: 3

Bathrooms: 2

Foundation: Crawl space or slab; basement option for fee

Materials List Available: No

Price Category: C

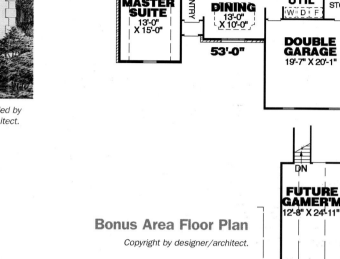

Images provided by designer/architect.

Bonus Area Floor Plan

Copyright by designer/architect.

Plan #321030

Dimensions: 61' W x 51' D

Levels: 1

Square Footage: 2,029

Bedrooms: 4

Bathrooms: 2

Foundation: Crawl space, slab, basement, or walkout

Materials List Available: Yes

Price Category: D

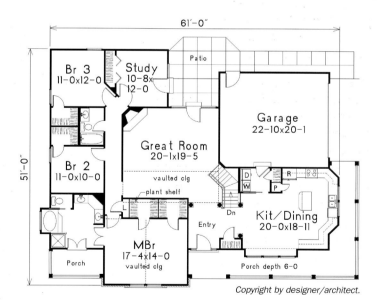

Images provided by designer/architect.

Copyright by designer/architect.

SMARTtip

Measuring Angles

A sure-fire way to accurately measure the wall-frame acute angle is to cut a piece of scrap lumber to emulate the angle, and then measure it.

design ideas for CREATIVE HOMEOWNER

Curb Appeal

architectural details I color and paint I landscaping and more

Megan Connelly

This article was reprinted from *Design Ideas for Curb Appeal* (Creative Homeowner 2006).

Hardscaping Your Yard

Landscape designs often benefit from vertical elements such as walls, fences, arches, arbors, pergolas, and decorative freestanding plant supports. Walls and fences help define boundaries while enclosing special spaces. Properly positioned, an arbor or arch is an eye-catching accent, adding visual drama to the scene and providing an attractive focal point or point of passage between two parts of the garden. A pergola transforms an ordinary path into a special, shaded, and sheltered passageway, while a freestanding plant support is like an exclamation point, drawing attention to itself and creating a pleasant focus.

As an added bonus, any one of these features provides an opportunity to grow and enjoy the wide range of climbing plants such as clematis, wisteria, climbing roses, honeysuckle, trumpet vine, and jasmine. These vertical plants add a sense of lushness to the garden as they scramble up walls and over trellised arches or droop heavy panicles of flowers through the open fretwork ceiling of a pergola. Here are some ideas for hardscaping your front yard with these elements.

Fences, opposite, not only serve as boundary markers, they are a design element in their own right. There are so many styles from which to choose that you should have no trouble finding one that is both functional and decorative. The posts on this classic style are topped with decorative finials.

The brick wall, above, that encloses this garden complements the brick pathway. Both have weathered to the point where they look as though they have always been part of the setting.

Consider installing a fence, below, as a backdrop to a group of lush plantings. This simple rail fence defines the garden path and separates the front yard from the side yard, but it also seems to support the flowering plants.

A traditional picket fence, right, serves as a backdrop for a group of border plants. In addition to their utilitarian functions, vertical elements such as fences and walls add texture and visual interest to a landscape.

The classic picket fence, below, can be used with a variety of house styles. A purely decorative section of fence spans an opening in a hedge that borders the front yard of this house.

Fence posts, bottom right, especially posts that mark an entry, can become focal points if you add special cap treatments or adorn one with fresh flowers.

Designing a Fence

Erecting a fence is the quickest and generally easiest way to define the boundary of your property. To be a successful part of a landscape design, a fence should be planned to complement the architecture of your house, possibly even echoing a distinctive design feature. Also bear in mind the character of your neighborhood and region. Your fence may be beautiful in and of itself but look out of place in the neighborhood where you live. In addition to style, other considerations for making a fence harmonious with its surroundings include height, color, and material.

With that in mind, the possibilities for fence designs are limitless. Traditional options include wrought iron, wooden pickets (or palings), stockade, split-rail, double- and triple-bar ranch fences, and even chain-link fences. Within those basic styles are many variations. For example, iron can be wrought in fanciful designs from modern clean-cut to the fancy curlicues of the Romanesque style. Picket points can take the form of arrows, fleurs-de-lis, or any other design. The pickets can be spaced in a variety of ways. Stockade fences can be closed- or open-board, or have angled paling boards. To add extra charm and interest, a solid wooden fence can be topped with lattice. The main components of a

board fence are pickets, horizontal rails, a top rail to protect the end grain of the pickets from moisture, the kickboard, and the support post.

Fence Anatomy

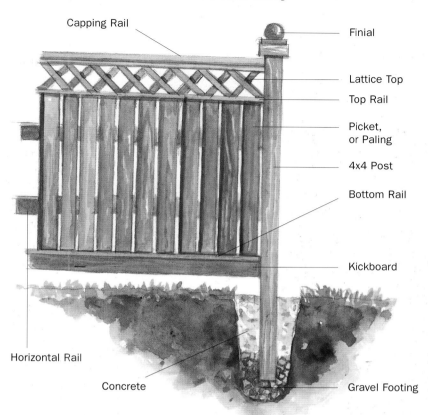

- Capping Rail
- Finial
- Lattice Top
- Top Rail
- Picket, or Paling
- 4x4 Post
- Bottom Rail
- Kickboard
- Horizontal Rail
- Concrete
- Gravel Footing

Building Fences on Slopes

A slope presents a special challenge for fence design as fence sections are generally straight and parallel with the ground. Three possible solutions include stepping the fence down the slope, allowing gaps to occur as the slope progresses downward; building the fence to follow the hillside so that the top of the fence is angled at the same degree as the slope; and custom-building the fence so each paling touches the ground, creating a wavy line across the fence top and bottom.

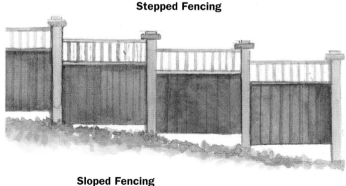

Stepped Fencing

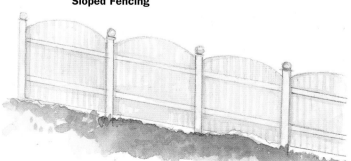

Sloped Fencing

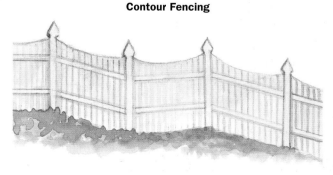

Contour Fencing

Designing a Gate

The garden gate meets many needs, from practical to aesthetic to psychological. It is a place of romance—where else would an ardent suitor steal a kiss or wait for a late-night romantic tryst but by the garden gate?

On the purely practical side, a gate allows passage to and between a front and back garden. This functional aspect is closely tied to a gate's symbolic meaning. A locked, solid gate set in a high wall or fence provides a sense of privacy, enclosure, and security. A gate with an open design, even when set into a solid wall, has a welcoming air about it.

An open gate beckons; a tall, solid gate adds mystery, suggesting the entrance to a secret garden. It can guide the eye to a focal point or add charm, intimacy, drama, or panache.

Gates, even short ones that stand only 3 feet high, serve as important transition points from the garden to the outside world or from one part of the garden to another. They define boundaries while linking the two areas together. For that reason, gates and pathways tend to go together in a landscape design.

Don't confine your gates to the perimeter of your property. Use them within your garden as well, to divide space visually and to mark the boundaries between different areas or garden rooms.

Gates come in a seemingly endless variety of styles and sizes. Massive wrought-iron gates mark the entrances to many large Victorian parks and private estates. Painted, slatted gates set in white picket fences tend to belong with small, intimate cottages or traditional country homes. The gate to a vegetable plot at the bottom of the garden might be rough-hewn, in keeping with an untreated wooden fence designed to keep out foraging wildlife. Japanese moon gates have cutout circles symbolic of the full moon. These circles may be open or filled in with a fretted design of wood or iron to add visual interest and increase security.

Formal front yards, above, require a distinctive-looking entrance. The metalwork shown here works well with the formal brick wall and posts topped with decorative urns.

Hanging a Gate

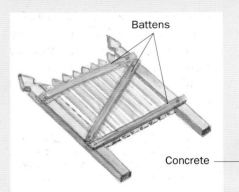

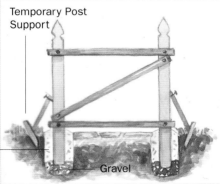

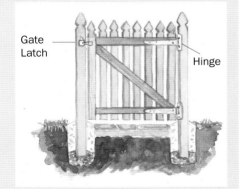

Step One: Space the Posts. Lay the gate on the ground, and position the posts on each side, allowing enough space for the hinges and latch. Make sure the tops and bottoms of the posts are even. Nail temporary battens onto the posts as shown. (The bottom batten should be at the bottom of the gate.)

Step Two: Set the Posts. Dig postholes. Set the posts on a gravel bed, making sure the bottom batten is 3 inches off the ground and that the posts are plumb and level. Secure the posts temporarily with braces and stakes, and then fill the holes with concrete. Check again for plumb and level before the concrete sets.

Step Three: Hang the Gate. When the concrete has completely cured, remove the braces and battens, attach the hinges (with the gate attached) to the post, and then attach the latch. The job is easier if one person holds the gate in position while the other person drills the screw holes and attaches the hardware.

Choose your gates to fit the style of your garden, but don't be afraid to have fun. For example, use a terra-cotta color to blend with a Spanish-style house, or set a light-colored gate set against a dark backdrop of heavy foliage.

Informal designs, above, put visitors at ease. This type of fence and gate is a good way to welcome visitors to a rear or side yard. It also helps support tall plants.

This distinctive gate, far left, is attached to a house of similar style. Look to the facade of the house and the landscaping style of the front yard when selecting a fence and gate style.

Gates, left, don't always need a fence. Here a decorative metal gate forms part of an arbor that is set in a hedge. This gate opens to a field beyond the garden.

The simple lattice design, above, of this fence is both appealing and practical. It not only encloses the garden but also serves as a trellis for climbing plants. A fence builder can create a custom design for you, or you can buy sections of fencing at home centers and fence speciality retailers.

This arbor and trellis, left, can serve as a destination in a large garden. You might find this type of structure in a front yard, but only in a very informal garden setting. Many large arbors contain a bench as part of the design. For interest, try placing a tall arbor in a rear or side yard that can be seen from the street.

Designing a Trellis

Trellises were a key element in Renaissance gardens and continued in popularity through the eighteenth century. Trellises enjoyed a resurgence of popularity in the late-nineteenth century, but never to the extent of earlier times. Trellises can lend an air of magic and mystery to a garden. Generally, we think of trellises in terms of the prefabricated sheets of diamond- or square-grid lattice and the fan-shaped supports for training climbers, both of which are readily available at home and garden centers in both wood and plastic. Lacking a pattern book, most gardeners are unaware of the incredible variety of designs, patterns, and optical illusions that can be created with trellises.

A trellis screen is a wonderfully airy way to achieve privacy or to partition off a space. The lath slats of lattice interrupt the view without totally obscuring it, creating the effect of a transparent curtain. Left bare, the pretty design of diamonds or squares makes an attractive effect. Covered in vines or decorated with hanging baskets, a trellis screen is enchanting.

The art of *treillage*, as the French call it, is not limited to screens. You can cover a bare wall or unattractive fence with a trellis pattern. Arrange the trellis pieces to create an optical illusion of an archway in the wall. Paint a realistic

Typical Trellis Designs

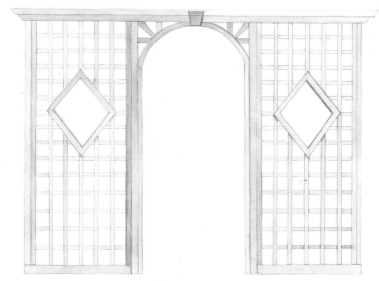

Trellis with Arched Entry

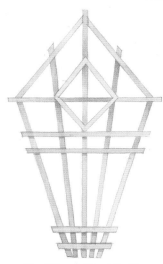

Traditional Wood Trellis

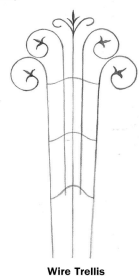

Wire Trellis

mural of the make-believe garden space beyond. Use a trellis for the walls of a gazebo to provide enclosure without being claustrophobic. Put a trellis screen with a pleasing, intricate pattern at the end of a walkway as a focal point.

Closely spaced horizontal slats, left, topped with decorative beams combine to form a handsome trellis and arbor that forms a border in this garden. The slats on the structure provide some privacy without impeding air flow into the garden. Decorative posts and beams add interest when seen from the street.

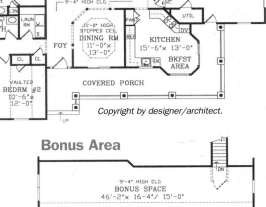

Copyright by designer/architect.

Images provided by designer/architect.

Rear Elevation

Plan #131047

Dimensions: 69'10" W x 51'8" D
Levels: 1
Square Footage: 1,793
Bedrooms: 3
Bathrooms: 2
Foundation: Crawl space, slab, or basement
Materials List Available: Yes
Price Category: D

Bonus Area

9'-4" HIGH CLG
BONUS SPACE
46'-2" x 16-4"/ 15'-0"

Plan #181085

Dimensions: 56'4" W x 44' D
Levels: 2
Square Footage: 2,183
Main Level Sq. Ft.: 1,232
Second Level Sq. Ft.: 951
Bedrooms: 3
Bathrooms: 2½
Foundation: Basement
Materials List Available: Yes
Price Category: D

Images provided by designer/architect.

Main Level Floor Plan

Upper Level Floor Plan

Copyright by designer/architect.

Plan #131030

Dimensions: 51' W x 41'10" D

Levels: 2

Square Footage: 2,470

Main Level Sq. Ft.: 1,290

Upper Level Sq. Ft.: 1,180

Bedrooms: 4

Bathrooms: 2½

Foundation: Crawl space, slab, basement, or walkout

Materials List Available: Yes

Price Category: F

This home, as shown in the photograph, may differ from the actual blueprints. For more detailed information, please check the floor plans carefully.

If high ceilings and spacious rooms make you happy, you'll love this gorgeous home.

Features:

- Family Room: An 18-ft. vaulted ceiling that's open to the balcony above, a corner fireplace, and a wall of windows make this room feel special.

- Dining Room: This formal room, which flows into the living room, also opens to the front porch and optional backyard deck.

- Kitchen: A bright breakfast room joins with this kitchen and opens to the backyard deck.

- Master Suite: You'll smile when you see the 11-ft. vaulted ceiling, stunning arched window, and two walk-in closets in the bedroom. A skylight lets natural light into the private bath, with its spa tub, separate shower, and dual-sink vanity.

- Bedrooms: To reach these three charming bedrooms, you'll admire the view into the family room below as you walk along the balcony hall.

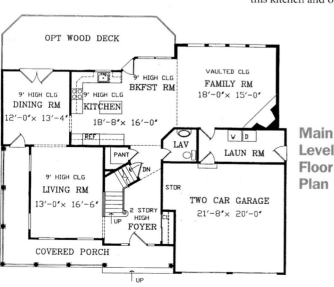

Main Level Floor Plan

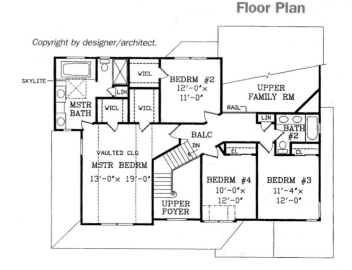

Upper Level Floor Plan

Copyright by designer/architect.

Plan #121047

Dimensions: 67'8" W x 57' D
Levels: 2
Square Footage: 3,072
Main Level Sq. Ft.: 2,116
Upper Level Sq. Ft.: 956
Bedrooms: 4
Bathrooms: 3½
Foundation: Slab
Materials List Available: Yes
Price Category: G

Images provided by designer/architect.

A long porch and a trio of roof dormers give this gracious home a sophisticated country look.

Features:

• Ceiling Height: 8 ft. unless otherwise noted.

• Balcony: This balcony overlooks the entry and the staircase hall.

• Dining Room: Columns and a cased opening lend elegance, making this the perfect venue for stylish dinner parties.

• Family Room: A cathedral ceiling gives this room a light and airy feel. The handsome fireplace framed by windows is sure to become a favorite family gathering place.

• Master Bedroom: This architecturally distinctive bedroom features a bayed sitting area and a tray ceiling.

• Bedrooms: One of the bedrooms enjoys a private bath, making it a perfect guest room. Other bedrooms feature walk-in closets.

Main Level Floor Plan

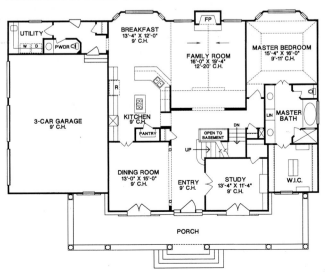

Upper Level Floor Plan

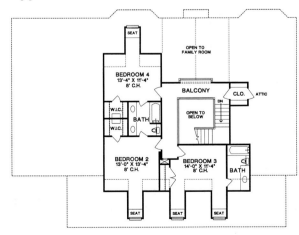

Copyright by designer/architect.

Plan #131002

Dimensions: 70'1" W x 60'7" D
Levels: 1
Square Footage: 1,709
Bedrooms: 3
Bathrooms: 2½
Foundation: Crawl space, slab, or basement
Materials List Available: Yes
Price Category: D

Images provided by designer/architect.

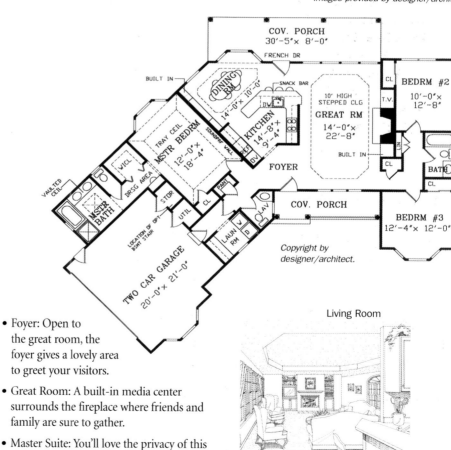

Rear View

Living Room

You'll love the way this angled ranch brings out the best in a corner lot or on a slope.

Features:

- Ceiling Height: 8 ft.

- Front Porch: Hang baskets of plants from the roof of this porch, which is just the right size for a couple of rockers and a side table.

- Dining Room: Well-placed windows flood this room with sunlight during the day and a built-in cabinet gives ample storage space for all your china, linens, and collectables.

- Foyer: Open to the great room, the foyer gives a lovely area to greet your visitors.

- Great Room: A built-in media center surrounds the fireplace where friends and family are sure to gather.

- Master Suite: You'll love the privacy of this somewhat isolated but easily accessed room. Decorate to show off the large bay window and tray ceiling, and enjoy the luxury of a compartmented bathroom.

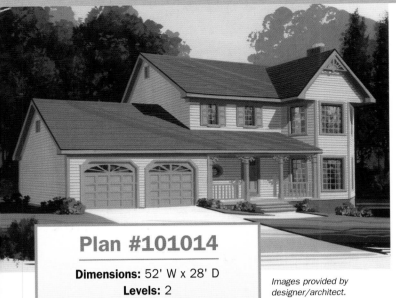

Plan #101014

Dimensions: 52' W x 28' D

Levels: 2

Square Footage: 1,598

Main Level Sq. Ft.: 812

Upper Level Sq. Ft.: 786

Bedrooms: 3

Bathrooms: 2½

Foundation: Slab, crawl space

Materials List Available: No

Price Category: C

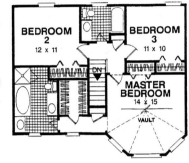

Main Level Floor Plan

DECK

STORAGE

KITCHEN 10 x 12

BREAKFAST 9 x 10

DINING 12 x 11

W D

GARAGE 20 x 21

UP

FAMILY ROOM 14 x 16

28

52

Images provided by designer/architect.

BEDROOM 2 12 x 11

BEDROOM 3 11 x 10

DN

MASTER BEDROOM 14 x 15

VAULT

Upper Level Floor Plan

Copyright by designer/architect.

Plan #181034

Dimensions: 60' W x 44' D

Levels: 2

Square Footage: 2,687

Main Level Sq. Ft.: 1,297

Upper Level Sq. Ft.: 1,390

Bedrooms: 3

Bathrooms: 2½

Foundation: Full basement

Materials List Available: Yes

Price Category: F

Images provided by designer/architect.

CAD FILE AVAILABLE

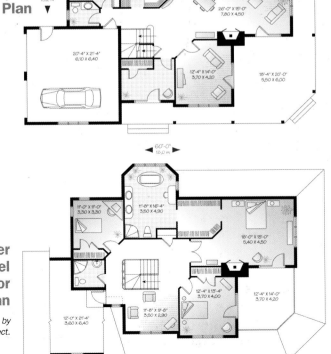

Main Level Floor Plan

44'-0"
13.2 m

11'-8" X 16'-4"
3.50 X 4.90

26'-0" X 15'-0"
7.80 X 4.50

20'-4" X 21'-4"
6.10 X 6.40

12'-4" X 14'-0"
3.70 X 4.20

18'-0" X 20'-0"
5.50 X 6.00

60'-0"
18.0 m

Upper Level Floor Plan

11'-0" X 11'-0"
3.30 X 3.30

11'-8" X 16'-4"
3.50 X 4.90

18'-0" X 15'-0"
5.40 X 4.50

12'-0" X 21'-4"
3.60 X 6.40

12'-4" X 13'-4"
3.70 X 4.00

12'-4" X 14'-0"
3.70 X 4.20

11'-8" X 9'-6"
3.50 X 2.90

Copyright by designer/architect.

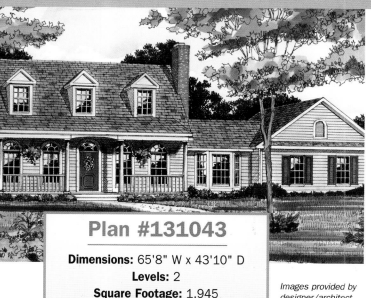

Plan #131043

Dimensions: 65'8" W x 43'10" D
Levels: 2
Square Footage: 1,945
Main Level Sq. Ft.: 1,375
Upper Level Sq. Ft.: 570
Bedrooms: 3
Bathrooms: 2½
Foundation: Crawl space, slab, or basement
Materials List Available: Yes
Price Category: D

Images provided by designer/architect.

Main Level Floor Plan

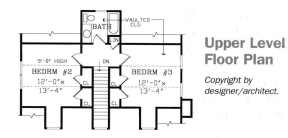

Upper Level Floor Plan

Copyright by designer/architect.

Plan #131035

Dimensions: 65'4" W x 45'10" D
Levels: 1
Square Footage: 1,892
Bedrooms: 3
Bathrooms: 2½
Foundation: Crawl space, slab, or basement
Materials List Available: Yes
Price Category: D

Images provided by designer/architect.

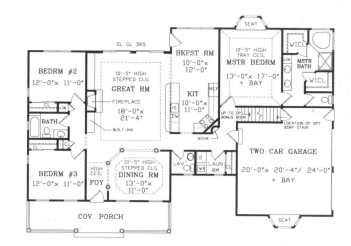

Rear Elevation

Bonus Area

Copyright by designer/architect.

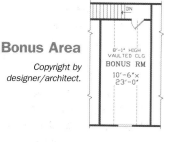

Plan #181151

Dimensions: 50' W x 46' D
Levels: 2
Square Footage: 2,283
Main Level Sq. Ft.: 1,274
Second Level Sq. Ft.: 1,009
Bedrooms: 3
Bathrooms: 2½
Foundation: Basement
Materials List Available: Yes
Price Category: E

Multiple porches, stately columns, and arched multi-paned windows adorn this country home.

CAD FILE AVAILABLE

Features:

- Ceiling Height: 8 ft. unless otherwise noted.

- Great Room: The second-floor mezzanine overlooks this great room. With its soaring ceiling, this dramatic room is the centerpiece of a spacious and flowing design that is just as suited to entertaining as it is to family life.

- Dining Area: Guests will naturally flow into this dining area when it is time to eat. After dinner they can step directly out onto the porch to enjoy coffee and dessert when the weather is fair.

- Kitchen: This efficient and well-designed kitchen has double sinks and offers a separate eating area for those impromptu family meals.

- Master Bedroom: This master retreat has a walk-in closet and its own sumptuous bath.

- Home Office: Whether you work at home or just need a place for the family computer and keeping track of family finances, this home office fills the bill.

Main Level Floor Plan

Upper Level Floor Plan

Plan #121083

Dimensions: 72' W x 45'4" D
Levels: 2
Square Footage: 2,695
Main Level Sq. Ft.: 1,881
Upper Level Sq. Ft.: 814
Bedrooms: 4
Bathrooms: 3½
Foundation: Basement
Materials List Available: Yes
Price Category: F

Images provided by designer/architect.

You'll love this home for its soaring entryway ceiling and well-designed layout.

Features:

- **Entry:** A balcony from the upper level looks down into this two-story, which features a decorative plant shelf.

- **Great Room:** Comfort is guaranteed in this large room, with its built-in bookcases framing a lovely fireplace and trio of transom-topped windows along one wall.

- **Living Room:** Save both this formal room and the formal dining room, both of which flank the entry, for guests and special occasions.

- **Kitchen:** This convenient work space includes a gazebo-shaped breakfast area where friends and family will gather at any time of day.

Main Level Floor Plan

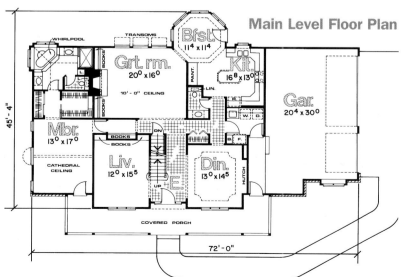

Upper Level Floor Plan

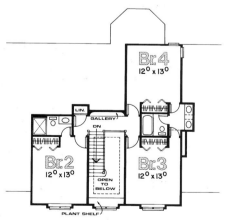

Copyright by designer/architect.

Images provided by designer/architect.

Plan #131001

Dimensions: 72'4" W x 32'4" D
Levels: 1
Square Footage: 1,615
Bedrooms: 3
Bathrooms: 2
Foundation: Crawl space, slab, basement, or walkout
Materials List Available: Yes
Price Category: D

Cathedral ceilings and illuminating skylights add drama and beauty to this practical ranch house.

Features:

- Ceiling Height: 8 ft.

- Front Porch: Watch the rain in comfort from the covered front porch.

- Foyer: The stone-tiled foyer flows into the living areas.

- Living Room: Oriented towards the front of the house, the living room opens to the dining room and shares a lovely three-sided fireplace with the family room.

- Family Room: Conveniently located to share the fireplace with the living room, this room is bright and cheery thanks to its skylights as well as the sliding glass doors that open onto the rear patio.

- Kitchen: An island makes this sunny room both efficient and attractive.

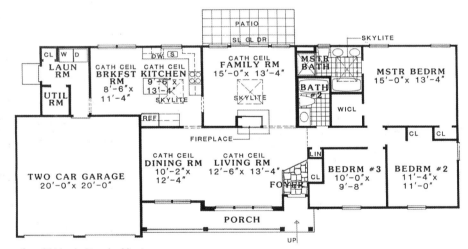

Copyright by designer/architect.

- Breakfast Nook: Located just off the kitchen, this area can serve double-duty as a spot for kitchen visitors to sit.

- Dining Room: The open design between the dining and living rooms adds to the spacious feeling that the cathedral ceiling creates in this area.

- Laundry Room: This area opens from the kitchen for convenience.

- Master Suite: A walk-in closet makes this room practical, but the master bathroom with a skylight, dual-sink vanity, soaking tub, and separate shower makes it luxurious.

- Bedrooms: The two additional bedrooms share a bathroom.

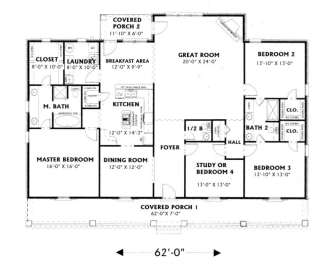

Copyright by designer/architect.

Images provided by designer/architect.

Plan #191027

Dimensions: 62' W x 42' D
Levels: 1
Square Footage: 2,354
Bedrooms: 4
Bathrooms: 2½
Foundation: Crawl space
Materials List Available: No
Price Category: E

Plan #201025

Dimensions: 62' W x 46' D
Levels: 1
Square Footage: 1,379
Bedrooms: 3
Bathrooms: 2
Foundation: Crawl space, slab
Materials List Available: Yes
Price Category: B

Images provided by designer/architect.

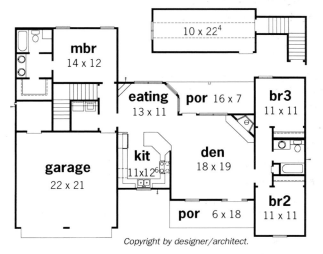

Copyright by designer/architect.

SMARTtip

Arrangement of Mantle Objects

On a fireplace mantle, group objects of different heights for visual interest—a straight line can be boring. Raise one or two pieces with a small pedestal or stand, and stagger the pieces from back to front. If you have three or more objects, make a triangle or overlapping triangles.

Plan #131051

Dimensions: 64'4" W x 53'4" D
Levels: 2
Square Footage: 2,431
Main Level Sq. Ft.: 1,293
Upper Level Sq. Ft.: 1,138
Bedrooms: 4
Bathrooms: 2½
Foundation: Crawl space, slab, or basement
Materials List Available: Yes
Price Category: F

Gracious and charming with a wraparound front porch and a backyard terrace, this home also has a ready-to-finish third floor all-purpose room and a full bath.

Features:

- Main Level Ceiling Height: 8 ft.

- Family Room: A comfortable space for the entire family to gather, this delightful room can be warmed by a heat-circulating fireplace.

- Dining Room: A cozy dinette boasts a sliding glass door with access to a gorgeous backyard terrace with an optional calm reflecting pool.

- Kitchen: Adjoining the dining area, the kitchen offers plenty of storage and counter space. The laundry room and half-bath are nearby for convenience.

- Garage: The garage is tucked way back to keep it from intruding into the traditional facade.

Main Level Floor Plan

Images provided by designer/architect.

This home, as shown in the photograph, may differ from the actual blueprints. For more detailed information, please check the floor plans carefully.

Rear Elevation

Upper Level Floor Plan

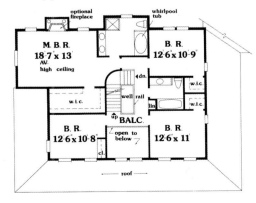

Optional 3rd Level Floor Plan

Copyright by designer/architect.

Plan #151006

Dimensions: 54'2" W x 52'10" D

Levels: 1

Square Footage: 1,758

Bedrooms: 3

Bathrooms: 2

Foundation: Crawl space, slab, basement, or walkout

CompleteCost List Available: Yes

Price Category: C

Images provided by designer/architect.

This home, as shown in the photograph, may differ from the actual blueprints. For more detailed information, please check the floor plans carefully.

You'll love the expansive feeling of the open, spacious rooms in this home and wonder how you ever did without the amenities it offers.

Features:

- **Foyer:** A foyer with a 10-ft. ceiling provides the perfect transition between the columned front porch and the interior of this home.

- **Great Room:** A fireplace, 9-ft. boxed ceiling, and access to the rear grilling porch and back yard make this room the heart of the home.

- **Dining Room:** The 10-ft. ceiling and boxed columns provide a touch of formality.

- **Kitchen:** Convenience marks this well-designed kitchen that opens to the breakfast room.

- **Master Suite:** With a 9-ft. boxed ceiling, this elegant room will be your favorite retreat. The bath has a whirlpool tub with glass blocks, a shower, and double vanities.

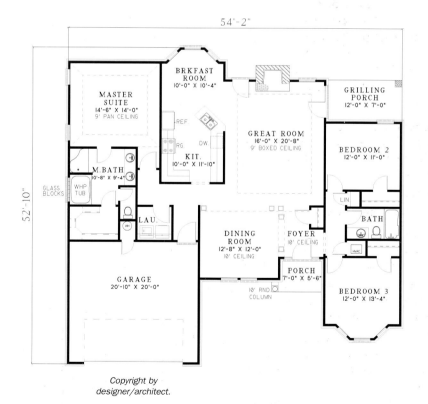

Copyright by designer/architect.

Plan #121014

Dimensions: 52' W x 47'4" D

Levels: 2

Square Footage: 1,869

Main Level Sq. Ft.: 1,421

Upper Level Sq. Ft.: 448

Bedrooms: 3

Bathrooms: 2½

Foundation: Basement

Materials List Available: Yes

Price Category: D

Images provided by designer/architect.

This compact home is packed with all the amenities you'll need for a gracious lifestyle.

Features:

- Ceiling Height: 8 ft. except as noted.
- Great Room: A soaring ceiling and six tall transom-topped windows make this a light and airy spot for entertaining.
- Formal Dining Room: This elegant room is ideal for entertaining dinner guests.

- Breakfast Area: This sunny area shares a see-through fireplace with the great room. It's the perfect place to start the day.
- Master Suite: Here are all the features you expect to find in large luxury homes. Wake up to tall, sloped ceilings, and enjoy the corner whirlpool, separate shower, and vanity. A large walk-in closet provides plenty of wardrobe storage.
- Attached Garage: The garage provides two bays of parking plus plenty of storage space.

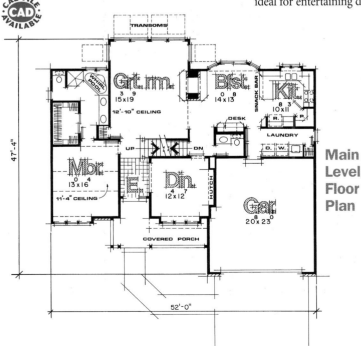

Main Level Floor Plan

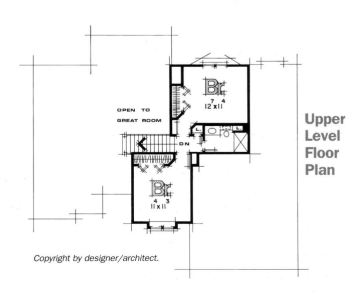

Upper Level Floor Plan

Copyright by designer/architect.

Plan #121006

Dimensions: 46' W x 58' D
Levels: 1
Square Footage: 1,762
Bedrooms: 3
Bathrooms: 2
Foundation: Slab
Materials List Available: Yes
Price Category: C

The entry has a trio of arched openings that leads you to other areas of this amenity-packed home.

Features:

- Ceiling Height: 8 ft. except as noted.

- Eating Bar: Conveniently located between the kitchen and family room, this is sure to be a favorite spot for informal entertaining and family gatherings.

- Family room: A wall of windows, a fireplace, and a vaulted ceiling stretching to 11 ft. work together to make this a bright and warm room.

- Kitchen: There's no shortage of counter space in this well-planned kitchen that features a center island in addition to the eating bar.

- Master Suite: Luxuriate at the end of the day in this large bedroom with its decorative tray ceiling and walk-in closet. Enjoy the pampering bath with its sunlit corner whirlpool flanked by vanities.

- Garage: Two bays provide room for cars and plenty of storage as well.

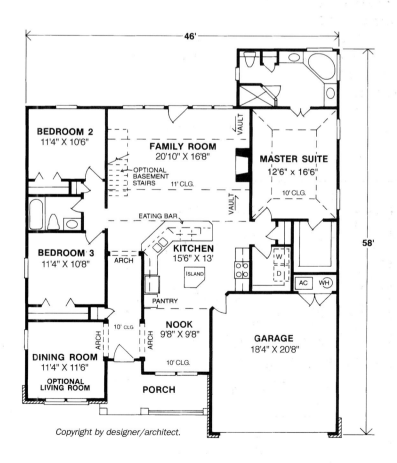

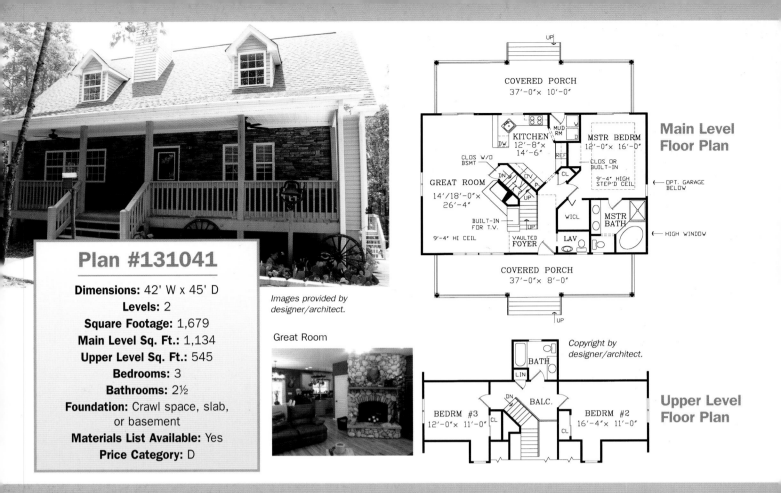

Plan #131041

Dimensions: 42' W x 45' D
Levels: 2
Square Footage: 1,679
Main Level Sq. Ft.: 1,134
Upper Level Sq. Ft.: 545
Bedrooms: 3
Bathrooms: 2½
Foundation: Crawl space, slab, or basement
Materials List Available: Yes
Price Category: D

Images provided by designer/architect.

Great Room

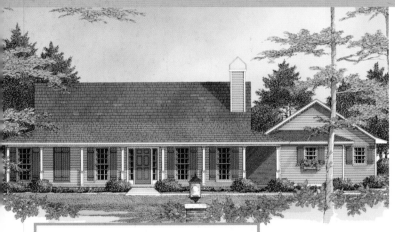

Main Level Floor Plan

COVERED PORCH
37'-0"x 10'-0"

KITCHEN
12'-8"x
14'-6"

MUD RM

MSTR BEDRM
12'-0"x 16'-0"

CLOS W/O BSMT

DW

REF

CLOS OR BUILT-IN

9'-4" HIGH STEP'D CEIL

← OPT. GARAGE BELOW

GREAT ROOM
14'/18'-0"x
26'-4"

UP

CL

WICL

MSTR BATH

BUILT-IN FOR T.V.

LAV

← HIGH WINDOW

9'-4" HI CEIL

VAULTED FOYER

COVERED PORCH
37'-0"x 8'-0"

UP

Copyright by designer/architect.

Upper Level Floor Plan

BATH

LIN

BEDRM #3
12'-0"x 11'-0"

CL

DN

BALC.

BEDRM #2
16'-4"x 11'-0"

CL

Plan #251004

Dimensions: 50'9" W x 42'1" D
Levels: 1
Square Footage: 1,550
Bedrooms: 3
Bathrooms: 2
Foundation: Crawl space, slab
Materials List Available: Yes
Price Category: C

Images provided by designer/architect.

CAD FILE AVAILABLE

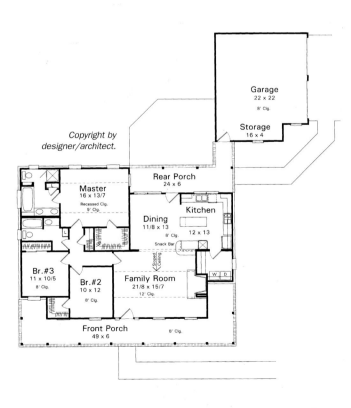

Copyright by designer/architect.

Garage
22 x 22
8' Clg.

Storage
16 x 4

Rear Porch
24 x 6

Master
16 x 13/7
Recessed Clg.
9' Clg.

Kitchen

Dining
11/8 x 13
8' Clg.

12 x 13

Snack Bar

Br.#3
11 x 10/5
8' Clg.

Br.#2
10 x 12
8' Clg.

Family Room
21/8 x 15/7
12' Clg.

Sloped Ceiling

W D

Front Porch
49 x 6
8' Clg.

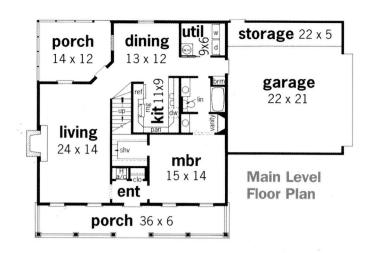

Main Level
Floor Plan

Images provided by designer/architect.

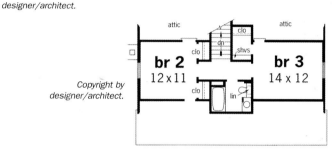

Upper Level
Floor Plan

Copyright by designer/architect.

Plan #211069

Dimensions: 58' W x 42' D
Levels: 1½
Square Footage: 1,600
Main Level Sq. Ft.: 1,136
Upper Level Sq. Ft.: 464
Bedrooms: 3
Bathrooms: 2
Foundation: Crawl space
Materials List Available: Yes
Price Category: C

Main Level
Floor Plan

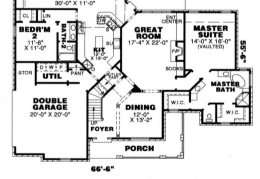

Images provided by designer/architect.

Upper Level
Floor Plan

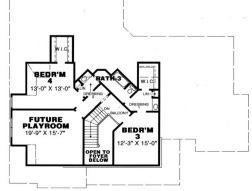

Copyright by designer/architect.

Plan #241014

Dimensions: 66'6" W x 55'6" D
Levels: 2
Square Footage: 3,046
Main Level Sq. Ft.: 2,292
Upper Level Sq. Ft.: 754
Bedrooms: 4
Bathrooms: 3
Foundation: Slab
Materials List Available: No
Price Category: G

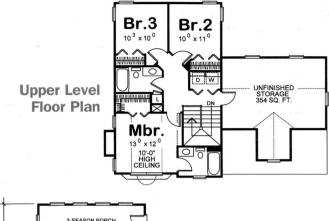

Upper Level Floor Plan

Br.3
10³ x 10⁰

Br.2
10⁰ x 11⁰

UNFINISHED STORAGE 354 SQ. FT.

Mbr.
13⁰ x 12⁰
10'-0" HIGH CEILING

DN

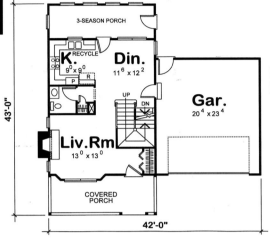

Plan #121036

Dimensions: 42' W x 43' D
Levels: 2
Square Footage: 1,297
Main Level Sq. Ft.: 603
Upper Level Sq. Ft.: 694
Bedrooms: 3
Bathrooms: 2½
Foundation: Basement
Materials List Available: Yes
Price Category: B

Images provided by designer/architect.

CAD FILE AVAILABLE

Main Level Floor Plan

Copyright by designer/architect.

3-SEASON PORCH

K.
9⁰ x 9⁰

RECYCLE

Din.
11⁶ x 12²

Gar.
20⁴ x 23⁴

UP

DN

Liv.Rm
13⁰ x 13⁰

COVERED PORCH

43'-0"

42'-0"

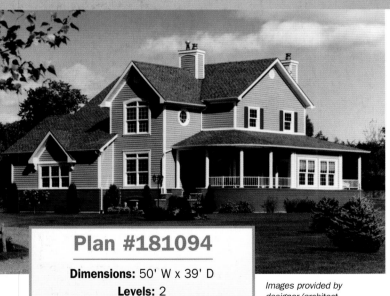

Main Level Floor Plan

39'-0"
11,7 m

50'-0"
15,0 m

Plan #181094

Dimensions: 50' W x 39' D
Levels: 2
Square Footage: 2,099
Main Level Sq. Ft.: 1,060
Upper Level Sq. Ft.: 1,039
Bedrooms: 4
Bathrooms: 2½
Foundation: Basement
Materials List Available: Yes
Price Category: D

Images provided by designer/architect.

CAD FILE AVAILABLE

Upper Level Floor Plan

Copyright by designer/architect.

Plan #131021

Dimensions: 60' W x 52'4" D
Levels: 2
Square Footage: 3,110
Main Level Sq. Ft.: 1,818
Upper Level Sq. Ft.: 1,292
Bedrooms: 5
Bathrooms: 2½
Foundation: Crawl space, slab, or basement
Materials List Available: Yes
Price Category: H

This home, as shown in the photograph, may differ from the actual blueprints. For more detailed information, please check the floor plans carefully.

Images provided by designer/architect.

Amenities abound in this luxurious two-story beauty with a cozy gazebo on one corner of the spectacular wraparound front porch. Comfort, functionality, and spaciousness characterize this home.

Features:

• Ceiling Height: 8 ft.

• Foyer: This two-story high foyer is breathtaking.

• Family Room: Roomy with open views of the kitchen, the family room has a vaulted ceiling and boasts a functional fireplace and a built-in entertainment center.

• Dining Room: Formal yet comfortable, this spacious dining room is perfect for entertaining family and friends.

• Kitchen: Perfectly located with access to a breakfast room and the family room, this U-shaped kitchen with large center island is charming as well as efficient.

• Master Suite: Enjoy this sizable room with a vaulted ceiling, two large walk-in closets, and a lovely compartmented bath.

Copyright by designer/architect.

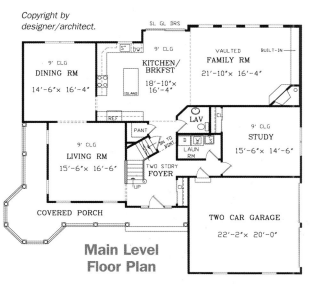

Main Level Floor Plan

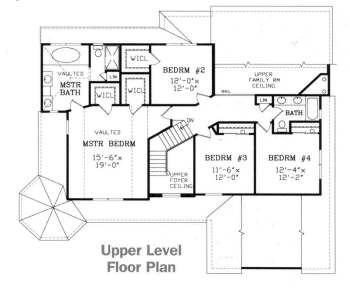

Upper Level Floor Plan

Plan #121037

Dimensions: 46' W x 47'10" D

Levels: 2

Square Footage: 2,292

Main Level Sq. Ft.: 1,158

Upper Level Sq. Ft.: 1,134

Bedrooms: 4

Bathrooms: 2½

Foundation: Basement

Materials List Available: Yes

Price Category: E

CAD FILE AVAILABLE

Images provided by designer/architect.

This convenient and comfortable home is filled with architectural features that set it apart.

Features:

- Ceiling Height: 8 ft. unless otherwise noted.

- Foyer: You'll know you have arrived when you enter this two-story area highlighted by a decorative plant shelf and a balcony.

- Great Room: Just beyond the entry is the great room where the warmth of the two-sided fireplace will attract family and friends to gather. A bay window offers a more intimate place to sit and converse.

- Hearth Room: At the other side of the fireplace, the hearth offers a cozy spot for smaller gatherings or a place to sit alone and enjoy a book by the fire.

- Breakfast Area: With sunlight streaming into its bay window, the breakfast area offers the perfect spot for informal family meals.

- Master Suite: This private retreat is made more convenient by a walk-in closet. It features its own tub and shower.

Main Level Floor Plan

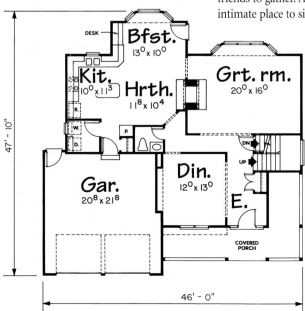

Upper Level Floor Plan

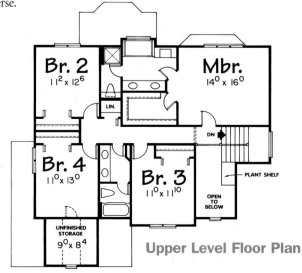

Copyright by designer/architect.

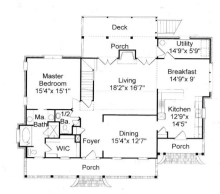

Main Level Floor Plan

Deck

Porch

Utility
14'9"x 5'9"

Master Bedroom
15'4"x 15'1"

Living
18'2"x 16'7"

Breakfast
14'9"x 9'

Kitchen
12'9"x 14'5"

Ma. Bath

1/2 Ba.

Dining
15'4"x 12'7"

WIC

Foyer

Porch

Porch

Copyright by designer/architect.

Plan #111009

Dimensions: 56' W x 49' D
Levels: 2
Square Footage: 2,514
Main Level Sq. Ft.: 1,630
Upper Level Sq. Ft.: 884
Bedrooms: 4
Bathrooms: 3½
Foundation: Basement
Materials List Available: No
Price Category: E

Upper Level Floor Plan

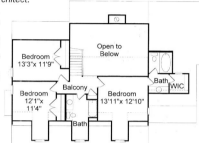

Bedroom
13'3"x 11'9"

Open to Below

Bath

Bedroom
12'1"x 11'4"

Balcony

Bedroom
13'11"x 12'10"

WIC

Bath

Bath

Basement Level Floor Plan

Future Gameroom
14'5"x 21'7"

Two-Car Garage

Plan #181078

Dimensions: 58' W x 40' D
Levels: 2
Square Footage: 2,292
Main Level Sq. Ft.: 1,266
Upper Level Sq. Ft.: 1,026
Bedrooms: 4
Bathrooms: 2½
Foundation: Full basement
Materials List Available: Yes
Price Category: E

CAD FILE AVAILABLE

40'-0"
12,0 m

12'-0" X 12'-4"
3,60 X 3,70

18'-4" X 14'-0"
5,50 X 4,20

17'-0" X 12'-0"
5,10 X 3,60

11'-0" X 13'-4"
3,30 X 4,00

20'-0" X 20'-0"
6,00 X 6,00

58'-0"
17,4 m

Main Level Floor Plan

Upper Level Floor Plan

17'-0" X 14'-0"
5,10 X 4,20

11'-0" X 10'-8"
3,30 X 3,20

11'-0" X 13'-4"
3,30 X 4,00

Copyright by designer/architect.

Plan #211127

Dimensions: 94' W x 71' D
Levels: 2
Square Footage: 5,474
Main Level Sq. Ft.: 4,193
Upper Level Sq. Ft.: 1,281
Bedrooms: 4
Bathrooms: 4 full, 2 half
Foundation: Slab, crawl space
Materials List Available: No
Price Category: I

Images provided by designer/architect.

This is a truly grand southern-style home, with stately columns and eye-pleasing symmetry.

Features:

• Ceiling Height: 12 ft.

• Foyer: A grand home warrants a grand entry, and here it is. The graceful curved staircase will impress your guests as they move from this foyer to the fireplace.

• Family Room: Great for entertaining, this family room features a vaulted ceiling. A handsome fireplace adds warmth and ambiance.

• Den: Another fireplace enhances this smaller and cozier den. Here the kids can play, supervised by the family chef working in the adjacent kitchen.

• Verandas: As is fitting for a gracious southern home, you'll find verandas at front and rear.

• Master Suite: A romantic third fireplace is found in this sprawling master bedroom. The master bath provides the utmost in privacy and organization.

Main Level Floor Plan

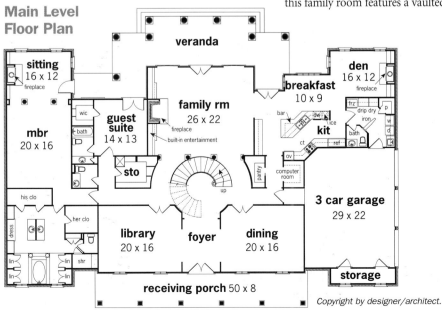

Copyright by designer/architect.

Upper Level Floor Plan

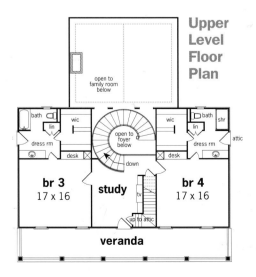

Rear View

Great Room

Kitchen

Dining Room

Master Bedroom

Master Bath

Plan #131004

Dimensions: 59'4" W x 35'8" D

Levels: 1

Square Footage: 1,097

Bedrooms: 3

Bathrooms: 2

Foundation: Crawl space, slab, or basement

Materials List Available: Yes

Price Category: B

Images provided by designer/architect.

This home, as shown in the photograph, may differ from the actual blueprints. For more detailed information, please check the floor plans carefully.

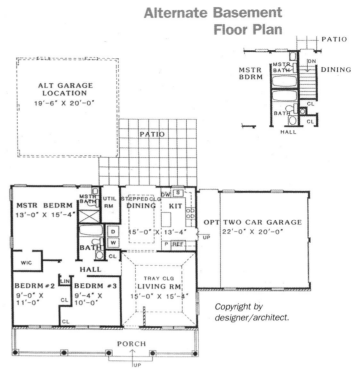

Alternate Basement Floor Plan

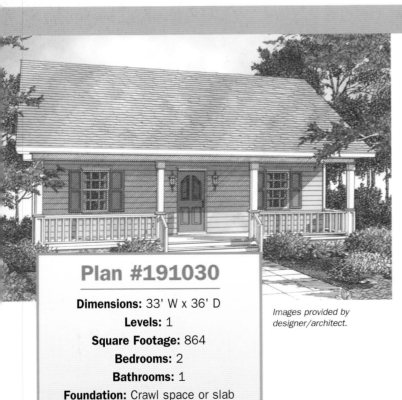

Plan #191030

Dimensions: 33' W x 36' D

Levels: 1

Square Footage: 864

Bedrooms: 2

Bathrooms: 1

Foundation: Crawl space or slab

Materials List Available: No

Price Category: A

Images provided by designer/architect.

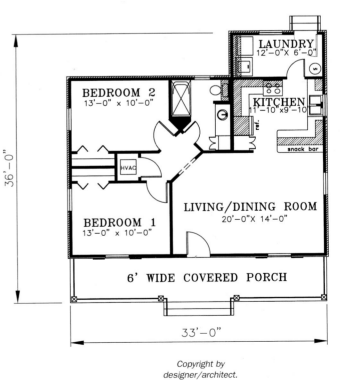

Main Level Floor Plan

Plan #181081

Dimensions: 58' W x 33' D

Levels: 2

Square Footage: 2,350

Main Level Sq. Ft.: 1,107

Second Level Sq. Ft.: 1,243

Bedrooms: 3

Bathrooms: 2½

Foundation: Basement

Materials List Available: Yes

Price Category: E

Images provided by designer/architect.

CAD FILE AVAILABLE

Upper Level Floor Plan

Copyright by designer/architect.

Plan #181120

Dimensions: 32' W x 40' D

Levels: 2

Square Footage: 1,480

Main Level Sq. Ft.: 1,024

Second Level Sq. Ft.: 456

Bedrooms: 2

Bathrooms: 2

Foundation: Basement

Materials List Available: Yes

Price Category: B

Images provided by designer/architect.

CAD FILE AVAILABLE

Main Level Floor Plan

Upper Level Floor Plan

Copyright by designer/architect.

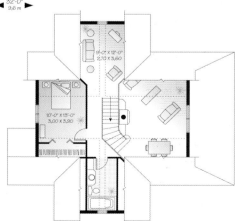

Plan #281004

Dimensions: 36' W x 50' D
Levels: 2
Square Footage: 1,426
Main Level Sq. Ft.: 1,086
Upper Level Sq. Ft.: 340
Bedrooms: 3
Bathrooms: 2½
Foundation: Walkout basement
Materials List Available: Yes
Price Category: B

Images provided by designer/architect.

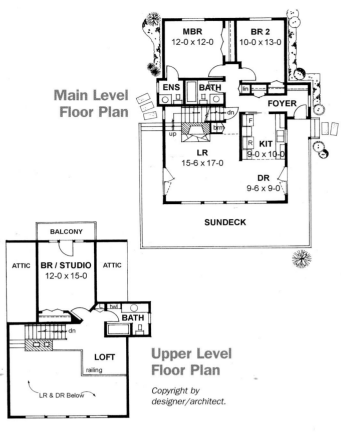

Main Level Floor Plan

MBR 12-0 x 12-0 · BR 2 10-0 x 13-0 · ENS · BATH · lin · FOYER · dn · brm · up · F · R · KIT 9-0 x 10-0 · LR 15-6 x 17-0 · DR 9-6 x 9-0 · SUNDECK

BALCONY · ATTIC · BR / STUDIO 12-0 x 15-0 · ATTIC · twl · BATH · dn · LOFT · railing · LR & DR Below

Upper Level Floor Plan

Copyright by designer/architect.

Plan #321009

Dimensions: 55'8" W x 46'4" D
Levels: 1
Square Footage: 2,295
Bedrooms: 3
Bathrooms: 2
Foundation: Basement
Materials List Available: Yes
Price Category: E

Images provided by designer/architect.

Rear View

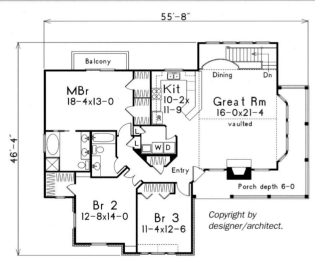

55'-8"

46'-4"

Balcony · MBr 18-4x13-0 · Kit 10-2x 11-9 · Dining · Dn · Great Rm 16-0x21-4 vaulted · W D · Entry · Br 2 12-8x14-0 · Br 3 11-4x12-6 · Porch depth 6-0

Copyright by designer/architect.

Optional Basement Level Floor Plan

Up · Garage 22-4x26-8 · Family 15-6x20-8

Plan #131056

Dimensions: 40' W x 54' D
Levels: 1.5
Square Footage: 1,396
Main Level Sq. Ft.: 964
Upper Level Sq. Ft.: 432
Bedrooms: 3
Bathrooms: 2
Foundation: Slab or basement
Materials List Available: Yes
Price Category: C

This ruggedly handsome home is a true A-frame. The elegance of the roof virtually meeting the ground and the use of rugged stone veneer and log-cabin siding make it stand out.

Features:

- Living Room: This area is the interior highlight of the home. The large, exciting space features a soaring ceiling, a massive fireplace, and a magnificent window wall to capture a view.

- Side Porch: The secondary entry from this side porch leads to a center hall that provides direct access to the first floor's two bedrooms, bathroom, kitchen, and living room.

- Kitchen: This kitchen is extremely efficient and includes a snack bar and access to the screened porch.

- Loft Area: A spiral stairway leads from the living room to this second-floor loft, which overlooks the living room. The area can also double as an extra sleeping room.

Images provided by designer/architect.

Main Level Floor Plan

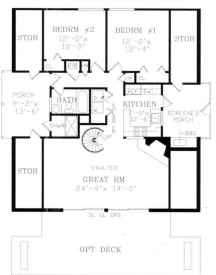

Upper Level Floor Plan

Copyright by designer/architect

Rear View

Great Room

Plan #151529

Dimensions: 43' W x 66'6" D
Levels: 1
Square Footage: 1,474
Bedrooms: 2
Bathrooms: 2
Foundation: Crawl space or slab
CompleteCost List Available: Yes
Price Category: B

This elegant design is reflective of the Arts and Crafts era. Copper roofing and carriage style garage doors warmly welcome guests into this split-bedroom plan.

Features:

- Great Room: With access to the grilling porch as a bonus, this large gathering area features a 10-ft.-high ceiling and a beautiful fireplace.

- Kitchen: This fully equipped island kitchen has a raised bar and a built-in pantry. The area is open to the great room and dining room, giving an open and airy feeling to the home.

- Master Suite: Located on the opposite side of the home from the secondary bedroom, this retreat offers a large sleeping area and two large closets. The master bath features a spa tub, a separate shower, and dual vanities.

- Bedroom: This secondary bedroom has a large closet and access to the full bathroom in the hallway.

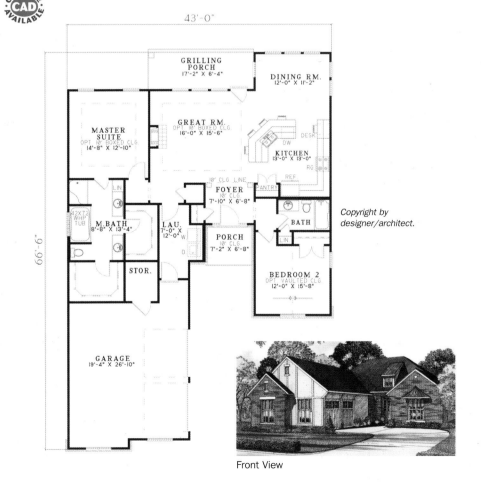

Front View

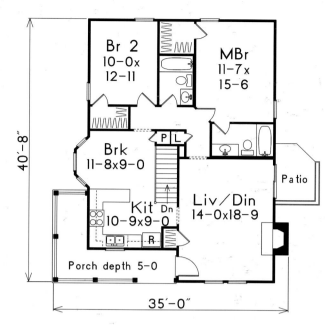

Images provided by designer/architect.

Plan #321040

Dimensions: 35' W x 40'8" D

Levels: 1

Square Footage: 1,084

Bedrooms: 2

Bathrooms: 2

Foundation: Basement

Materials List Available: Yes

Price Category: B

Br 2
10-0x
12-11

MBr
11-7 x
15-6

Brk
11-8x9-0

PL

Patio

Kit
10-9x9-0

Dn

R

Liv/Din
14-0x18-9

40'-8"

35'-0"

Porch depth 5-0

Copyright by designer/architect.

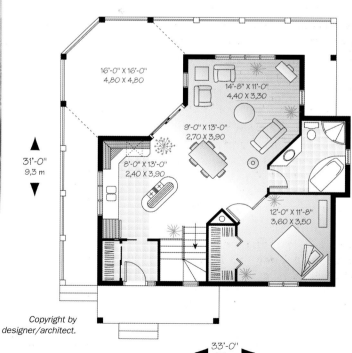

Images provided by designer/architect.

CAD FILE AVAILABLE

Plan #181145

Dimensions: 33' W x 31' D

Levels: 1

Square Footage: 840

Bedrooms: 1

Bathrooms: 1

Foundation: Full basement with walkout

Materials List Available: Yes

Price Category: A

16'-0" X 16'-0"
4,80 X 4,80

14'-8" X 11'-0"
4,40 X 3,30

9'-0" X 13'-0"
2,70 X 3,90

8'-0" X 13'-0"
2,40 X 3,90

12'-0" X 11'-8"
3,60 X 3,50

31'-0"
9,3 m

33'-0"
9,9 m

Copyright by designer/architect.

Plan #271053

Dimensions: 70' W x 34' D
Levels: 2
Square Footage: 2,458
Main Level Sq. Ft.: 1,067
Upper Level Sq. Ft.: 346
Bedrooms: 3
Bathrooms: 2½
Foundation: Crawl space or daylight basement
Materials List Available: No
Price Category: E

The octagonal shape and window-filled walls of this home create a powerful interior packed with panoramic views.

Features:

- Great Room: Straight back from the angled entry, this room is brightened by sunlight through windows and sliding glass doors. Beyond the doors, a huge wraparound deck offers plenty of space for tanning or relaxing. A spiral staircase adds visual interest.

- Kitchen: This efficient space includes a convenient pantry.

- Master Suite: On the upper level, this romantic master suite overlooks the great room below. Several windows provide scenic outdoor views. A walk-in closet and a private bath round out this secluded haven.

- Basement: The optional basement includes a recreation room, as well as an extra bedroom and bath.

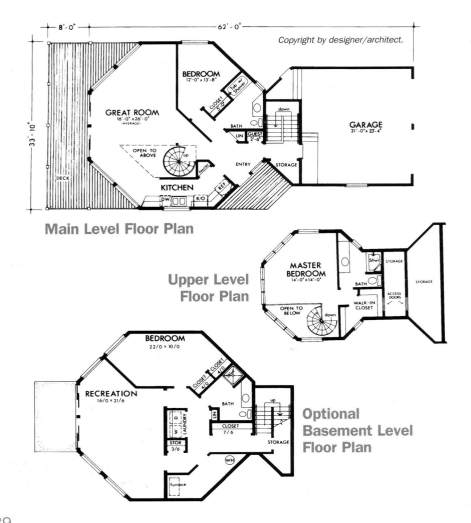

Main Level Floor Plan

Upper Level Floor Plan

Optional Basement Level Floor Plan

Plan #131008

Dimensions: 45'4" W x 36'4" D
Levels: 1
Square Footage: 1,299
Bedrooms: 3
Bathrooms: 2
Foundation: Crawl space, basement
Materials List Available: Yes
Price Category: C

Images provided by designer/architect.

Build this home in a vacation spot or any other location where you'll treasure the convenience of having three different outdoor entrances.

Features:

- Ceiling Height: 8 ft.

- Living Room: Sliding glass doors open onto the large deck area and serve to let bright, natural light stream into the home during the day. Add drapes to keep the house cozy at night and on cloudy winter days.

- Kitchen: Shaped like a galley, this kitchen is so well designed that you'll love working in it. Counter space and cabinets add to its practicality, and a windowed nook makes it charming.

- Master Suite: Enjoy the private bath attached to the bedroom in this quiet area.

- Additional Bedrooms: These nicely sized rooms share another full bathroom.

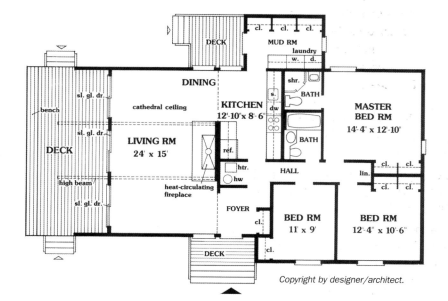

Copyright by designer/architect.

Rear View

Plan #121013

Dimensions: 40' W x 55'8" D
Levels: 1
Square Footage: 1,375
Bedrooms: 1
Bathrooms: 2
Foundation: Basement
Materials List Available: Yes
Price Category: B

This convenient open plan is well-suited to retirement or as a starter home.

Features:

- Ceiling Height: 8 ft., unless otherwise noted.

- Den: To the left of the entry, French doors lead to a den that can convert to a second bedroom.

- Kitchen: A center island doubles as a snack bar while the breakfast area includes a pantry and a desk for compiling shopping lists and menus.

- Open Plan: The sense of spaciousness is enhanced by the large open area that includes the family room, kitchen, and breakfast area.

- Family Room: A handsome fireplace invites family and friends to gather in this area.

- Porch: Step through the breakfast area to enjoy the fresh air on this secluded porch.

- Master Bedroom: This distinctive bedroom features a boxed ceiling. It's served by a private bath with a walk-in closet.

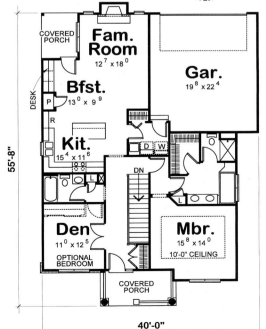

CAD FILE AVAILABLE

Copyright by designer/architect.

SMARTtip

Paint Color Choices for Your Home

Earth tones are easy to decorate with because they are neutral colors. Use neutral or muted tones, such as light grays, browns, or greens with either lighter or darker shades for accenting.

Use bright colors sparingly, to catch the eye. Painting the front door a bright color creates a cheerful entryway.

Investigate home shows, magazines, and houses in your area for color ideas. Paint suppliers can also give you valuable tips on appropriate color schemes.

Colors that look just right on a color card may need to be toned down for painting large areas. If in doubt, buy a quart of paint and test it.

Plan #451223

Dimensions: 71'6" W x 87'6" D
Levels: 2
Square Footage: 3,650
Main Level Sq. Ft.: 2,106
Upper Level Sq. Ft.: 272
Lower Level Sq. Ft.: 1,272
Bedrooms: 3
Bathrooms: 3½
Foundation: Crawl space
Materials List Available: No
Price Category: H

This timber-frame log home would look great in a neighborhood or in the backcountry.

Features:

- **Great Room:** The cozy fireplace, which is flanked by built-ins, makes this two-story gathering area special. The wet bar here features a serving shelf to the rear deck.

- **Kitchen:** This Island kitchen makes the most of its built-in pantry, and its raised bar is open to the great room and dining area. The utility room with washer and dryer are just a few steps away.

- **Master Suite:** The romantic fireplace in the bedroom is just the start in this retreat, which also provides access to the rear deck. The master bath features a spa tub, dual vanities, and a separate shower.

- **Lower Level:** This area offers the option of an additional bedroom, a guest suite, and a recreation room. The mechanical room is also on this level.

Images provided by designer/architect.

**Main Level
Floor Plan**

**Upper Level
Floor Plan**

**Basement Level
Floor Plan**

Copyright by designer/architect.

Plan #161037

Dimensions: 46' W x 59'4" D
Levels: 1
Square Footage: 2,469
Main Level Sq. Ft.: 1,462
Basement Level Sq. Ft.: 1,007
Bedrooms: 2
Bathrooms: 2½
Foundation: Walkout; basement for fee
Materials List Available: Yes
Price Category: E

Images provided by designer/architect.

A brick-and-stone facade welcomes you into this lovely home, which is designed to fit into a narrow lot.

Features:

- **Foyer:** This entrance, with vaulted ceiling, introduces the graciousness of this home.

- **Great Room:** A vaulted center ceiling creates the impression that this large great room and dining room are one space, making entertaining a natural in this area.

- **Kitchen:** Designed for efficiency with ample storage and counter space, this kitchen also allows casual dining at the counter.

- **Master Suite:** A tray ceiling sets this room off from the rest of the house, and the lavishly equipped bathroom lets you pamper yourself.

- **Lower Level:** Put extra bedrooms or a library in this finished area, and use the wet bar in a game room or recreation room.

Dining Room

Rear Elevation

Main Level Floor Plan

Optional Screened Porch 12 x 12
Deck
Copyright by designer/architect.
Dining 13' x 15'4"
Great Room 15' x 18'6"
Master Bedroom 16'4" x 14'
Kitchen 13' x 12'6"
Foyer
Dress.
Bath
Laun.
walk-in closet
Porch
Garage 22'2" x 26'5"
59'4"
46'

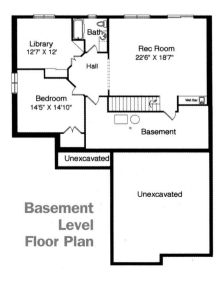

Basement Level Floor Plan

Library 12'7" X 12'
Bath
Hall
Rec Room 22'6" X 18'7"
Bedroom 14'5" X 14'10"
Wet Bar
Basement
Unexcavated
Unexcavated

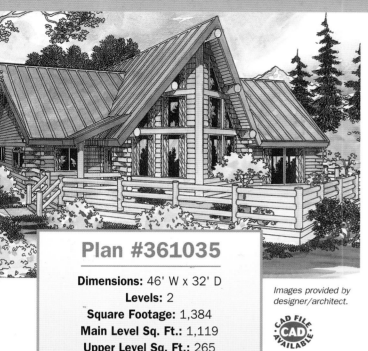

Plan #361035

Dimensions: 46' W x 32' D
Levels: 2
Square Footage: 1,384
Main Level Sq. Ft.: 1,119
Upper Level Sq. Ft.: 265
Bedrooms: 2
Bathrooms: 2
Foundation: Basement
Material List Available: No
Price Category: B

Images provided by designer/architect.

CAD FILE AVAILABLE

Main Level Floor Plan

Upper Level Floor Plan

Copyright by designer/architect.

Plan #181013

Dimensions: 44' W x 30' D
Levels: 1
Square Footage: 1,147
Bedrooms: 3
Bathrooms: 1
Foundation: Full basement
Materials List Available: Yes
Price Category: B

Images provided by designer/architect.

CAD FILE AVAILABLE

Copyright by designer/architect.

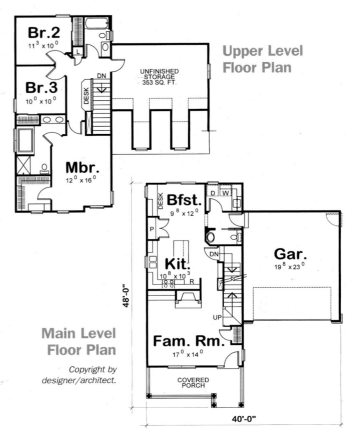

Upper Level Floor Plan

Br.2
11³ x 10⁰

Br.3
10⁰ x 10⁰

DESK

DN

UNFINISHED STORAGE 353 SQ. FT.

Mbr.
12⁰ x 16⁰

Bfst.
9⁸ x 12⁰

DESK

P

D W

Kit.
10⁸ x 10³

R

DN

UP

Gar.
19⁸ x 23⁰

Fam. Rm.
17⁰ x 14⁰

COVERED PORCH

48'-0"

40'-0"

Main Level Floor Plan

Plan #121045

Dimensions: 40' W x 48' D
Levels: 2
Square Footage: 1,575
Main Level Sq. Ft.: 787
Upper Level Sq. Ft.: 788
Bedrooms: 3
Bathrooms: 2½
Foundation: Basement
Materials List Available: Yes
Price Category: C

Images provided by designer/architect.

This home, as shown in the photograph, may differ from the actual blueprints. For more detailed information, please check the floor plans carefully.

Copyright by designer/architect.

Plan #111010

Dimensions: 34' W x 38' D
Levels: 3
Square Footage: 1,804
Main Level Sq. Ft.: 731
Upper Level Sq. Ft.: 935
Third Level Sq.Ft.: 138
Bedrooms: 3
Bathrooms: 3
Foundation: Piers
Materials List Available: No
Price Category: D

Images provided by designer/architect.

Third Level Floor Plan

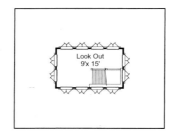

Look Out
9'x 15'

Main Level Floor Plan

Deck
14'x 10'

Kitchen
10'6"x 13'9"

Dining
9'x 13'8"

Living
14'x 19'

Screen Porch
19'6"x 10'

Copyright by designer/architect.

Side View

Upper Level Floor Plan

Bedroom
11'6"x 11'

Master Bedroom
18'6"x 15'

Bedroom
12'x 10'

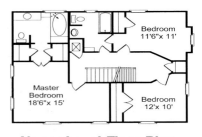

Plan #291015

Dimensions: 88'6" W x 58'3" D
Levels: 1.5
Square Footage: 2,901
Main Level Sq. Ft.: 2,078
Upper Level Sq. Ft.: 823
Bedrooms: 3
Bathrooms: 2½
Foundation: Basement
Materials List Available: No
Price Category: F

Images provided by designer/architect.

Upon entering this home, a cathedral-like timber-framed interior fills the eye.

Features:

- Great Room: This large gathering area's ceiling rises up two stories and is open to the kitchen. The beautiful fireplace is the focal point of this room.

- Kitchen: This island kitchen is open to the great room and the breakfast nook. Warm woods of all species enhance the great room and this space.

- Master Suite: This suite has a sloped ceiling and adjoins a luxurious master bath with twin walk-in closets that open to a sunroom with a private balcony.

- Upper Level: This upper level has an open lounge that leads to two bedrooms with vaulted ceilings and a generous second bath.

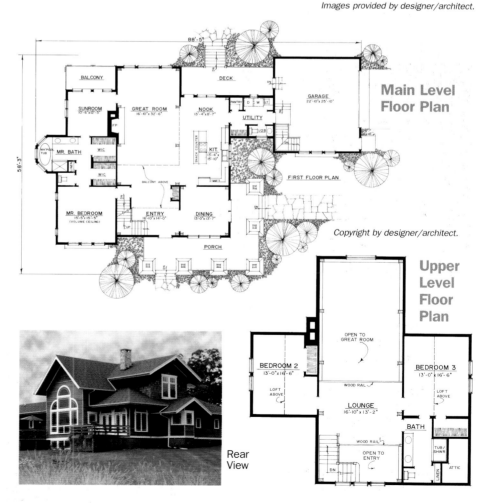

Main Level Floor Plan

Copyright by designer/architect.

Upper Level Floor Plan

Rear View

Plan #271086

Dimensions: 56'6" W x 67'6" D

Levels: 2

Square Footage: 1,910

Main Level Sq. Ft.: 1,324

Upper Level Sq. Ft.: 586

Bedrooms: 3

Bathrooms: 2

Foundation: Crawl space, daylight basement

Materials List Available: Yes

Price Category: D

Images provided by designer/architect.

A passive-solar sunroom is the highlight of this popular home and helps to minimize heating costs.

Features:

- Living/Dining Area: This expansive space is brightened by numerous windows and offers panoramic views of the outdoor scenery. A handsome woodstove gives the area a delightful ambiance, especially when the weather outside is frightful. Your dining table goes in the corner by the sun room.

- Kitchen: This room's efficient design keeps all of the chef's supplies at the ready. A snack bar could be used to help serve guests during parties.

- Bedrooms: With three bedrooms to choose from, all of your family members will be able to find secluded spots of their very own.

- Lower Level: This optional space includes a recreation room with a second woodstove. Let the kids gather here and make as much noise as they want.

Main Level Floor Plan

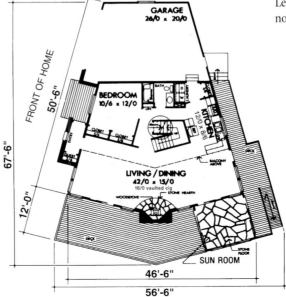

Optional Basement Level Floor Plan

Copyright by designer/architect.

Upper Level Floor Plan

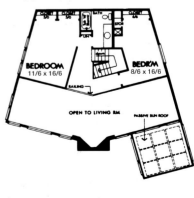

Plan #441028

Dimensions: 53'6" W x 73' D
Levels: 2
Square Footage: 3,165
Main Level Sq. Ft.: 1,268
Upper Level Sq. Ft.: 931
Lower Level Sq. Ft.: 966
Bedrooms: 4
Bathrooms: 3½
Foundation: Slab
Materials List Available: No
Price Category: G

Arts and Crafts style meets hillside design. The result is this stunning design, which fits perfectly on a sloped site.

CAD FILE AVAILABLE

Images provided by designer/architect.

Features:

- Porch: This covered porch introduces the front entry but also allows access to a mud-room and the three-car garage beyond.

- Great Room: This room is vaulted and has a fireplace, media center, and window seat in a corner window area—a cozy place to read or relax.

- Dining Room: The recess in this room is ideal for a hutch, and the double French doors open to the wide lower deck.

- Upper Level: This floor holds the two family bedrooms with walk-in closets, the shared bathroom, and the master suite. A spa tub and vaulted salon with private deck appoint the suite.

- Lower Level: This floor features another bedroom, with its full bathroom; the recreation room, which has a fireplace and wet bar; and the wine cellar.

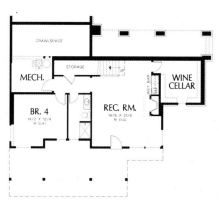

Lower Level Floor Plan
Copyright by designer/architect.

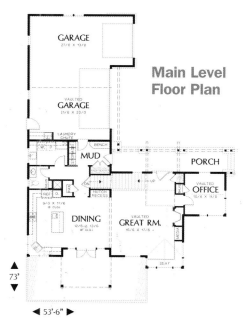

Main Level Floor Plan

73'

53'-6"

Upper Level Floor Plan

Plan #111047

Dimensions: 36' W x 54' D
Levels: 2
Square Footage: 1,863
Main Level Sq. Ft.: 1,056
Upper Level Sq. Ft.: 807
Bedrooms: 4
Bathrooms: 3
Foundation: Pier
Materials List Available: No
Price Category: D

Designed for a coastline, this home is equally appropriate as a year-round residence or a vacation retreat.

Features:

- **Orientation:** The rear-facing design gives you an ocean view and places the most attractive side of the house where beach-goers can see it.

- **Entryway:** On the waterside, a large deck with a covered portion leads to the main entrance.

- **Carport:** This house is raised on piers that let you park underneath it and that protect it from water damage during storms.

- **Living Room:** A fireplace, French doors, and large windows grace this room, which is open to both the kitchen and the dining area.

- **Master Suite:** Two sets of French doors open to a balcony on the ocean side, and the suite includes two walk-in closets and a fully equipped bath.

Main Level Floor Plan

Upper Level Floor Plan

Copyright by designer/architect.

Plan #181117

Dimensions: 33' W x 26' D
Levels: 2
Square Footage: 1,325
Main Level Sq. Ft.: 741
Upper Level Sq. Ft.: 584
Bedrooms: 2
Bathrooms: 1½
Foundation: Walkout basement
Materials List Available: Yes
Price Category: B

Images provided by designer/architect.

CAD FILE AVAILABLE

Main Level Floor Plan

Upper Level Floor Plan

Copyright by designer/architect.

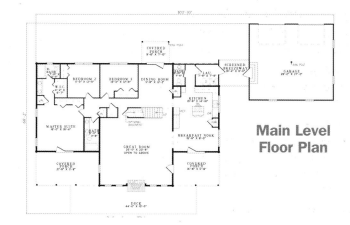

Plan #151791

Dimensions: 103'10" W x 68'2" D
Levels: 1.5
Square Footage: 2,660
Main Level Sq. Ft.: 2,360
Upper Level Sq. Ft.: 300
Bedrooms: 3
Bathrooms: 2½
Foundation: Crawl space
CompleteCost List Available: Yes
Price Category: F

Images provided by designer/architect.

Main Level Floor Plan

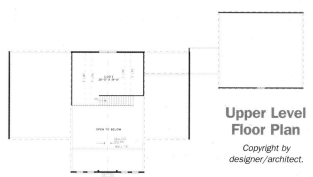

Upper Level Floor Plan

Copyright by designer/architect.

Main Level Floor Plan

Plan #391001

Dimensions: 32' W x 40' D
Levels: 2
Square Footage: 2,015
Main Level Sq. Ft.: 1,280
Upper Level Sq. Ft.: 735
Bedrooms: 3
Bathrooms: 2½
Foundation: Crawl space
Materials List Available: Yes
Price Category: D

Images provided by designer/architect.

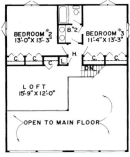

Upper Level Floor Plan

Copyright by designer/architect.

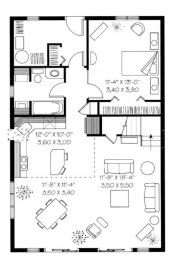

Main Level Floor Plan

Plan #181111

Dimensions: 24'8" W x 38'4" D
Levels: 2
Square Footage: 1,304
Main Level Sq. Ft.: 945
Upper Level Sq. Ft.: 359
Bedrooms: 2
Bathrooms: 1
Foundation: Crawl space
Materials List Available: Yes
Price Category: B

Images provided by designer/architect.

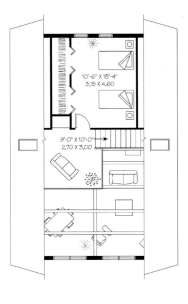

Upper Level Floor Plan

Copyright by designer/architect.

Plan #271013

Dimensions: 43' W x 46' D
Levels: 2
Square Footage: 1,498
Main Level Sq. Ft.: 1,044
Upper Level Sq. Ft.: 454
Bedrooms: 2
Bathrooms: 2½
Foundation: Basement
Materials List Available: Yes
Price Category: B

Smart in looks, function, and cost, this design is filled with flexible spaces.

Features:

• Great Room: Straight ahead from the entry, this broad space serves as one large, flexible living space. It features a cathedral ceiling, a built-in wet bar, a cozy fireplace, and lots of glass overlooking the backyard deck.

• Kitchen/Breakfast: There's space enough here for morning meals. The pass-through to the great room is a bonus.

• Master Bedroom: Main-floor accessibility combines with a window seat, walk-in closet, and private bath to deliver a getaway that is worth the wait.

• Secondary Bedrooms: An upper-floor bedroom and a loft share a full bath. The loft can be framed in to create a study or media room, or simply keep it open and let the kids use it as a playroom.

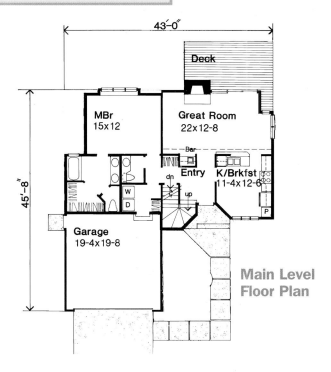

Main Level Floor Plan

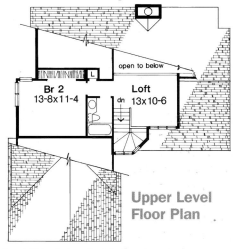

Upper Level Floor Plan

Copyright by designer/architect.

Plan #271052

Dimensions: 57' W x 67' D
Levels: 2
Square Footage: 1,779
Main Level Sq. Ft.: 1,309
Upper Level Sq. Ft.: 470
Bedrooms: 3
Bathrooms: 2
Foundation: Crawl space, daylight basement
Materials List Available: Yes
Price Category: C

Images provided by designer/architect.

Designed for relaxation, this home offers a gigantic deck and an irresistible spa room.

Features:

• Great Room: A covered porch welcomes guests into the entry hall and this spectacular great room beyond. Outlined by windows and sliding glass doors, this great room offers panoramic views of scenic beauty. Step outside onto the deck to commune with nature one on one.

• Kitchen: This U-shaped kitchen flows into a cozy breakfast nook. A formal dining room is just steps away.

• Master Suite: This main-floor master suite features direct access to a passive-solar spa room and a sunning area beyond. A walk-in closet and a window seat round out the suite.

• Secondary Bedrooms: On the upper floor, a balcony hall overlooks the great room, while leading to these two good-sized bedrooms. A hall bath is located between them.

Basement Level Floor Plan

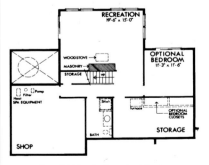

Copyright by designer/architect.

Main Level Floor Plan

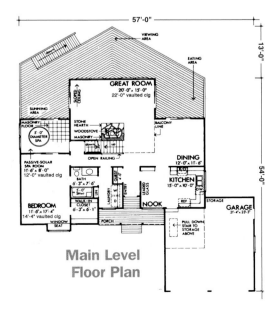

Upper Level Floor Plan

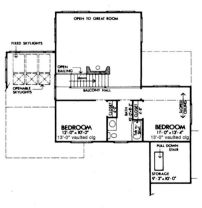

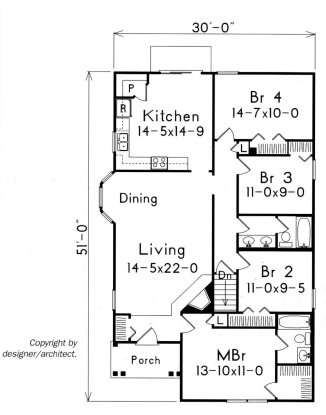

30'-0"

51'-0"

P
R
Kitchen
14-5x14-9

Dining

Living
14-5x22-0

Dn

Porch

Br 4
14-7x10-0

Br 3
11-0x9-0

Br 2
11-0x9-5

MBr
13-10x11-0

Images provided by designer/architect.

Copyright by designer/architect.

Plan #321038

Dimensions: 30' W x 51' D
Levels: 1
Square Footage: 1,452
Bedrooms: 4
Bathrooms: 2
Foundation: Basement
Materials List Available: Yes
Price Category: B

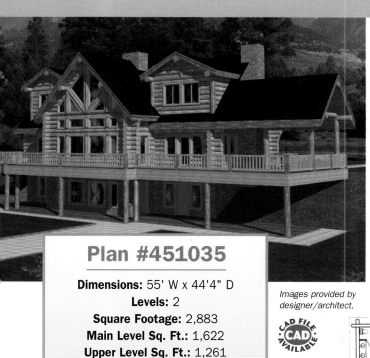

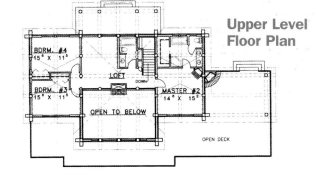

Upper Level Floor Plan

BDRM. #4
15' X 11'

BDRM. #3
15' X 11'

LOFT
DOWN

OPEN TO BELOW

MASTER #2
14' X 15'

OPEN DECK

Basement Level Floor Plan

UTILITY   SAUNA   GUEST BATH   WET BAR   mechanical / storage

OFFICE
15' X 13'10

SEWING
14' X 19'4

FAMILY ROOM
22'8 X 18'4

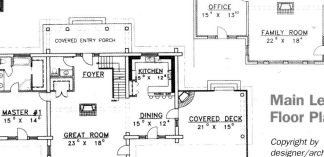

COVERED ENTRY PORCH

FOYER

KITCHEN
15' X 12'

MASTER #1
15' X 14'

GREAT ROOM
23' X 18'

DINING
15' X 12'

COVERED DECK
21' X 15'

OPEN DECK

Main Level Floor Plan

Copyright by designer/architect.

Plan #451035

Dimensions: 55' W x 44'4" D
Levels: 2
Square Footage: 2,883
Main Level Sq. Ft.: 1,622
Upper Level Sq. Ft.: 1,261
Bedrooms: 4
Bathrooms: 3½
Foundation: Walkout basement
Materials List Available: No
Price Category: F

Images provided by designer/architect.

CAD FILE AVAILABLE

Kitchen Cabinets

Of all the rooms in a house, kitchens present unique decorating challenges because so much tends to happen in these spaces. In addition to preparing meals, most families use kitchens as gathering and entertaining areas. Kitchens need to be functional, comfortable, and inviting.

Who can't relate to this scenario: you turn on the oven to preheat it, but wait, did you take out the large roasting pan first?

How about the lasagna dish, muffin tins, pizza stone, and cookie sheets that are in there, too? Now where can you put everything that was in the oven while the casserole is baking and the countertop is laden with the rest of tonight's dinner ingredients? Good cabinetry outfitted with an assortment of organizing options can help you there. It can make your kitchen more efficient and a whole lot neater while establishing a style, or "look," for the room.

Cabinet Construction

Basically, cabinets are constructed in one of two ways: framed or frameless. Framed cabinets have a traditional look, with a full frame across the face of the cabinet box that may show between closed doors. This secures adjacent cabinets and strengthens wider cabinet boxes with a center rail. Hinges on framed cabinets may or may not be visible around doors when they are closed. The door's face may be ornamented with raised or recessed panels, trimmed or framed panels, or a framed-glass panel with or without muntins (the narrow vertical and horizontal strips of wood that divide panes of glass).

Frameless Cabinets. Also known as European-style cabinets, although American manufacturers also make them, frameless cabinets are built without a face frame and sport a clean, contemporary look, often not befitting a Southern or Country style. There's no trim or molding with this simple design. Close-fitting doors cover the entire front of the box, no ornamentation appears on the face of the doors, and hinges are typically hidden inside the cabinet box.

Selecting Cabinets

Choosing one type over another is generally a matter of taste, although framed units offer slightly less interior space. But the quality of construction is a factor that should always be taken into consideration. How do you judge it? Solid wood is too expensive for most of today's budgets, but it might be used on just the doors and frames. More typical is plywood box construction, which offers good structural support and solid wood on the doors and frames. To save money, cabinetmakers sometimes use strong plywood for support elements, such as the box and frame, and medium-density fiberboard for other parts, such as doors and drawer fronts. In

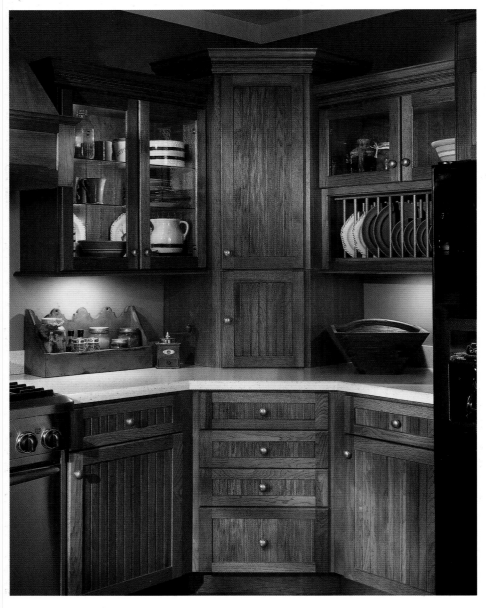

yet another alternative, good-quality laminate cabinets can be made with high-quality, thick particleboard underneath the laminate finish.

Quality Points. There are other things to look for in cabinet construction. They include dovetail or mortise-and-tenon joinery and solidly mortised hinges. Also, make sure that the interior of every cabinet is well finished, with adjustable shelves that are a minimum ⅝ inch thick to prevent bowing.

Bead-board paneled doors, opposite, are at home in Southern-style kitchens.

Framed cabinets, above, offer a traditional look to an otherwise modern kitchen.

Country-style designs have many attributes of Cottage decor, right.

Unless you have the time and skill to build the cabinets yourself or can hire someone else to do it, you'll have to purchase them in one of four ways. **Knockdown cabinetry** (also known as RTA, ready to assemble) is shipped flat and, sometimes, unfinished because you put the pieces together. **Stock cabinetry** comes in standard sizes but limited styles and colors; it is often available on the spot or can be delivered quickly. Like stock, **semicustom cabinetry** comes in standard styles, but it is manufactured to fit a homeowner's specific size and finish needs. **Custom cabinetry** is not limited in terms of style or size because it is built to the designer's specifications.

The Decorative Role of Cabinets

The look you create in your kitchen will be largely influenced by the cabinetry you select. Finding a style that suits you and how you will use your new kitchen is similar to shopping for furniture. In fact, don't be surprised to see many furniture details dressing up the cabinets on view in showrooms and home centers today.

Details That Stand Out. Besides architectural elements such as fluted pilasters, corbels, moldings, and bull's-eye panels, look for details such as fretwork, rope motifs, gingerbread trim, balusters, composition ornamentation (it looks like carving), even footed cabinets that mimic separate furniture pieces. If your taste runs toward less fussy design, you'll also find handsome door and drawer styles that feature minimal decoration, if any. Woods and finishes are just as varied, and range from informal looks in birch, oak, ash, and maple to rich mahogany and cherry. Laminate finishes, though less popular than they were a decade ago, haven't completely disappeared from the marketplace, but an array of colors has replaced the once-ubiquitous almond and white finishes.

Color

Color is coming on strong on wood cabinetry, too. Accents in one, two, or more hues are pairing with natural wood tones. White-painted cabinets take on a warmer

glow with tinted shades of this always popular neutral. Special "vintage" finishes, such as translucent color glazes, continue to grow in popularity, as do distressed finishing techniques such as wire brushing and rubbed-through color that add both another dimension and the appeal of handcraftmanship, even on mass-produced items.

If you're shy about using color on such a high-ticket item as cabinetry, try it as an accent on molding, door trim, or island cabinetry. Just as matched furniture suites have become passé in other rooms of the house, the same is true for the kitchen,

where mixing several looks can add sophistication and visual interest.

Cabinet Hardware

Another way to emphasize your kitchen's style is with hardware. From exquisite reproductions in brass, pewter, wrought iron, or ceramic to handsome bronze, chrome, nickel, glass, steel, plastic, rubber, wood, or stone creations, a smorgasbord of shapes and designs is available. Some pieces are highly polished; others are matte-finished, smooth, or hammered. Some are abstract or geometrical; others are simple,

elegant shapes. Whimsical designs take on the forms of animals or teapots, vegetables or flowers. Even just one or two great-looking door or drawer pulls can be showstoppers in a kitchen that may otherwise be devoid of much personality. Like mixing cabinet finishes, a combination of two hardware styles—perhaps picked up from other materials in the room—makes a big design statement. As the famed architect Mies Van der Rohe once stated, "God is in the details," and the most perfect detail in your new kitchen may be the artistic hardware that you select.

Cabinet style will set the tone for the design of the entire kitchen. The simple door styles keeps the room at left airy and casual.

The rustic look of the cabinets above is tailor-made for any Country style kitchen.

Color accents, such as the splash of color on the kitchen island shown right,can customize any simple cabinet design.

Cabinet hardware should complement the cabinet door and drawer designs, but it should also be easy for everyone in the household to grasp, above.

Kitchen storage comes in a variety of forms, including cabinets, drawers, pullout extensions, and the glass-front bins shown to the right.

Besides looks, consider the function of a pull or knob. You have to be able to grip it easily and comfortably. If your fingers or hands get stiff easily, or if you have arthritis, select C- or U-shaped pulls. If you like a knob, try it out in the showroom to make sure it isn't slippery or awkward when you grab it. Knobs and pulls can be inexpensive if you can stick to unfinished ones that you can paint in an accent color picked up from the tile or wallpaper. If you don't plan to buy new cabinets, changing the hardware on old ones can redefine their style. The right knob or pull can suggest any one of a number of vintage looks or decorative styles, from Colonial to Victorian, and reinforce your decor.

Types of Storage

Storage facilities can make or break a kitchen, so choose the places you'll put things with care. Here's a look at a few alternatives:

Pantries. How often you shop and how many groceries you typically bring home determine the amount of food storage space your family needs. If you like to stock up or take advantage of sales, add a pantry to your kitchen. To maximize a pantry's convenience, plan shallow, 6-inch-deep shelves so that cans and packages will never be stored more than two deep. This way, you'll easily be able to see what you've got on hand. Pantries range in size from floor-to-ceiling models to narrow units designed to fit between two standard-size cabinets.

Appliance Garages. Appliance garages make use of dead space in a corner, but they can be installed anywhere in the vertical space between wall-mounted cabinets and the countertop. A tambour (rolltop) door hides small appliances like a food processor or anything else you want within reach but hidden from view.

Lazy Susans and Carousel Shelves. Rotating shelves like lazy Susans and carousels maximize dead corner storage and put items like dishes or pots and pans within easy reach. A lazy Susan rotates 360 degrees, so just spin it to find what you're looking for. Carousel shelves, which attach to two right-angled doors, rotate 270 degrees; open the doors, and the shelves swing out allowing you to reach items easily.

Pivoting Shelves. Door-mounted shelves and in-cabinet swiveling shelf units offer easy access to kitchen supplies. Taller units serve as pantries that hold a great deal in minimal space.

Pullout Tables and Trays. In tight kitchens, pullout tables and trays are excellent ways to gain eating space or an extra work surface. Pullout cutting boards come in handy near cooktops, microwaves, and food prep areas. Pullout tea carts are also available.

Customized Organizers. If you decide to use value-priced cabinets or choose to forego the storage accessories offered by manufacturers, consider refitting their interiors with cabinet organizers you purchase yourself. These plastic, plastic-coated wire, or enameled-steel racks and hangers are widely available at department stores, hardware stores, and home centers.

Some of these units slide in and out of base cabinets, similar to the racks in a dishwasher. Others let you mount shallow drawers to the undersides of wall cabinets. Still others consist of stackable plastic bins with plenty of room to hold kitchen sundries.

Beware of the temptation to over-specialize your kitchen storage facilities. Sizes and needs for certain items change, so be sure to allot at least 50 percent of your kitchen's storage to standard cabinets with one or more movable shelves. And don't forget to allow for storing recyclable items.

Today's cabinets can be customized with storage accessories, right.

Full-height pantries, above, provide a number of different types of storage near where you need the items. This pantry is next to the food-prep area.

Base cabinets can be outfitted with accessories for kitchen storage or for wet bar storage as shown in the cabinet below.

Storage Checklist

Here's a guide to help you get your storage needs in order.

■ **Do you like kitchen gadgets?**
Plan drawer space, countertop sorters, wall magnets, or hooks to keep these items handy near where you often use them.

■ **Do you own a food processor, blender, mixer, toaster oven, electric can opener, knife sharpener, juicer, coffee maker, or coffee mill?**
If you're particularly tidy, you may want small appliances like these tucked away in an appliance garage or cupboard to be taken out only when needed. If you pre-fer to have frequently used machines sitting on the counter, ready to go, plan enough space, along with conveniently located electrical outlets.

■ **Do you plan to store large quantities of food?**
Be sure to allow plenty of freezer, bin, and shelf space for the kind of food shopping you do.

■ **Do you intend to do a lot of freezing or canning?**
Allow a work space and place to stow equipment. Also plan adequate storage for the fruits of your labor—an extra stand-alone freezer, a good-sized food safe in the kitchen, or a separate pantry or cellar.

■ **Do you bake often?**
Consider a baking center that can house your equipment and serve as a separate baking-ingredients pantry.

■ **Do you collect pottery, tinware, or anything else that might be displayed in the kitchen?**
Soffits provide an obvious place to hang small objects like collectible plates. Eliminating soffits provides a shelf on top of the wall cabinets for larger lightweight objects like baskets. Open shelving, glass-front cupboards, and display cabinets are other options.

■ **Do you collect cookbooks?**
If so, you'll need expandable shelf space and perhaps a bookstand.

Personal Profile of You and Your Family

■ **How tall are you and everyone else who will use your kitchen?**
Adjust your counter and wall-cabinet heights to suit. Multilevel work surfaces for special tasks are a necessity for good kitchen design.

■ **Do you or any of your family members use a walker, leg braces, or a wheelchair?**
Plan a good work height, knee space, grab bars, secure seating, slide-out work

boards, and other convenience features to make your kitchen comfortable for all who will use it.

Fold-down ironing boards, above left, are a true luxury. If you have the space, install one near the kitchen or laundry room.

■ **Are you left- or right-handed?**
Think about your natural motion when you choose whether to open cupboards or refrigerator doors from the left or right side, whether to locate your dishwasher to the left or right of the sink, and so on.

Corner cabinets often contain storage space you can't reach. Make it accessible by installing swing-out shelves, above right, or a lazy Susan.

Glass doors put your kitchen items on display. The owners of the kitchen below chose distinctive pottery and glassware for their glass-door cabinets.

■ **How high can you comfortably reach?**
If you're tall, hang your wall cabinets high. If you're petite, you may want to hang the cabinets lower and plan a spot to keep a step stool handy.

■ **Can you comfortably bend and reach for something in a base cabinet? Can you lift heavy objects easily and without strain or pain?**
If your range is limited in these areas, be sure to plan roll-out shelving on both upper and lower tiers of your base cabinets. Also, look into spring-up shelves designed to lift mixer bases or other heavy appliances to counter height.

■ **Do you frequently share cooking tasks with another family member?**
If so, you may each prefer to have your own work area.

Plan #121063

Dimensions: 84' W x 52' D
Levels: 2
Square Footage: 3,473
Main Level Sq. Ft.: 2,500
Upper Level Sq. Ft.: 973
Bedrooms: 4
Bathrooms: 3½
Foundation: Basement
Materials List Available: Yes
Price Category: G

Images provided by designer/architect.

Enjoy the many amenities in this well-designed and gracious home.

Features:

• Entry: A large sparkling window and a tapering split staircase distinguish this lovely entryway.

• Great Room: This spacious great room will be the heart of your new home. It has a 14-ft. spider-beamed window that serves to highlight its built-in bookcase, built-in entertainment center, raised hearth fireplace,

wet bar, and lovely arched windows topped with transoms.

• Kitchen: Anyone who walks into this kitchen will realize that it's designed for both convenience and efficiency.

• Master Suite: The tiered ceiling in the bedroom gives an elegant touch, and the bay window adds to it. The two large walk-in closets and the spacious bath, with columns setting off the whirlpool tub and two vanities, complete this dream of a suite.

Main Level Floor Plan

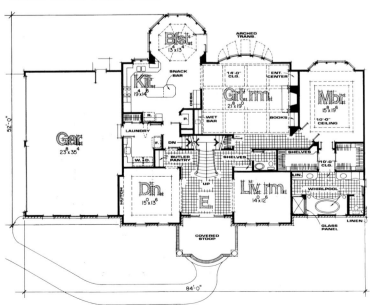
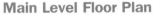

Upper Level Floor Plan

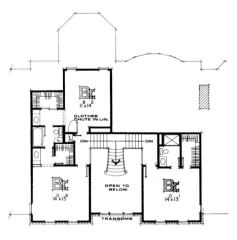

Copyright by designer/architect.

Plan #151018

Dimensions: 69' W x 69'10" D

Levels: 2

Square Footage: 2,755

Main Level Sq. Ft.: 2,406

Upper Level Sq. Ft.: 349

Bedrooms: 3

Bathrooms: 4½

Foundation: Crawl space, slab, or basement

CompleteCost List Available: Yes

Price Category: F

Images provided by designer/architect.

Treasure the countless amenities that make this home ideal for a family and welcoming to guests.

Features:

- **Great Room:** A gas fireplace and built-in shelving beg for a warm, comfortable decorating scheme.

- **Kitchen:** An island counter here opens to the breakfast room, and a swinging door leads to the dining room with its formal entry columns.

- **Laundry Room:** You'll wonder how you ever kept the laundry organized without this room and its built-in ironing board and broom closet.

- **Master Suite:** Atrium doors to the porch are a highlight of the bedroom, with its two walk-in closets, a corner whirlpool tub with glass blocks, and a separate shower.

- **Bedrooms:** These large rooms will surely promote peaceful school-day mornings for the children because each room has both a private bath and a walk-in closet.

Main Level Floor Plan

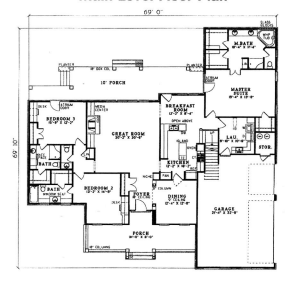

Upper Level Floor Plan

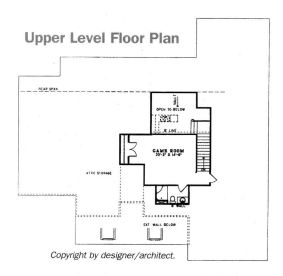

Copyright by designer/architect.

Plan #161114

Dimensions: 50' W x 36'8" D
Levels: 2
Square Footage: 2,246
Main Level Sq. Ft.: 1,072
Upper Level Sq. Ft.: 1,174
Bedrooms: 4
Bathrooms: 2½
Foundation: Basement
Material List Available: Yes
Price Category: E

A covered porch says "welcome" as you approach this delightful traditionally styled home.

Images provided by designer/architect.

Features:

- **Great Room:** This large gathering room, with its corner fireplace, draws you in to share good times. Open to the breakfast room and kitchen, it allows friends and family to flow among all three spaces.

- **Dining Room:** This formal dining room showcases a dropped soffit around the perimeter to give dimension to the ceiling treatment and add drama to your dining. The triple window allows an abundance of natural light.

- **Master Suite:** Located on the upper level with the secondary bedrooms, this retreat offers privacy. The master bath boasts a double-bowl vanity and a whirlpool tub to offer luxury and comfort to the homeowner.

- **Garage:** This front-loading two-car garage features an additional storage area in the rear.

Rear Elevation

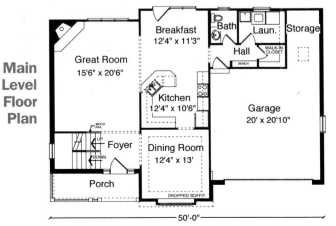

Main Level Floor Plan

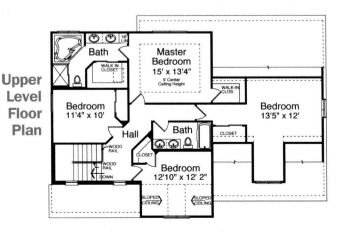

Upper Level Floor Plan

Copyright by designer/architect.

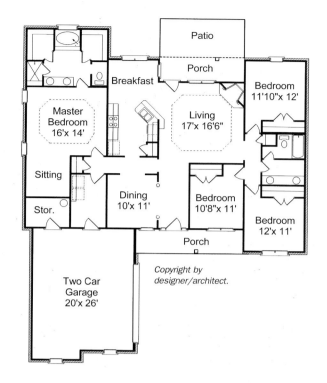

Plan #111015

Dimensions: 64' W x 58' D

Levels: 1

Square Footage: 2,208

Bedrooms: 4

Bathrooms: 2

Foundation: Slab

Materials List Available: No

Price Category: E

Images provided by designer/architect.

Copyright by designer/architect.

Plan #191013

Dimensions: 74' W x 69' D

Levels: 1

Square Footage: 2,293

Bedrooms: 3

Bathrooms: 3

Foundation: Crawl space or slab

Material List Available: No

Price Category: E

Images provided by designer/architect.

Copyright by designer/architect.

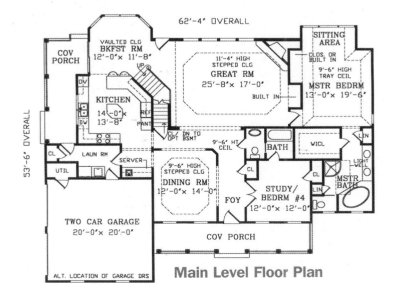

Plan #131027

Dimensions: 62'4" W x 53'6" D
Levels: 2
Square Footage: 2,567
Main Level Sq. Ft.: 2,017
Upper Level Sq. Ft.: 550
Bedrooms: 4
Bathrooms: 3
Foundation: Crawl space, slab, or basement
Materials List Available: Yes
Price Category: F

Images provided by designer/architect.

The features of this home are so good that you may have trouble imagining all of them at once.

Features:

- Great Room: Imagine a stepped ceiling, corner fireplace, built-media center, and wall of windows with a glass door to the backyard—in one room.

- Dining Room: A stepped ceiling and server with a sink add to the elegance of this formal room.

- Breakfast Room: Eat at the bar this room shares with the island kitchen, and admire the 12-ft. cathedral ceiling and bayed group of 8- and 9-ft. windows. Or go through the sliding glass door to the covered side porch.

- Master Suite: The bedroom has a tray ceiling and cozy sitting area, and a whirlpool tub, shower, and walk-in closet are in the skylighted bath.

- Optional Study: The private bath in bedroom 2 makes it ideal for a study or home office.

- Bonus Room: Enjoy the extra 300 sq. ft.

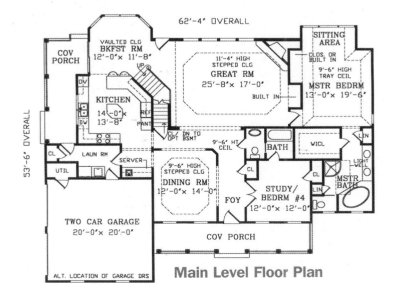

Main Level Floor Plan

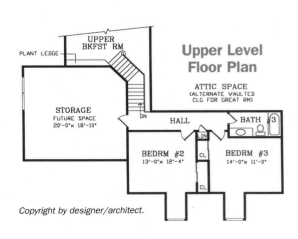

Upper Level Floor Plan

Copyright by designer/architect.

Plan #221050

Dimensions: 70' W x 48' D
Levels: 2
Square Footage: 2,683
Main Level Sq. Ft.: 1,426
Upper Level Sq. Ft.: 1, 257
Bedrooms: 4
Bathrooms: 3½
Foundation: Basement
Materials List Available: No
Price Category: F

An unusual blend of stucco and stone makes this home appealing to family and friends.

CAD FILE AVAILABLE CAD

Images provided by designer/architect.

Features:

- **Family Room:** You'll love the view of the backyard through the large bank of windows; the fireplace will add a touch of elegance to this gathering area.

- **Formal Entertaining:** Designed with entertaining in mind, the formal living room and the formal dining room are located at the entry to allow flow between them.

- **Kitchen:** This kitchen features a walk-in pantry and an eat-in island, and it flows directly into the adjacent breakfast nook. On nice days eat outside on the deck located off the breakfast nook.

- **Master Suite:** Located on the upper level along with three secondary bedrooms this retreat offers a large walk-in closet. The master bath boasts a Jacuzzi tub, stall shower, and dual vanities.

- **Secondary Bedrooms:** Bedroom 4 features a large walk-in closet and a private bathroom. Bedrooms 2 and 3 share a common bathroom.

Rear Elevation

Main Level Floor Plan

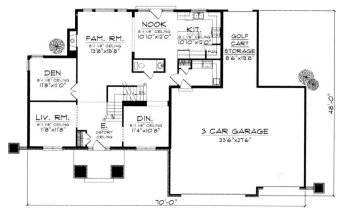

Upper Level Floor Plan
Copyright by designer/architect.

Plan #101022

Dimensions: 66'2" W x 62' D

Levels: 1

Square Footage: 1,992

Bedrooms: 3

Bathrooms: 3

Foundation: Crawl space, slab, or basement

Materials List Available: Yes

Price Category: D

Images provided by designer/architect.

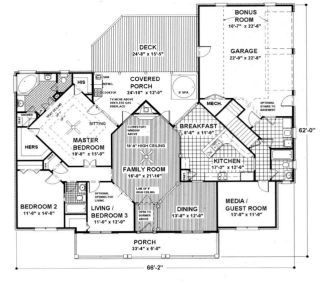

Copyright by designer/architect.

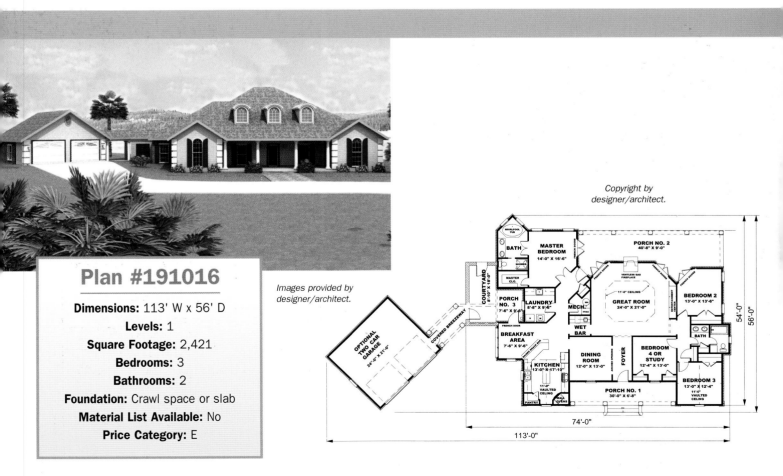

Plan #191016

Dimensions: 113' W x 56' D

Levels: 1

Square Footage: 2,421

Bedrooms: 3

Bathrooms: 2

Foundation: Crawl space or slab

Material List Available: No

Price Category: E

Images provided by designer/architect.

Copyright by designer/architect.

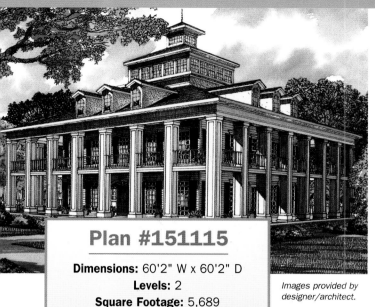

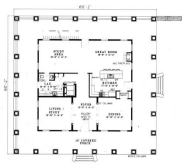

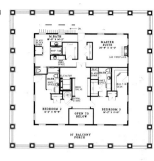

Main Level Floor Plan

Upper Level Floor Plan

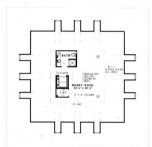

Basement Level Floor Plan

Bonus Area Floor Plan

Images provided by designer/architect.

Copyright by designer/architect.

Plan #151115

Dimensions: 60'2" W x 60'2" D

Levels: 2

Square Footage: 5,689

Main Level Sq. Ft.: 1,600

Upper Level Sq. Ft.: 1,530

Lower Level Sq. Ft.: 2,559

Bedrooms: 5

Bathrooms: 5½

Foundation: Walkout

CompleteCost List Available: Yes

Price Category: J

CAD FILE AVAILABLE · CAD

Main Level Floor Plan

Upper Level Floor Plan

Copyright by designer/architect.

Images provided by designer/architect.

Plan #111024

Dimensions: 46'10" W x 68'5" D

Levels: 2

Square Footage: 2,356

Main Level Sq. Ft.: 1,516

Upper Level Sq. Ft.: 840

Bedrooms: 4

Bathrooms: 2½

Foundation: Slab

Materials List Available: No

Price Category: E

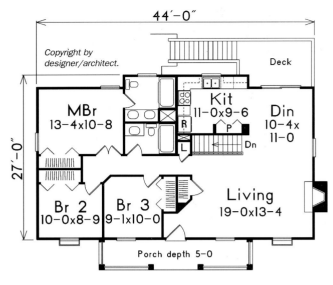

Copyright by designer/architect.

Deck

MBr
13-4x10-8

Kit
11-0x9-6

Din
10-4x
11-0

Br 2
10-0x8-9

Br 3
9-1x10-0

Living
19-0x13-4

Dn

44'-0"

27'-0"

Porch depth 5-0

Images provided by designer/architect.

Plan #321022

Dimensions: 44' W x 27' D
Levels: 1
Square Footage: 1,140
Bedrooms: 3
Bathrooms: 2
Foundation: Basement
Materials List Available: Yes
Price Category: B

SMARTtip

Basement Moldings

Keep moldings simple in a basement with lower ceilings. Elaborate moldings around the ceiling or floor can shorten the height of the room.

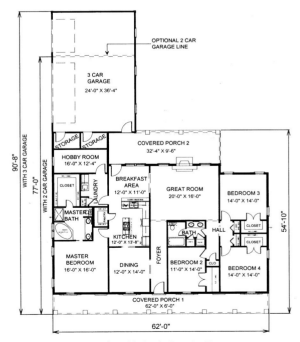

OPTIONAL 2 CAR GARAGE LINE

3 CAR GARAGE
24'-0" X 36'-4"

STORAGE STORAGE

HOBBY ROOM
16'-0" X 12'-4"

CLOSET

LAUNDRY

MASTER BATH

MASTER BEDROOM
16'-0" X 16'-0"

KITCHEN
12'-0" X 13'-8"

BREAKFAST AREA
12'-0" X 11'-0"

DINING
12'-0" X 14'-0"

FOYER

COVERED PORCH 2
32'-4" X 9'-6"

GREAT ROOM
20'-0" X 16'-0"

BATH

BEDROOM 2
11'-0" X 14'-0"

HALL

CLO

BEDROOM 3
14'-0" X 14'-0"

CLOSET

CLOSET

BEDROOM 4
14'-0" X 14'-0"

COVERED PORCH 1
62'-0" X 6'-0"

90'-8"
WITH 3 CAR GARAGE

77'-0"
WITH 2 CAR GARAGE

54'-10"

62'-0"

Copyright by designer/architect.

Plan #191014

Dimensions: 62' W x 90'8" D
Levels: 1
Square Footage: 2,435
Bedrooms: 4
Bathrooms: 2
Foundation: Crawl space or slab
Material List Available: No
Price Category: E

Images provided by designer/architect.

Plan #311003

Dimensions: 70'10" W x 65'4" D
Levels: 2
Square Footage: 2,428
Main Level Sq. Ft.: 2,348
Upper Level Sq. Ft.: 80
Bedrooms: 3
Bathrooms: 2½
Foundation: Crawl space, slab, or basement
Materials List Available: Yes
Price Category: E

Images provided by designer/architect.

Main Level Floor Plan

Bath 16-2x16-1
Patio
Garage 24-6x21-2
Sitting 12-10x9-8
Porch 20-2x10-0
Owner's Bedroom 16-2x15-3
Greatroom 18-0x17-2
Laun. 7-3x6-0
Kitchen 17-0x11-8
Bedroom 11-3x14-3
Bedroom 11-7x12-3
Foyer
Dining 14-0x12-6
Brkfst 11-3x10-0
Porch 36-0x8-2

Upper Level Floor Plan

Copyright by designer/architect.

Future 21-8x12-0
Open to Below
Future 13-5x12-0
Balcony
Future 35-5x11-4

Plan #101005

Dimensions: 63' W x 57'2" D
Levels: 1
Square Footage: 1,992
Bedrooms: 3
Bathrooms: 2½
Foundation: Crawl space, slab, or basement
Materials List Available: Yes
Price Category: D

Images provided by designer/architect.

CAD FILE AVAILABLE

Copyright by designer/architect.

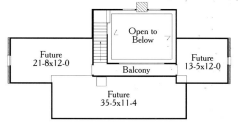

SCREENED PORCH 15'4" x 13'10"
DECK 11'0" x 7'6"
14' CEILING
SITTING
BEDROOM 3 13'0" x 11'0"
BRKFST 11'0" x 10'10"
MASTER SUITE 21'4" x 15'0"
8' HIGH OPENING
FAMILY ROOM 16'0" x 24'1"
KITCHEN 13'8" x 9'6"
10' CEILING
OPTIONAL STAIRS TO BASEMENT
LINEN
13'-10" CEILING
DINING 11'0" x 12'0"
TRAY CEILING
57'-2"
BEDROOM 2 13'0" x 11'0"
13'-4" CEILING
9' CEILING
LIVING 11'0" x 12'0"
PORCH 15'4" x 5'4"
3 CAR GARAGE 21'4" x 29'10"
2 CAR GARAGE OPTION
63'-0"

Rear View

Plan #151101

Dimensions: 87'10" W x 54'6" D
Levels: 1
Square Footage: 2,804
Bedrooms: 4
Bathrooms: 2½
Foundation: Slab
CompleteCost List Available: Yes
Price Category: F

This one-story home has everything you would find in a two-story house and more. This home plan is keeping up with the times.

CAD FILE AVAILABLE

Features:

- **Porches:** The long covered front porch is perfect for sitting out on warm evenings and greeting passersby. The back grilling porch, which opens through French doors from the great room, is great for entertaining guests with summer barbecues.

- **Utility:** Accessible from outside as well as the three-car garage, this small utility room is a multipurpose space. Through the breakfast area is the unique hobby/laundry area, a room made large enough for both the wash and the family artist.

- **Cooking and Eating Areas:** In one straight shot, this kitchen flows into both the sunlit breakfast room and the formal dining room,

for simple transitions no matter the meal. The kitchen features tons of work and storage space, as well as a stovetop island with a seated snack bar and a second eating bar between the kitchen and breakfast room.

- **Study:** For bringing work home with you or simply paying the bills, this quiet study sits off the foyer through French doors.

- **Master Suite:** A triplet of windows allows the

morning sun to shine in on this spacious, relaxing area. The full master bath features two separate vanities, a glass shower, a whirlpool tub, and a large walk-in closet.

- **Secondary Bedrooms:** Two of the three bedrooms include computer centers, keeping pace with the technological times, and all three share access to the second full bathroom, with its dual sinks and whirlpool tub.

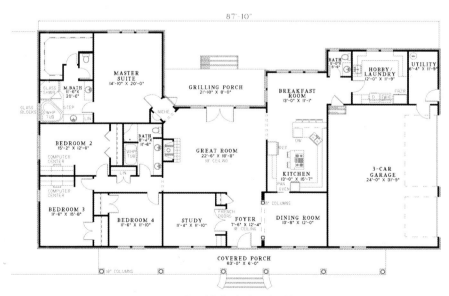

Copyright by designer/architect.

Plan #271096

Dimensions: 66' W x 98' D
Levels: 2
Square footage: 3,190
Main Level Sq. Ft.: 2,152
Upper Level Sq. Ft.: 1,038
Bedrooms: 4
Bathrooms: 3½
Foundation: Crawl space
Materials List Available: No
Price Category: G

Images provided by designer/architect.

This traditional home contains quite possibly everything you're dreaming of, and even more!

Features:

- **Formal Rooms:** These living and dining rooms flank the entry foyer, making a large space for special occasions.

- **Family Room:** A fireplace is the highlight of this spacious area, where the kids will play with their friends and watch TV.

- **Kitchen:** A central island makes cooking a breeze. The adjoining dinette is a sunny spot for casual meals.

- **Master Suite:** A large sleeping area is followed by a deluxe private bath with a whirlpool tub and a walk-in closet. Step through a French door to the backyard, which is big enough to host a deck with an inviting hot tub!

- **Guest Suite:** One bedroom upstairs has its own private bath, making it perfect for guests.

- A future room above the garage awaits your decision on how to use it.

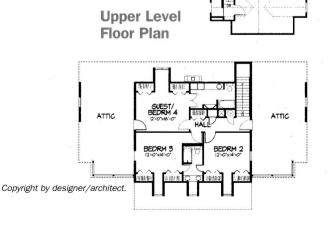

Copyright by designer/architect.

Plan #141022

Dimensions: 90' W x 93' D
Levels: 1
Square Footage: 2,911
Bedrooms: 3
Bathrooms: 2½
Foundation: Basement
Materials List Available: No
Price Category: F

Second-floor dormers accent this charming country ranch, which features a gracious porch that spans its entire front. A detached garage, connected by a covered extension, creates an impressive, expansive effect.

Features:

- **Living Room:** As you enter the foyer, you are immediately drawn to this dramatic, bayed living room.

- **Study:** Flanking the foyer, this cozy study features built-in shelving and a direct-vent fireplace.

- **Kitchen:** From a massive, partially covered deck, a wall of glass floods this spacious kitchen, breakfast bay, and keeping room with light.

- **Master Suite:** Enjoy the complete privacy provided by this strategically located master suite.

- **Guest Quarters:** You can convert the bonus room, above the garage, into a guest apartment.

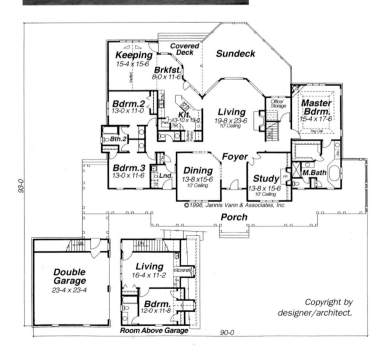

Rear View

Copyright by designer/architect.

Plan #131046

Dimensions: 68' W x 57'6" D
Levels: 2
Square Footage: 2,245
Main Level Sq. Ft.: 1,720
Upper Level Sq. Ft.: 525
Bedrooms: 3
Bathrooms: 2½
Foundation: Crawl space, slab, or basement
Materials List Available: Yes
Price Category: F

You'll love the mixture of country charm and contemporary amenities in this lovely home.

Features:

- Porch: The covered wraparound porch spells comfort, and the arched windows spell style.

- Great Room: Look up at the 18-ft. vaulted ceiling and the balcony that looks over this room from the upper level, and then notice the wall of windows and the fireplace that's set into a media wall for decorating ease.

- Kitchen: This roomy kitchen is also designed for convenience, thanks to its ample counter space and work island.

- Breakfast Room: The kitchen looks out to this lovely room, with its vaulted ceiling and sliding French doors that open to the rear covered porch.

- Master Bedroom: A 10-ft-ceiling and a dramatic bay window give character to this charming room.

Images provided by designer/architect.

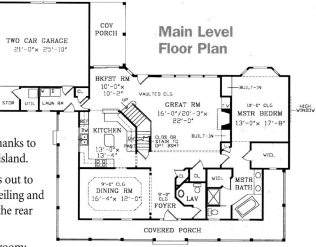

Main Level Floor Plan

Upper Level Floor Plan

Copyright by designer/architect.

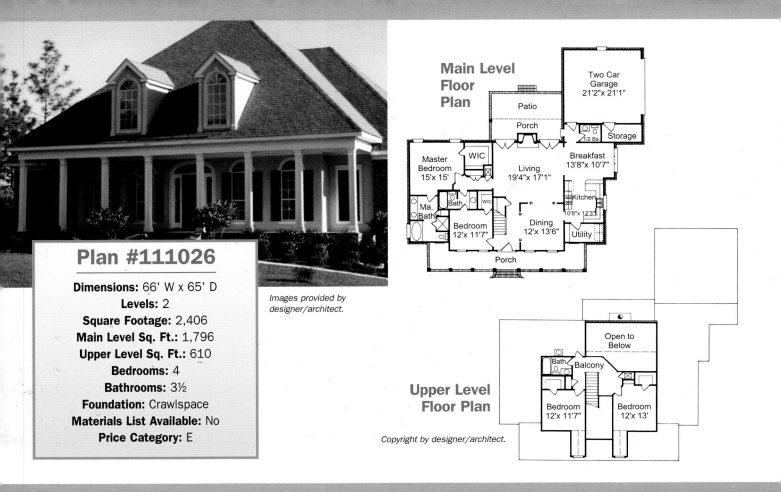

Plan #111026

Dimensions: 66' W x 65' D
Levels: 2
Square Footage: 2,406
Main Level Sq. Ft.: 1,796
Upper Level Sq. Ft.: 610
Bedrooms: 4
Bathrooms: 3½
Foundation: Crawlspace
Materials List Available: No
Price Category: E

Images provided by designer/architect.

Main Level Floor Plan

Two Car Garage 21'2"x 21'1"
Patio
Porch
½ Ba
Storage
Master Bedroom 15'x 15'
WIC
Living 19'4"x 17'1"
Breakfast 13'8"x 10'7"
Ma. Bath
Bath
WIC
Kitchen 10'8"x 12'3"
Bedroom 12'x 11'7"
Dining 12'x 13'6"
Utility
Porch

Upper Level Floor Plan

Open to Below
Bath
Balcony
Bedroom 12'x 11'7"
Bedroom 12'x 13'

Copyright by designer/architect.

Plan #151432

Dimensions: 27' W x 54' D
Levels: 2
Square Footage: 1,672
Main Level Sq. Ft.: 1,140
Lower Level Sq. Ft.: 532
Bedrooms: 3
Bathrooms: 2½
Foundation: Crawl space or slab; basement or walkout for fee
CompleteCost List Available: Yes
Price Category: C

Images provided by designer/architect.

Main Level Floor Plan

27'-0"
54'-0"
MASTER SUITE 13'-8" X 14'-0" 10' BOXED CEILING
GLASS SHWR
WHP TUB
KID'S NOOK
BENCH / STORAGE HANGING
KITCHEN 10'-0" X 14'-2"
REF
LIVING RM. 14'-0" X 14'-4"
8" COLUMNS
DINING 10'-0" X 13'-0"
COVERED PORCH 14'-0" X 8'-0"

Upper Level Floor Plan

ATTIC STORAGE
BATH
BEDROOM 2 11'-8" X 12'-0"
BEDROOM 3 12'-0" X 13'-5"
PORCH 14'-8" X 8'-0"

Copyright by designer/architect.

Plan #121050

Dimensions: 64' W x 50' D
Levels: 1
Square Footage: 1,996
Bedrooms: 2
Bathrooms: 2
Foundation: Basement
Materials List Available: Yes
Price Category: D

This compact design includes features usually reserved for larger homes and has styling that is typical of more-exclusive home designs.

Features:

- **Entry:** As you enter this home, you'll see the formal living and dining rooms—both with special ceiling detailing—on either side.

- **Great Room:** Located in the rear of the home for convenience, this great room is likely to be your favorite spot. The fireplace is framed by transom-topped windows, so you'll love curling up here, no matter what the weather or time of day.

- **Kitchen:** Ample counter and cabinet space make this kitchen a dream in which to work.

- **Master Suite:** A tray ceiling and lovely corner windows create an elegant feeling in the bedroom, and two walk-in closets make it easy to keep this space tidy and organized. The private bath has a skylight, corner whirlpool tub, and two separate vanities.

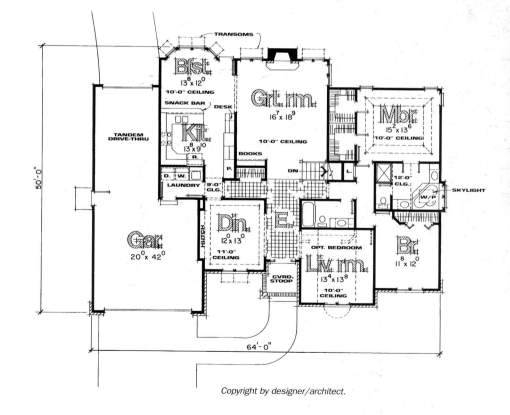

Plan #121074

Dimensions: 68'8" W x 47'8" D

Levels: 2

Square Footage: 2,486

Main Level Sq. Ft.: 1,829

Upper Level Sq. Ft.: 657

Bedrooms: 4

Bathrooms: 2½

Foundation: Basement

Materials List Available: Yes

Price Category: E

Images provided by designer/architect.

Enjoy the natural light that streams through the many lovely windows in this well-designed home.

Features:

- Living Room: This room is sure to be your family's headquarters, thanks to the lovely 15-ft. ceiling, stacked windows, central location, and cozy fireplace.

- Dining Room: A boxed ceiling adds formality to this well-positioned room.

- Kitchen: The island cooktop in this kitchen is so large that it includes a snack bar area. A pantry gives ample storage space, and a built-in desk—where you can set up a computer station or a record-keeping area—adds efficiency.

- Master Suite: For the sake of privacy, this master suite is located on the opposite side of the home from the other living areas. You'll love the roomy bedroom and luxuriate in the private bath with its many amenities.

Main Level Floor Plan

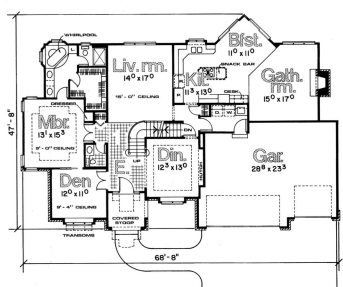

Upper Level Floor Plan

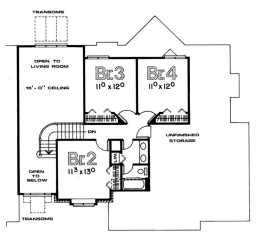

Copyright by designer/architect.

Plan #101019

Dimensions: 58'4" W x 55'2" D

Levels: 2

Square Footage: 2,954

Main Level Sq. Ft. 2093

Upper Level Sq. Ft. 861

Bedrooms: 4

Bathrooms: 3½

Foundation: Crawl space, slab, or basement

Materials List Available: No

Price Category: F

Images provided by designer/architect.

This luxurious home features a spectacular open floor plan and a brick exterior.

Features:

• Ceiling Height: 9 ft. unless otherwise noted.

• Foyer: This inviting two-story foyer, which vaults to 18 ft., will greet guests with an impressive "welcome."

• Dining Room: To the right of the foyer is this spacious dining room surrounded by decorative columns.

• Family Room: There's plenty of room for all kinds of family activities in this enormous room, with its soaring two-story ceiling.

• Master Suite: This sumptuous retreat boasts a tray ceiling. Optional pocket doors provide direct access to the study. The master bath features his and her vanities and a large walk-in closet.

• Breakfast Area: Perfect for informal family meals, this bayed breakfast area has real flair.

• Secondary Bedrooms: Upstairs are three large bedrooms with 8-ft. ceilings. One has a private bath.

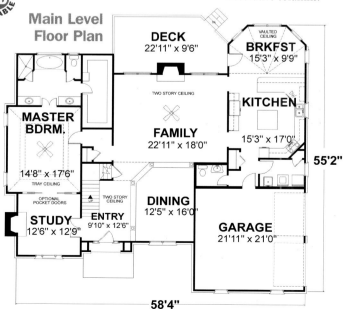

Main Level Floor Plan

DECK 22'11" x 9'6"

BRKFST 15'3" x 9'9" — VAULTED CEILING

KITCHEN 15'3" x 17'0"

TWO STORY CEILING

MASTER BDRM. 14'8" x 17'6" — TRAY CEILING

FAMILY 22'11" x 18'0"

OPTIONAL POCKET DOORS

STUDY 12'6" x 12'9"

ENTRY 9'10" x 12'6" — TWO STORY CEILING

DINING 12'5" x 16'0"

GARAGE 21'11" x 21'0"

55'2"

58'4"

Upper Level Floor Plan

OPEN BELOW

BEDRM 4 13'0" x 11'6"

OPEN BELOW

BEDRM 2 12'5" x 12'5"

BEDRM 3 11'3" x 17'1"

PLANT SHELF

Copyright by designer/architect.

Plan #151002

Dimensions: 67' W x 66' D

Levels: 1

Square Footage: 2,444

Bedrooms: 3

Bathrooms: 2½

Foundation: Crawl space, slab, or basement

CompleteCost List Available: Yes

Price Category: E

Images provided by designer/architect.

This gracious, traditional home is designed for practicality and convenience.

Features:

- Ceiling Height: 9 ft. except as noted below.

- Great Room: This room is ideal for entertaining, thanks to its lovely fireplace and French doors that open to the covered rear porch. Built-in cabinets give convenient storage space.

- Family Room: With access to the kitchen as well as the rear porch, this room will become your family's "headquarters."

- Study: Enjoy the quiet in this room with its 12-ft. ceiling and doorway to a private patio on the side of the house.

- Dining Room: Take advantage of the 8-in. wood columns and 12-ft. ceilings to create a formal dining area.

- Kitchen: An eat-in bar is a great place to snack, and the handy computer nook allows the kids to do their homework while you cook.

- Breakfast Room: Opening from the kitchen, this area gives added space for the family to gather any time.

- Master Suite: Featuring a 10-ft. boxed ceiling, the master bedroom also has a door way that opens onto the covered rear porch. The master bathroom has a step-up whirlpool tub, separate shower, and twin vanities with a makeup area.

Copyright by designer/architect.

Plan #161016

Dimensions: 59'4" W x 58'8" D
Levels: 2
Square Footage: 2,101
Main Level Sq. Ft.: 1,626
Upper Level Sq. Ft.: 475
Bedrooms: 3
Bathrooms: 2½
Foundation: Basement;
crawl space option available for fee
Materials List Available: Yes
Price Category: D

Note: Home in photo reflects a modified garage entrance.

Images provided by designer/architect.

Features:

• **Great Room:** Made for relaxing and entertaining, the great room is sunken to set it off from the rest of the house. A balcony from the second floor looks down into this spacious area, making it easy to keep track of the kids while they are playing.

• **Kitchen:** Convenience marks this well laid-out kitchen where you'll love to cook for guests and for family.

• **Master Bedroom:** A vaulted ceiling complements the unusual octagonal shape

of the master bedroom. Located on the first floor, this room allows some privacy from the second floor bedrooms. It is also ideal for anyone who no longer wishes to climb stairs to reach a bedroom.

You'll love the exciting roofline that sets this elegant home apart from its neighbors as well as the embellished, solid look that declares how well-designed it is—from the inside to the exterior.

CAD FILE AVAILABLE

Rear Elevation

Main Level Floor Plan

Deck

Bath

Sunken Great Room 16-10 x 21

Breakfast 9-2 x 16

Kitchen 8 x 13-4

Walk-in closet

Dining Room 16 x 11-8

Foyer

Master Bedroom 14 x 17-4

Slope ceiling   Slope ceiling

Bath

Hall

Laundry

Two-car Garage 21 x 20-8

58'-8"

59'-4"

Copyright by designer/architect.

Upper Level Floor Plan

Bedroom 15 x 10-8

Great Room Below

Bath

Bedroom 14 x 10-6

Foyer Below

Plan #121019

Dimensions: 70' W x 60' D
Levels: 2
Square Footage: 3,775
Main Level Sq. Ft.: 1,923
Upper Level Sq. Ft.: 1,852
Bedrooms: 4
Bathrooms: 3
Foundation: Basement
Materials List Available: Yes
Price Category: H

The grand exterior presence is carried inside, beginning with the dramatic curved staircase.

Features:

• Ceiling Height: 8 ft.

• Den: French doors lead to this sophisticated den, with its bayed windows and wall of bookcases.

• Living Room: A curved wall and a series of arched windows highlight this large space.

• Formal Dining Room: This room shares the curved wall and arched windows found in the living room.

• Screened Porch: This huge space features skylights and is accessible by another French door from the dining room.

• Family Room: Family and guests alike will be drawn to this room, with its trio of arched windows and fireplace flanked by bookcases.

• Kitchen: An island adds convenience and distinction to this large, functional kitchen.

• Garage: This spacious three-bay garage provides plenty of space for cars and storage.

Main Level Floor Plan

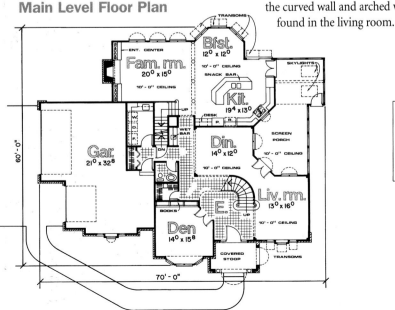

Upper Level Floor Plan

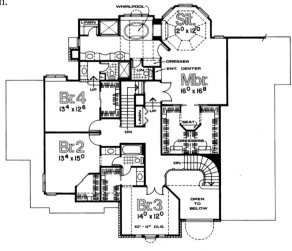

Copyright by designer/architect.

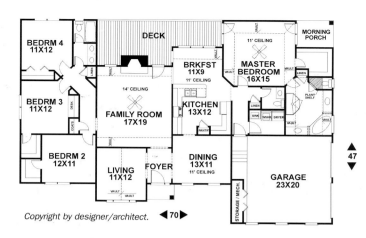

Copyright by designer/architect. ◀70▶

47

Plan #101010

Dimensions: 70' W x 47' D
Levels: 1
Square Footage: 2,187
Bedrooms: 4
Bathrooms: 2½
Foundation: Crawl space, slab, or basement
Materials List Available: Yes
Price Category: D

Images provided by designer/architect.

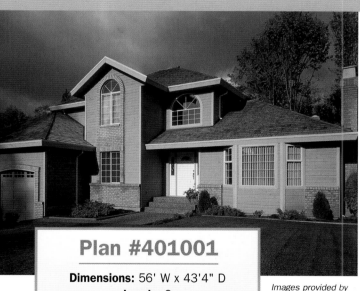

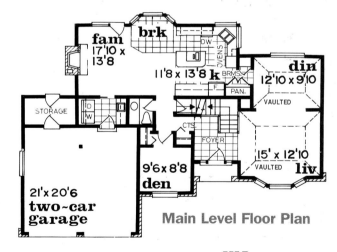

Main Level Floor Plan

Plan #401001

Dimensions: 56' W x 43'4" D
Levels: 2
Square Footage: 2,071
Main Level Sq. Ft.: 1,204
Upper Level Sq. Ft.: 867
Bedrooms: 3
Bathrooms: 2½
Foundation: Basement
Materials List Available: Yes
Price Category: D

Images provided by designer/architect.

CAD FILE AVAILABLE

Upper Level Floor Plan

Copyright by designer/architect.

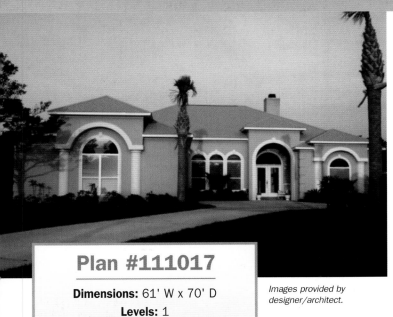

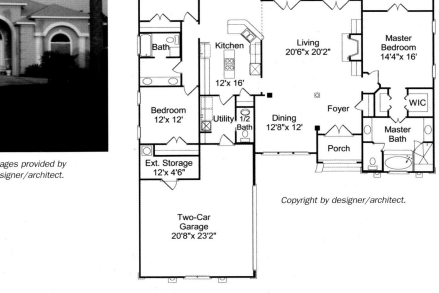

Plan #111017

Dimensions: 61' W x 70' D
Levels: 1
Square Footage: 2,323
Bedrooms: 3
Bathrooms: 2½
Foundation: Monolithic slab
Materials List Available: No
Price Category: E

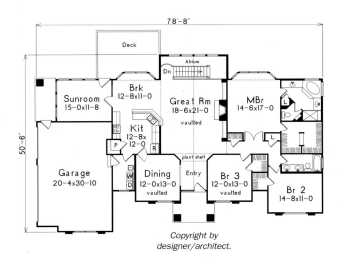

Plan #321037

Dimensions: 78'8" W x 50'6" D
Levels: 1
Square Footage: 2,397
Bedrooms: 3
Bathrooms: 2
Foundation: Basement or walkout
Materials List Available: Yes
Price Category: E

Optional Basement Level Floor Plan

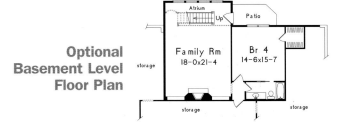

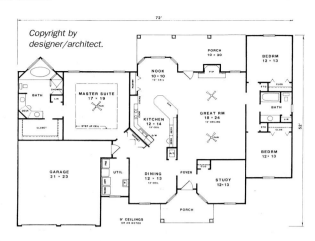

Plan #171004

Dimensions: 72' W x 52' D
Levels: 1
Square Footage: 2,256
Bedrooms: 3
Bathrooms: 2
Foundation: Crawl space, slab
Materials List Available: Yes
Price Category: E

SMARTtip

Windows – Privacy

You can easily stencil a work of art onto a windowpane, perhaps only as a border around the edge. Choose or create a design that gives you as little or as much privacy and light control as you need. Use a ready-made stencil or a piece of openwork fabric such as lace, or mask a design onto the glass using tape and a razor knife. Then apply glass paint or frosted glass spray, referring to the instructions and guidelines that come with the product.

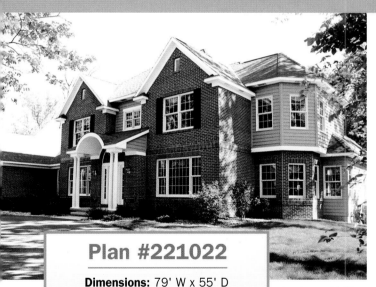

Main Level Floor Plan

Upper Level Floor Plan

Plan #221022

Dimensions: 79' W x 55' D
Levels: 2
Square Footage: 3,382
Main Level Sq. Ft.: 2,376
Upper Level Sq. Ft.: 1,006
Bedrooms: 4
Bathrooms: 3½
Foundation: Basement
Materials List Available: No
Price Category: G

Plan #121065

Dimensions: 62' W x 55'4" D

Levels: 2

Square Footage: 3,407

Main Level Sq. Ft.: 1,719

Upper Level Sq. Ft.: 1,688

Bedrooms: 4

Bathrooms: 2½

Foundation: Basement

Materials List Available: Yes

Price Category: G

Images provided by designer/architect.

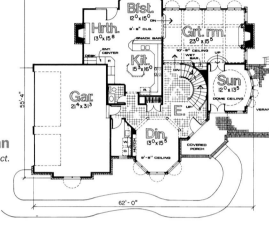

Upper Level Floor Plan

Main Level Floor Plan

Copyright by designer/architect.

Plan #211011

Dimensions: 84' W x 54' D

Levels: 1

Square Footage: 2,791

Bedrooms: 3 or 4

Bathrooms: 2

Foundation: Slab or crawl space

Materials List Available: Yes

Price Category: F

Images provided by designer/architect.

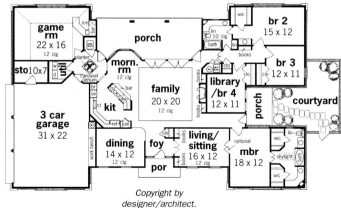

Copyright by designer/architect.

Plan #121073

Dimensions: 70' W x 52' D
Levels: 2
Square Footage: 2,579
Main Level Sq. Ft.: 1,933
Upper Level Sq. Ft.: 646
Bedrooms: 4
Bathrooms: 2½
Foundation: Basement
Materials List Available: Yes
Price Category: E

Images provided by designer/architect.

Main Level Floor Plan

Upper Level Floor Plan
Copyright by designer/architect.

Plan #151007

Dimensions: 54'2" W x 56'2" D
Levels: 1
Square Footage: 1,787
Bedrooms: 3
Bathrooms: 2
Foundation: Crawl space, slab, basement, or walkout
CompleteCost List Available: Yes
Price Category: C

Images provided by designer/architect.

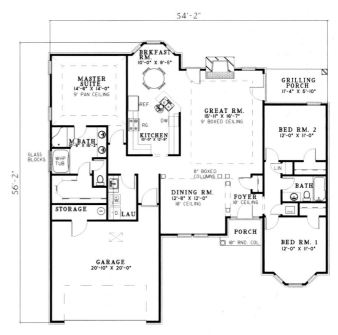

Copyright by designer/architect.

Plan #121082

Dimensions: 68'8" W x 60' D
Levels: 2
Square Footage: 2,932
Main Level Sq. Ft.: 2,084
Upper Level Sq. Ft.: 848
Bedrooms: 4
Bathrooms: 3½
Foundation: Basement
Materials List Available: Yes
Price Category: F

Enjoy the spacious covered veranda that gives this house so much added charm.

Features:

- **Great Room:** A volume ceiling enhances the spacious feeling in this room, making it a natural gathering spot for friends and family. Transom-topped windows look onto the veranda, and French doors open to it.

- **Den:** French doors from the entry lead to this room, with its unusual ceiling detail, gracious fireplace, and transom-topped windows.

- **Hearth Room:** Three skylights punctuate the cathedral ceiling in this room, giving it an extra measure of light and warmth.

- **Kitchen:** This kitchen is a delight, thanks to its generous working and storage space.

Main Level Floor Plan

Upper Level Floor Plan

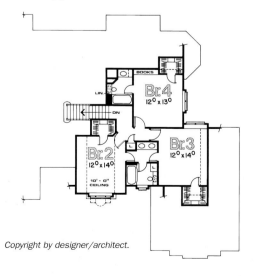

Plan #161001

Dimensions: 67'2" W x 47' D
Levels: 1
Square Footage: 1,782
Bedrooms: 3
Bathrooms: 2
Foundation: Basement
Materials List Available: Yes
Price Category: C

CAD FILE AVAILABLE

An all-brick exterior displays the solid strength that characterizes this gracious home.

Features:

- **Great Room:** A feeling of spaciousness permeates the gathering area created by the foyer, great room, and dining room. Multiple windows provide natural light that dances along a sloped ceiling, spilling onto decorative columns and a fireplace.

- **Breakfast Area:** A continuation of the sloped ceiling leads to the breakfast area where French doors open to a screened porch.

- **Kitchen:** An abundance of cabinets and counter space are the hallmarks of this large kitchen with its easy access to a spacious laundry room and storage area.

- **Master Suite:** A tray ceiling and spacious walk-in closet in the master bedroom, along with a whirlpool tub and double-bowl vanity in the bathroom, enable you to pamper yourself.

Images provided by designer/architect.

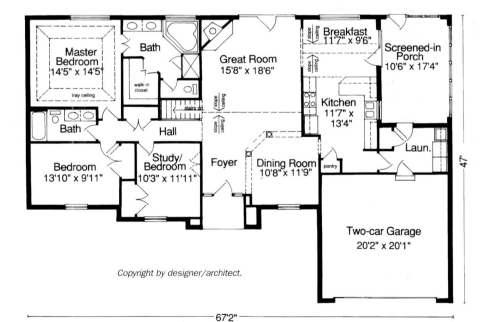

Copyright by designer/architect.

Great Room/Foyer

Rear Elevation

Plan #151004

Dimensions: 64'8" W x 62'1" D

Levels: 1

Square Footage: 2,107

Bedrooms: 4

Bathrooms: 2½

Foundation: Crawl space, slab, or basement

CompleteCost List Available: Yes

Price Category: D

You'll love the spacious feeling in this comfortable home designed for a family.

Features:

- Foyer: A 10-ft. ceiling greets you in this home.

- Great Room: A 10-ft. ceiling complements this large room, with its fireplace, built-in cabinets, and easy access to the rear covered porch.

- Dining Room: The 9-ft. boxed ceiling in this large room helps to create a beautiful formal feeling.

- Kitchen: The island in this kitchen is open to the breakfast room for true convenience.

- Breakfast Room: Morning light will stream through the bay window here.

- Master Suite: A 9-ft. pan ceiling adds a distinctive note to this room with access to the rear porch. In the bath, you'll find a whirlpool tub, separate shower, double vanities, and two walk-in closets.

Plan #121023

Dimensions: 85'5" W x 74'8" D
Levels: 2
Square Footage: 3,904
Main Level Sq. Ft.: 2,813
Upper Level Sq. Ft.: 1,091
Bedrooms: 4
Bathrooms: 3½
Foundation: Basement
Materials List Available: Yes
Price Category: H

Images provided by designer/architect.

Spacious and gracious, here are all the amenities you expect in a fine home.

Features:

• Ceiling Height: 8 ft. except as noted.

• Foyer: This magnificent entry features a graceful curved staircase with balcony above.

• Sunken Living Room: This sunken room is filled with light from a row of bowed windows. It's the perfect place for social gatherings both large and small.

• Den: French doors open into this truly distinctive den with its 11-ft. ceiling and built-in bookcases.

• Formal Dining Room: Entertain guests with style and grace in this dining room with corner column.

• Master Suite: Another set of French doors leads to this suite that features two walk-in closets, a whirlpool flanked by vanities, and a private sitting room with built-in bookcases.

Main Level Floor Plan

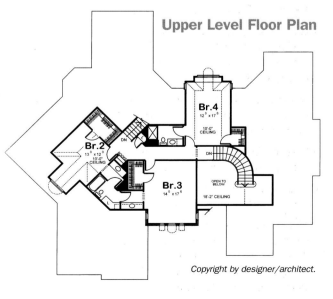

Upper Level Floor Plan

Copyright by designer/architect.

Images provided by designer/architect.

Copyright by designer/architect.

garage
22 x 22

sto 16 x 6

porch 30 x 8

br 3
12 x 12

dining
13 x 12

util 8 x 8

living
18 x 21

eating
10 x 12

bar

mbr
16 x 14

kit
12x13

foy 13 x 5

br 2
12 x 12

Plan #211002

Dimensions: 68' W x 62' D

Levels: 1

Square Footage: 1,792

Bedrooms: 3

Bathrooms: 2

Foundation: Crawl space

Materials List Available: Yes

Price Category: C

Plan #151011

Dimensions: 59'6" W x 74'4" D

Levels: 2

Square Footage: 3,437

Main Level Sq. Ft.: 2,184

Upper Level Sq. Ft.: 1,253

Bedrooms: 5

Bathrooms: 4

Foundation: Crawl space or slab; basement or daylight basement for fee

CompleteCost List Available: Yes

Price Category: G

**Main Level
Floor Plan**

**Upper Level
Floor Plan**

Images provided by designer/architect.

Copyright by designer/architect.

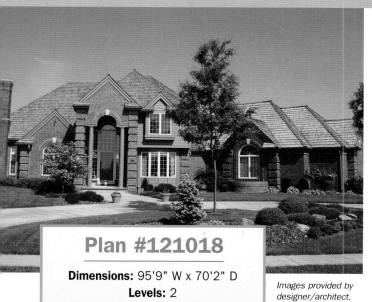

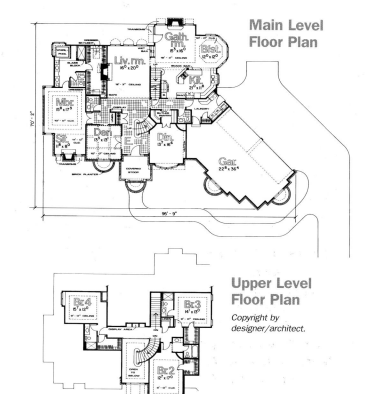

Main Level Floor Plan

Images provided by designer/architect.

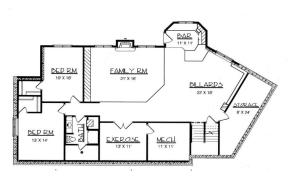

Upper Level Floor Plan

Copyright by designer/architect.

Plan #121018

Dimensions: 95'9" W x 70'2" D
Levels: 2
Square Footage: 3,950
Main Level Sq. Ft.: 2,839
Upper Level Sq. Ft.: 1,111
Bedrooms: 4
Bathrooms: 4 full, 2 half
Foundation: Basement
Materials List Available: Yes
Price Category: H

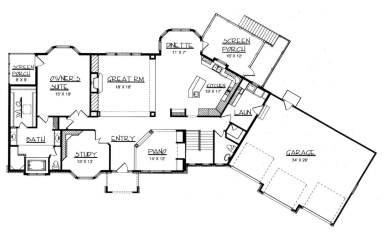

Optional Basement Level Floor Plan

Plan #271079

Dimensions: 104' W x 55' D
Levels: 1
Square Footage: 2,228
Bedrooms: 1-3
Bathrooms: 1½
Foundation: Daylight basement
Materials List Available: No
Price Category: E

Images provided by designer/architect.

Copyright by designer/architect.

Planning Your Landscape

Fringe tree

Spirea

Spreading English yew

Landscapes change over the years. As plants grow, the overall look evolves from sparse to lush. Trees cast cool shade where the sun used to shine. Shrubs and hedges grow tall and dense enough to provide privacy. Perennials and ground covers spread to form colorful patches of foliage and flowers. Meanwhile, paths, arbors, fences, and other structures gain the patina of age.

Constant change over the years—sometimes rapid and dramatic, sometimes slow and subtle—is one of the joys of landscaping. It is also one of the challenges. Anticipating how fast plants will grow and how big they will eventually get is difficult, even for professional designers, and was a major concern in formulating the designs for this article.

To illustrate the kinds of changes to expect in a planting, these pages show one of the designs at three different "ages." Even though a new planting may look sparse at first, it will soon fill in. And because of careful spacing, the planting will look as good in ten to fifteen years as it does after three to five. It will, of course, look different, but that's part of the fun.

At Planting—Here's how the corner might appear in spring immediately after planting. The fence and mulch look conspicuously fresh, new, and unweathered. The fringe tree is only 4 to 5 ft. tall, with trunks no thicker than broomsticks. (With this or other trees, you can buy bigger specimens to start with, but they're a lot more expensive and sometimes don't perform as well in the long run.) The spireas and spreading English yews, transplanted from 2-gal. nursery containers, spread 12 to 18 in. wide. The perennials, transplanted from quart- or gallon-size containers, are just low tufts of foliage now, but they grow fast enough to produce a few flowers the first summer.

Three to Five Years—The fringe tree has grown about 6 in. taller every year but is still quite slender. Some trees would grow faster, as much as 1 to 2 ft. a year. The spireas, like many fast-growing shrubs, have reached almost full size. From now on, they'll get thicker but not much taller. The slower-growing English yews make a series of low mounds; you still see them as individuals, not a continuous patch. Most perennials, such as the coneflowers, Shasta daisies, daylilies, and dianthus shown here, grow so crowded after a few years that they need to be divided and replanted.

Ten to Fifteen Years—The fringe tree is becoming a fine specimen, 10 to 12 ft. wide and tall. Unless you prune away enough of its lower limbs to let some sunlight in, the spireas will gradually stop blooming, get weaker, and need to be replaced with shade-tolerant shrubs such as more English yews or with shade-loving perennials and ferns. The original English yews will have formed a continuous ground cover by now and may have spread enough to limit the space available for perennials. Since the perennials get divided every few years anyway, it's no trouble to rearrange or regroup them, as shown here.

Fringe tree

Three to Five Years

Spreading
English yew

Spirea

Coneflower

Shasta daisy

Dianthus

Daylily

Fringe tree

Ten to Fifteen Years

Spreading
English yew

First Impressions

Make a pleasant passage to the front door

First impressions are as important in the home landscape as they are on a blind date or a job interview. Why wait until a visitor reaches the front door to extend a warm greeting? Instead let your landscape offer a friendly welcome and a helpful "Please come this way." Well-chosen plants and a revamped walkway not only make a visitor's short journey a pleasant one, they can also enhance your home's most public face and help settle it comfortably in its immediate surroundings.

The ample bluestone walkway in this design invites visitors to stroll side by side through a small garden from the driveway to the entrance. The path is positioned to put the front door in full view of arriving guests. Its generous width allows for informal gatherings as guests arrive and leave, and well-chosen plants encourage lingering there to enjoy them.

Three small trees grace the entrance with spring and summer flowers, light shade, and superb fall color. Most of the perennials and shrubs are evergreen and look good year-round, providing a fine background to the flowers and an attractive foil to the fall color. In the winter, colorful tree bark and bright berries make gazing out the windows a pleasure.

Plants & Projects

The predominantly evergreen foliage comes in a surprising range of blues and greens, accented by white and blue flowers in spring and summer. Once established, the planting requires regular pruning and shearing but little else.

A **Serviceberry** *Amelanchier × grandiflora* (use 1) This small deciduous, often multitrunked tree greets spring with clusters

'Natchez' crape myrtle **C**

See site plan for **K**

White evergreen azalea **B**

'Big Blue' lilyturf **D**

'Blue Prince' holly **H**

Blue oat grass **I**

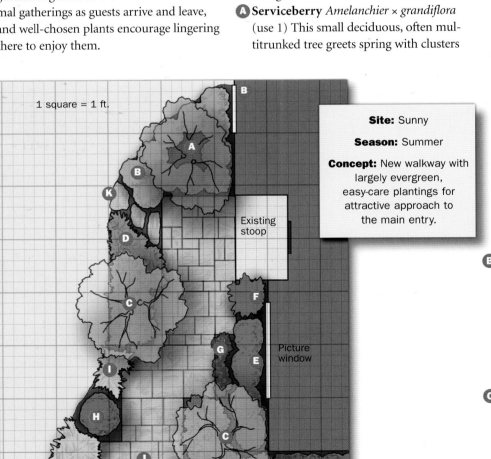

1 square = 1 ft.

Existing stoop

Picture window

Driveway

Site: Sunny

Season: Summer

Concept: New walkway with largely evergreen, easy-care plantings for attractive approach to the main entry.

of white flowers. Edible blue-purple berries ripen in June or July; bright foliage enlivens the autumn.

B **White evergreen azalea** *Rhododendron* (use 11) Low, mounding shrubs form a soft skirt beneath the serviceberry by the door. Try the cultivar 'Helen Curtis', with white flowers in mid to late spring.

C **'Natchez' crape myrtle** *Lagerstroemia indica* (use 2) Flanking the walk, these small multitrunked trees bear pure white crepe-papery flowers for weeks in summer. Colorful fall leaves drop to reveal attractive flaking bark in winter.

A Serviceberry

G Christmas rose

F Heavenly bamboo

E 'Otto Luyken' cherry laurel

D 'Big Blue' lily-turf

C 'Natchez' crape myrtle

H 'Blue Prince' holly

D **'Big Blue' lilyturf** *Liriope muscari* (use 40)
These grassy evergreen perennials carpet the ground beneath the crape myrtles. Small spikes of blue flowers in summer produce shiny blue-black berries in fall. Brighten up spring by underplanting 75 white daffodil bulbs (*Narcissus*) in each lilyturf bed.

E **'Otto Luyken' cherry laurel** (use 4) *Prunus laurocerasus*
This evergreen shrub has thick glossy leaves and fragrant white spring flowers.

Prune to form a neat block of greenery below the windows.

F **Heavenly bamboo**
Nandina domestica (use 1)
An evergreen shrub that packs four seasons of interest into the narrow space by the door. Tiers of lacy foliage turn from copper to green to rich crimson or purple. Summer's white flowers give way to heavy sprays of shiny red berries that may last until spring.

G **Christmas rose** *Helleborus niger* (use 5)
Tucked in by the walk, this

evergreen ground cover offers fine-toothed dark green leaves and white cup-size blossoms in winter and early spring. Underplant 20 white Grecian windflower bulbs (*Anemone blanda*) to add to the spring display.

H **'Blue Prince' holly** *Ilex × meserveae* (use 5)
An excellent evergreen foundation shrub between the drive and house; one is also used as a shaped specimen next to the walk. Features glossy blue-green foliage and purple twigs.

Maintained by regular pruning.

I **Blue oat grass**
Helictotrichon sempervirens (use 10)
The formality of the sheared holly is set off nicely by this small island of clump-forming grass. Blue-gray foliage looks good all year.

J **Walkway**
Rectangular flagstones in random sizes; bluestone shown here.

K **Steppingstones**
Fieldstones provide easy access to the lawn.

A Step Up

Plant a foundation garden

Homes on raised foundations usually have foundation plantings. These simple skirtings of greenery hide unattractive concrete-block underpinnings and help overcome the impression that the house is hovering a few feet above the ground. Useful as these plantings are, they are too often just monochromatic expanses of clipped junipers, dull as dishwater. But, as this design shows, a durable, low-maintenance foundation planting can be more varied, more colorful, and more fun.

Because a foundation planting should look good year-round, the design is anchored by a row of cherry laurels, broad-leaved evergreens covered each spring by heavily scented flowers. A small garden of shrubs, perennials, and a graceful arching grass will catch the eye of visitors approaching the front door. Colorful perennials bloom from spring to fall along the edge of the bed. At the far end is a tidy viburnum, whose spicy-scented flowers will encourage springtime strolls around that corner of the house.

Plants and Projects

From spring to fall, something is always blooming here, but foliage texture and color play an even greater role than flowers in this design. From the slender, shimmering leaves of Japanese silver grass rising behind mounded barberries, to furry lamb's ears, feathery coreopsis, and fleshy sedum, textures abound, colored in a variety of reds, greens, and silvers. Winter offers glossy green cherry laurels, the tawny leaves and striking seed heads of silver grass, and the rich russets of the sedum. Other than an annual cutback in spring and a little pruning to shape the viburnum, the planting requires little maintenance.

'Autumn Joy' sedum **E**

'Crimson Pygmy' **C**
Japanese barberry

Lamb's ears **I**

A **Korean spice viburnum**
Viburnum carlesii (use 1 plant)
At the corner of the house, this deciduous shrub produces spicy-scented flowers in spring (preceded by pretty pink buds) and dense green foliage in summer and fall. Shape by annual pruning.

B **'Otto Luyken' cherry laurel** (use 4) *Prunus laurocerasus*
The glossy dark leaves and spreading habit of these evergreen shrubs will clothe the foundation year-round. As a bonus, spring produces a profusion of fragrant white flowers in spikes.

C **'Crimson Pygmy' Japanese barberry** (use 3) *Berberis thunbergii*
A compact deciduous shrub with small, teardrop-shaped maroon leaves that turn crimson in fall, when they are joined by bright red berries.

D **'Morning Light' Japanese silver grass** (use 1)
Miscanthus sinensis
A rustling sentinel by the door, this grass is silvery all summer, then turns tawny after frost. Its fluffy seed heads last through the winter.

E **'Autumn Joy' sedum** (use 3)
Sedum
Flat-topped flower clusters emerge in late summer above clumps of fleshy gray-green leaves, turning from white through shades of ever deeper pink to rust-colored seed heads that can stand through the winter.

F **'East Friesland' salvia** (use 4) *Salvia × superba*
Shown off against the green backdrop, reddish purple flower spikes cover these perennials off and on from May through fall.

G **'Longwood Blue' bluebeard** (use 1) *Caryopteris × clandonensis*
A small deciduous shrub with silvery gray foliage and fringed blue flowers from late summer to frost.

H **'Moonbeam' coreopsis** (use 4) *Coreopsis verticillata*
A perennial with fine foliage and tiny pale yellow flowers from July into September.

I **Lamb's ears** (use 3) *Stachys byzantina*
A perennial with fuzzy silver-white leaves. Use the large-leaved, wide-spreading cultivar 'Helene von Stein' (sometimes called 'Big Ears').

J **'Big Blue' lilyturf** (use 4)
Liriope muscari
This grasslike evergreen perennial under the viburnum has dark blue flowers in summer.

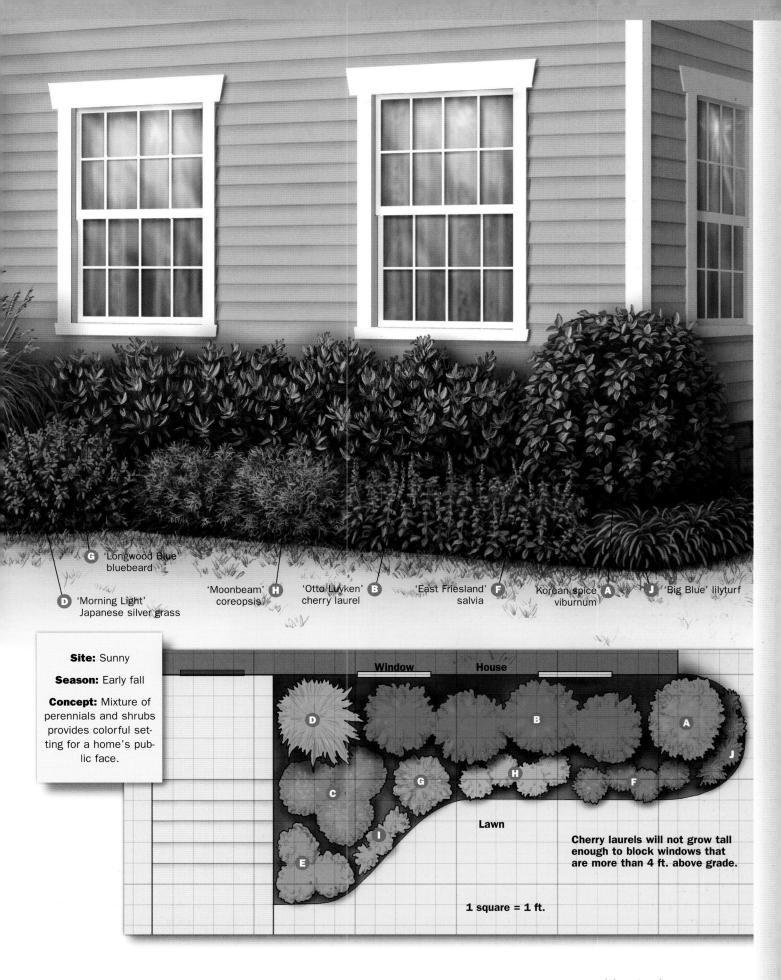

G 'Longwood Blue' bluebeard

D 'Morning Light' Japanese silver grass

'Moonbeam' coreopsis H

'Otto Luyken' cherry laurel B

'East Friesland' salvia F

Korean spice viburnum A

J 'Big Blue' lilyturf

Site: Sunny

Season: Early fall

Concept: Mixture of perennials and shrubs provides colorful setting for a home's public face.

Window   House

D

B

A

J

H

G

C

F

Lawn

I

E

Cherry laurels will not grow tall enough to block windows that are more than 4 ft. above grade.

1 square = 1 ft.

Up Front and Formal

Seasonal color brightens sheared symmetry

Formal gardens have a special appeal. Their simple geometry can be soothing in a hectic world, and the look is timeless, never going out of style. The front yard of a classical house, like the one shown here, with two identical rectangles of lawn either side of a central entry walk invites a formal makeover. (A house with a symmetrical facade in any style has similar potential.)

The layout of this elegant design keys off of and reinforces the symmetry of the house facade. Evergreens around the perimeter define the space, creating a sense of enclosure without shutting out the view of the street, or the view from it. The lawn has disappeared, replaced by rectangular flower beds. Framed with lilyturf, a low-growing evergreen perennial, the beds showcase seasonal plantings of colorful annuals. In the center of the design, a wide brick walkway forms a small courtyard, a pleasing setting for chatting with guests as they arrive or depart.

The design is easily altered to accommodate the character of your site and gardening preferences. The rectangular beds can be expanded or reduced to fit properties of differing sizes without losing the composition's balanced proportions. Dressed flagstones, neatly raked gravel, or precast pavers may be more in keeping with the materials used on your home's facade. If replanting annuals several times a year is more work than you care to tackle, you can substitute perennials such as 'Monch' aster, 'Dropmore' catmint, or 'May Night' salvia, which bloom through most of the summer. Finally, if you're a traditionalist, consider replacing the lilyturf edging with a low boxwood hedge.

Plants and Projects

The evergreens in this design display a mixture of hues, from the dark blue-green 'Blue Princess' hollies to the bright green yews. Against this neatly clipped and subdued

'Foster #2' holly **B**

See site plan for **H**

'Hatfield' **A**
hybrid yew

'Big Blue' **F**
lilyturf

background the bright-colored annuals and red fall berries are a striking sight. While the evergreens are dependable problem-free performers, you'll need to attend to them regularly with clippers to keep them in shape.

A **'Hatfield' hybrid yew** (use 6) *Taxus × media*
A slow-growing evergreen trained and sheared to form a dense hedge 4 ft. tall and 3 ft. wide.

B **'Foster #2' holly** (use 2) *Ilex × attenuata*
Pruned to form slender cones 12 ft. tall, these evergreen trees emphasize the corners of the house. Slim, spiny evergreen leaves look good year-round; masses of red berries enliven the winter scene.

C **'Blue Princess' holly** (use 4) *Ilex × meserveae*

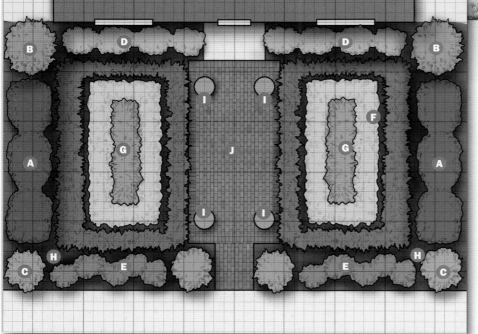

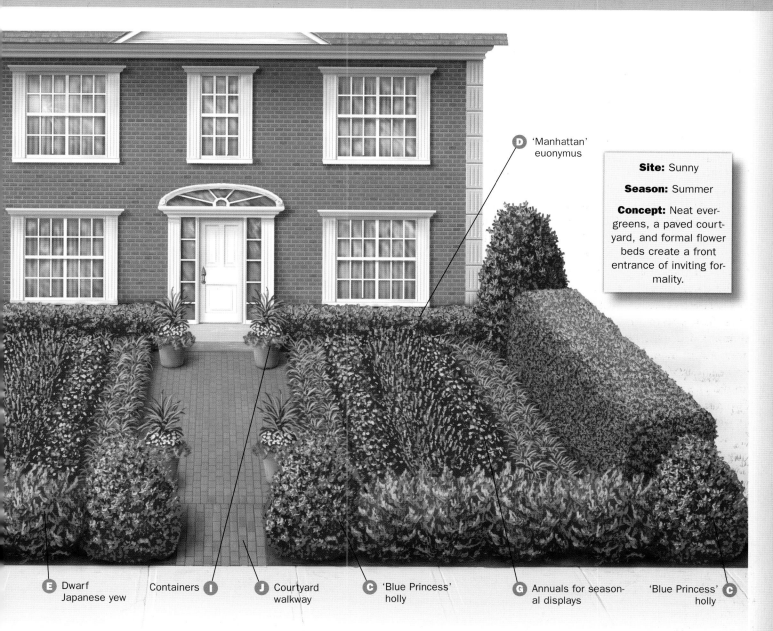

Site: Sunny

Season: Summer

Concept: Neat evergreens, a paved courtyard, and formal flower beds create a front entrance of inviting formality.

D 'Manhattan' euonymus

E Dwarf Japanese yew   **Containers** **I**   **J** Courtyard walkway   **C** 'Blue Princess' holly   **G** Annuals for seasonal displays   'Blue Princess' **C** holly

Waist-high sheared cones of lustrous dark blue-green leaves mark the front corners of the design and the entrance to the "courtyard." In fall and winter, these evergreen shrubs glow with abundant crops of bright red berries. (If there are no 'Blue Prince' hollies in your neighborhood, plant these pollinators at the corners to ensure berry production.)

D **'Manhattan' euonymus** (use 8) *Euonymus kiautschovicus* These evergreen shrubs are sheared to form a block of greenery beneath the windows. Leaves hold their color

through the region's mild winters; they're sprinkled in fall with eye-catching pinkish orange fruits.

E **Dwarf Japanese yew** (use 10) *Taxus cuspidata 'Nana'*, These compact evergreen shrubs contribute a modestly "natural" note in this geometric design. Their dense spreading form needs only a little pruning to keep the plants about a foot lower than the nearby hollies.

F **'Big Blue' lilyturf** (use 92) *Liriope muscari* Planted about 1 ft. apart, these evergreen perennials outline the annual beds with

a continuous ribbon of grassy foliage. Spikes of small blue flowers rise above the leaves in late summer.

G **Annuals for seasonal displays** Possibilities are endless for creating a different carpet of color in these little "rooms" each season. To get started, try tulips in spring, a mixture of pink geraniums and blue salvias for summer (shown here), chrysanthemums for fall, and ornamental cabbage for winter.

H **'Bronze Beauty' bugleweed** (as needed) *Ajuga reptans* Planted as a ground cover under hedges and shrubs,

these vigorous perennials will form a handsome carpet of purple-bronze foliage. May be shaded out as shrubs mature.

I **Containers** Fill pots or urns with annuals to suit your taste. Here we show impatiens and trailing variegated vinca clustered around a dracaena spike. Change these seasonally, too, if you wish.

J **Courtyard walkway** Select hard surface material to complement your house. Brick (shown here) or rectangular flagstones in random sizes reinforce the formal lines of the design.

Plan #161029

Dimensions: 87' W x 82' D
Levels: 2
Square Footage: 4,470
Main Level Sq. Ft.: 3,300
Upper Level Sq. Ft.: 1,170
Bedrooms: 4
Bathrooms: 3 full, 2 half
Foundation: Basement
Materials List Available: Yes
Price Category: I

This gracious home is so impressive — inside and out — that it suits the most discriminating tastes.

Features:

- Foyer: A balcony overlooks this gracious area decorated by tall columns.

- Hearth Room: Visually open to the kitchen and the breakfast area, this room is ideal for any sort of gathering.

- Great Room: Colonial columns also form the entry here, and a magnificent window treatment that includes French doors leads to the terrace.

- Library: Built-in shelving adds practicality to this quiet retreat.

- Kitchen: Spread out on the oversized island with a cooktop and seating.

- Additional Bedrooms: Walk-in closets and private access to a bath define each bedroom.

Main Level Floor Plan

Upper Level Floor Plan

Copyright by designer/architect.

Plan #151253

Dimensions: 61'8" W x 75' D
Levels: 2
Square Footage: 4,882
Main Level Sq. Ft.: 2,583
Upper Level Sq. Ft.: 2,299
Bedrooms: 6
Bathrooms: 6½
Foundation: Slab
CompleteCost List Available: Yes
Price Category: I

Images provided by designer/architect.

Luxury abounds in this six-bedroom home for larger families. You'll find lavish comforts throughout the design.

CAD FILE AVAILABLE CAD

Features:

- **Living Room:** This open room hosts a bar and wine storage for entertaining family and friends. The two-story space boasts a dramatic fireplace and access to the rear covered porch.

- **Family Room:** An open snack bar faces this room, which will become a favorite for the family to enjoy a movie and popcorn. On nice days or evenings you can step out the double doors and onto the rear covered porch.

- **Master Suite:** This private oasis features a large sleeping area, a sitting area, and an exercise room complete with a sauna and

steam room. The large master bath features a spa tub, dual vanities, a separate shower, and a private lavatory area.

- **Bedrooms:** Five additional bedrooms, each with a private full bathroom, complete the floor plan. Two bedrooms are located on the first level, with the remaining three on the upper level with the master suite.

Rear View.

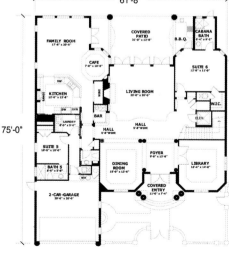

Main Level Floor Plan

Upper Level Floor Plan

Copyright by designer/architect.

Plan #131032

Dimensions: 69'2" W x 46' D
Levels: 2
Square Footage: 2,455
Main Level Sq. Ft.: 1,499
Upper Level Sq. Ft.: 956
Bedrooms: 4
Bathrooms: 3
Foundation: Crawl space, slab, or basement
Materials List Available: Yes
Price Category: F

Images provided by designer/architect.

If you love Victorian styling, you'll be charmed by the ornate, rounded front porch and the two-story bay that distinguish this home.

Features:

• Living Room: You'll love the 13-ft. ceiling in this room, as well as the panoramic view it gives of the front porch and yard.

• Kitchen: Sunlight streams into this room, where an angled island with a cooktop eases both prepping and cooking.

• Breakfast Room: This room shares an eating bar with the kitchen, making it easy for the family to congregate while the family chef is cooking.

• Guest Room: Use this lovely room on the first level as a home office or study if you wish.

• Master Suite: The dramatic bayed sitting area with a high ceiling has an octagonal shape that you'll adore, and the amenities in the private bath will soothe you at the end of a busy day.

Rear View

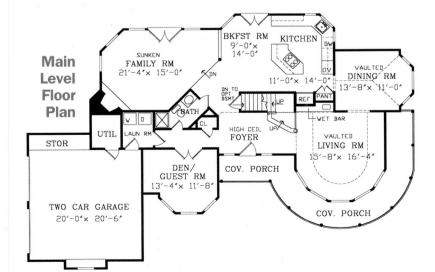

Main Level Floor Plan

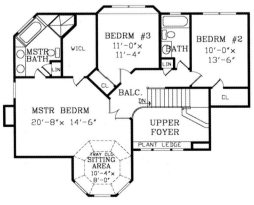

Upper Level Floor Plan

Copyright by designer/architect.

Main Level Floor Plan

Images provided by designer/architect.

Rear View

Basement Level Floor Plan

Plan #161100

Dimensions: 89' W x 59'2" D

Levels: 1

Square Footage: 5,377

Main Level Sq. Ft.: 2,961

Basement Level Sq. Ft.: 2,416

Bedrooms: 3

Bathrooms: 2 full, 2 half

Foundation: Walkout; basement for fee

Material List Available: No

Price Category: J

Main Level Floor Plan

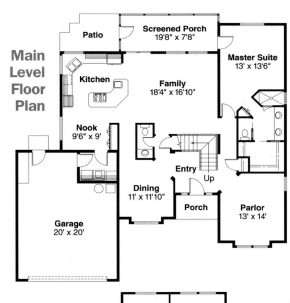

Images provided by designer/architect.

Plan #361267

Dimensions: 55' W x 56' D

Levels: 2

Square Footage: 2,051

Main Level Sq. Ft.: 1,628

Upper Level Sq. Ft.: 423

Bedrooms: 3

Bathrooms: 2½

Foundation: Slab

Material List Available: No

Price Category: D

Upper Level Floor Plan

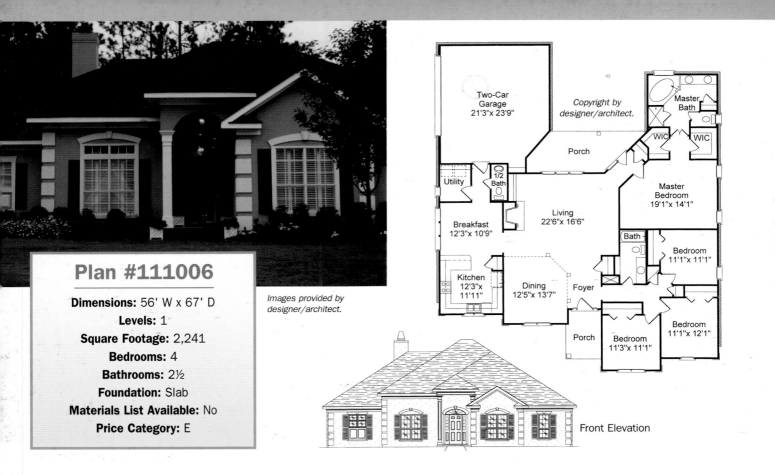

Plan #111006

Dimensions: 56' W x 67' D

Levels: 1

Square Footage: 2,241

Bedrooms: 4

Bathrooms: 2½

Foundation: Slab

Materials List Available: No

Price Category: E

Images provided by designer/architect.

Copyright by designer/architect.

Front Elevation

Plan #161019

Dimensions: 54'6" D x 41'10" W

Levels: 2

Square Footage: 2,428

Main Level Sq. Ft.: 1,309

Upper Level Sq. Ft.: 1,119

Bedrooms: 4

Bathrooms: 2½

Foundation: Basement

Materials List Available: No

Price Category: E

Images provided by designer/architect.

Copyright by designer/architect.

Main Level Floor Plan

Upper Level Floor Plan

Plan #481034

Dimensions: 84'8" W x 77'8" D
Levels: 2
Square Footage: 2,830
Main Level Sq. Ft.: 1,673
Upper Level Sq. Ft.: 1,157
Bedrooms: 3
Bathrooms: 2½
Foundation: Walkout
Materials List Available: No
Price Category: F

This European-influenced two-story home has stone accents and wide board siding.

Images provided by designer/architect.

Features:

• Great Room: The fireplace, flanked by built-in cabinets, is the focal point of this gathering area. Because the area is located just off the foyer, your guests can easily enter this area.

• Dining Room: This formal dining area features a built-in cabinet and a 9-ft.-high ceiling. The triple window has a view of the front yard.

• Kitchen: This large island kitchen is a bonus in any home. Open to the dinette and the great room, the area has a light and open feeling. The built-in pantry is ready to store all of your supplies.

• Master Suite: Occupying most of the upper level, this retreat boasts a vaulted ceiling in the sleeping area and a large walk-in closet. The master bath features his and her vanities and a large stall shower.

Rear View

Main Level Floor Plan

Upper Level Floor Plan

Copyright by designer/architect.

Plan #401050

Dimensions: 81' W x 61' D
Levels: 2
Square Footage: 6,841
Main Level Sq. Ft.: 2,596
Upper Level Sq. Ft.: 2,233
Finished Basement Sq. Ft.: 2,012
Bedrooms: 4
Bathrooms: 3 full, 2 half
Foundation: Basement
Materials List Available: Yes
Price Category: I

This grand two-story European home is adorned with a facade of stucco and brick, meticulously appointed with details for gracious living.

Features:

- Foyer: Guests enter through a portico to find this stately two-story foyer.

- Living Room: This formal area features a tray ceiling and a fireplace and is joined by a charming dining room with a large bay window.

- Kitchen: A butler's pantry joins the dining room to this gourmet kitchen, which holds a separate wok kitchen, an island work center, and a breakfast room with double doors that lead to the rear patio.

- Family Room: Located near the kitchen, this room enjoys a built-in aquarium, media center, and fireplace.

- Den: This room with a tray ceiling, window seat, and built-in computer center is tucked in a corner for privacy.

- Master Suite: The second floor features this spectacular space, which has a separate sitting room, an oversized closet, and a bath with a spa tub.

Images provided by designer/architect.

Upper Level Floor Plan

Main Level Floor Plan
Copyright by designer/architect.

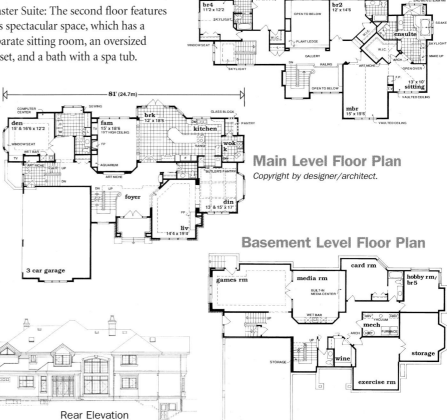

Basement Level Floor Plan

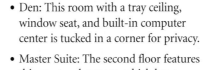

Rear Elevation

Plan #391050

Dimensions: 67' W x 51' D

Levels: 2

Square Footage: 2,674

Main Level Sq. Ft.: 1,511

Upper Level Sq. Ft.: 1,163

Bedrooms: 3

Bathrooms: 2½

Foundation: Crawl space, slab, or basement

Materials List Available: Yes

Price Category: F

This home, as shown in the photograph, may differ from the actual blueprints. For more detailed information, please check the floor plans carefully.

This home truly transforms tutor styling for today. Charming Old World half-timbering dramatizes exterior dormers and the deeply recessed pillared porch, while New World surprises fill the interior.

Features:

- Kitchen: Beyond the living room and study and past the double-entry stairway, this elaborately open-ended kitchen feeds into other important spaces, including the breakfast room, which is bathed in natural light on three sides as it looks out on the patio and three-season porch.

- Family Room: This open family room is also a big draw, with its fireplace, two-story cathedral ceilings, and porch access.

- Master Suite: The second level, enjoying the spacious aura of the vaulted ceiling, high lights this master suite, with its generous windowing, spectacular closeting, and bathroom with tub situated in a wide windowed corner.

- Bedrooms: Two additional bedrooms feature plentiful closeting and pretty front-view windows (one with window seat) and share a second full bath.

Main Level Floor Plan

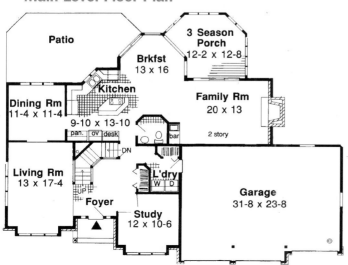

Upper Level Floor Plan

Copyright by designer/architect.

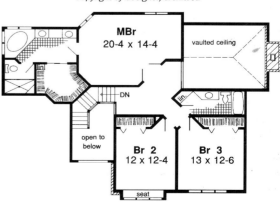

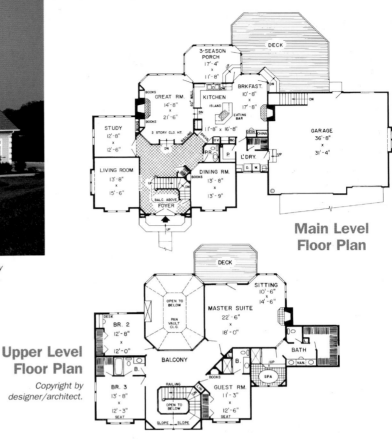

Plan #391018

Dimensions: 93' W x 54' D
Levels: 2
Square Footage: 3,746
Main Level Sq. Ft.: 1,978
Upper Level Sq. Ft.: 1,768
Bedrooms: 4
Bathrooms: 3½
Foundation: Basement
Materials List Available: Yes
Price Category: H

Images provided by designer/architect.

Main Level Floor Plan

Upper Level Floor Plan

Copyright by designer/architect.

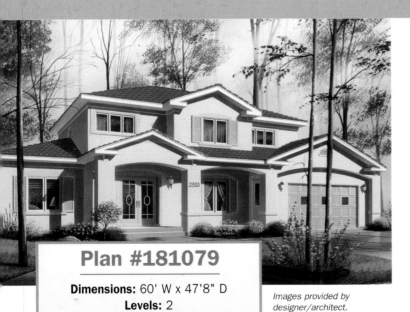

Plan #181079

Dimensions: 60' W x 47'8" D
Levels: 2
Square Footage: 3,016
Main Level Sq. Ft.: 1,716
Upper Level Sq. Ft.: 1,300
Bedrooms: 6
Bathrooms: 4½
Foundation: Crawl space
Materials List Available: Yes
Price Category: G

Images provided by designer/architect.

CAD FILE AVAILABLE

Main Level Floor Plan

Upper Level Floor Plan

Copyright by designer/architect.

Plan #161105

Dimensions: 90'2" W x 104'5" D

Levels: 2

Square Footage: 6,806

Main Level Sq. Ft.: 4,511

Upper Level Sq. Ft.: 2,295

Bedrooms: 4

Bathrooms: 4 full, 2 half

Foundation: Walkout basement

Material List Available: No

Price Category: K

The opulence and drama of this European-inspired home features a solid brick exterior with limestone detail, arched dormers, and a parapet.

CAD FILE AVAILABLE

Images provided by designer/architect.

Features:

- Foyer: A large octagonal skylight tops a water fountain feature displayed in this exquisite entryway. The formal dining room and library flank the entry and enjoy a 10-ft. ceiling height.

- Family Living Area: The gourmet kitchen, breakfast area, and cozy hearth room comprise this family activity center of the home. Wonderful amenities such as a magnificent counter with seating, a celestial ceiling over the dining table, an alcove for an entertainment center, a stone-faced wood-burning fireplace, and access to the rear porch enhance the informal area.

- Master Suite: This luxurious suite enjoys a raised ceiling, a seating area with bay window, and access to the terrace. The dressing room pampers the homeowner with a whirlpool tub, a ceramic tile shower enclosure, two vanities, and a spacious walk-in closet.

- Upper Level: Elegant stairs lead to the second-floor study loft and two additional bedrooms, each with a private bathroom and large walk-in closet. On the same level, and located for privacy, the third bedroom serves as a guest suite, showcasing a cozy sitting area and private bathroom.

Copyright by designer/architect.

Upper Level Floor Plan

Main Level Floor Plan

Optional Basement Level Floor Plan

Plan #161103

Dimensions: 89'10" W x 89'4" D
Levels: 2
Square Footage: 5,633
Main Level Sq. Ft.: 3,850
Upper Level Sq. Ft.: 1,783
Bedrooms: 4
Bathrooms: 3½
Foundation: Walkout; basement for fee
Material List Available: No
Price Category: J

The brick and stone exterior, with its arches and balcony overlooking the entry, creates a home that showcases artistic and historic architectural elements.

CAD FILE AVAILABLE

Features:

- Kitchen: The heart of the home centers around this gourmet kitchen, which features a large island and a breakfast area that opens to a delightful terrace. The adjacent hearth room boasts a cozy fireplace.

- Master Suite: This main-level retreat has private access to the rear porch and a stepped ceiling in the sleeping area. The master bath will pamper you with amenities such as a platform whirlpool tub and a two-person shower.

- Secondary Bedrooms: Three bedrooms are located on the upper level and each have a walk-in closets. Two bedrooms share a Jack-and-Jill bathroom, while the third has a private bathroom.

- Lower Level: For fun times, this lower level is finished to provide a wet bar, a billiard room, and a recreation room. Future expansion can include an additional bedroom and an exercise room.

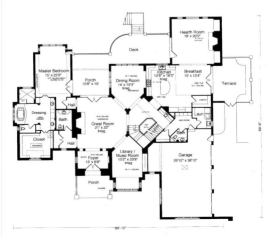

Main Level Floor Plan

Upper Level Floor Plan

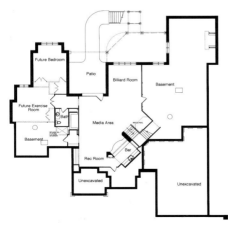

Optional Basement Level Floor Plan

Copyright by designer/architect.

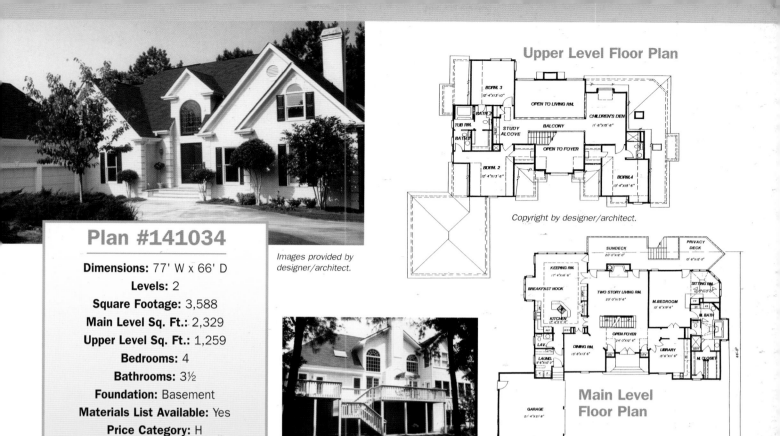

Upper Level Floor Plan

Copyright by designer/architect.

Images provided by designer/architect.

Main Level Floor Plan

Plan #141034

Dimensions: 77' W x 66' D
Levels: 2
Square Footage: 3,588
Main Level Sq. Ft.: 2,329
Upper Level Sq. Ft.: 1,259
Bedrooms: 4
Bathrooms: 3½
Foundation: Basement
Materials List Available: Yes
Price Category: H

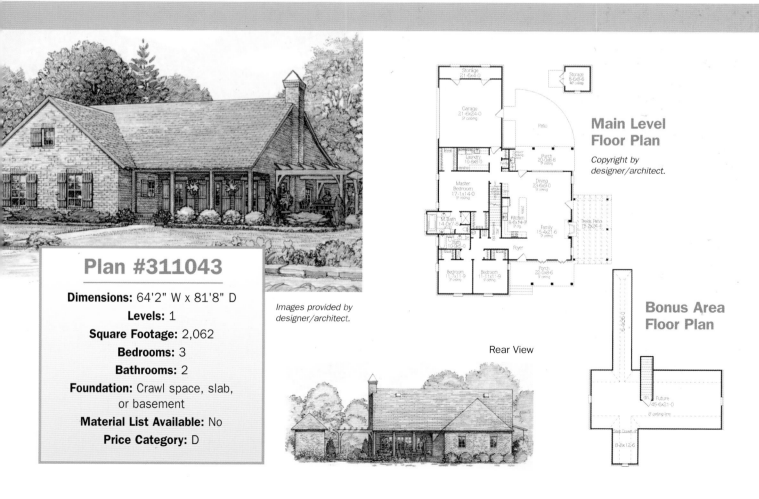

Main Level Floor Plan

Copyright by designer/architect.

Bonus Area Floor Plan

Plan #311043

Dimensions: 64'2" W x 81'8" D
Levels: 1
Square Footage: 2,062
Bedrooms: 3
Bathrooms: 2
Foundation: Crawl space, slab, or basement
Material List Available: No
Price Category: D

Images provided by designer/architect.

Rear View

Main Level Floor Plan

Dressing
walk-in closet
Great Room
16' x 19'6"
Breakfast
14' x 11'2"
Hearth Room
17' x 14'10"
Master Bedroom
14' x 14'1"
Foyer
Kitchen
Laun.
Sitting Area
11'2" x 9'4"
Porch
Dining Room
12' x 13'10"
Two-car Garage
21' x 20'4"

48'

63'4"

Rear Elevation

Images provided by
designer/architect.

Upper Level Floor Plan

Great Room
Below
Balcony
Bedroom
17' x 12'6"
Bedroom
10' x 13'10"
Bath
Bedroom
12' x 10'6"
slope ceiling   slope ceiling

Copyright by designer/architect.

Plan #161041

Dimensions: 63'4" W x 48' D

Levels: 2

Square Footage: 2,738

Main Level Sq. Ft.: 1,915

Upper Level Sq. Ft.: 823

Bedrooms: 4

Bathrooms: 3½

Foundation: Basement

Materials List Available: Yes

Price Category: F

Plan #171018

Dimensions: 48' W x 72' D

Levels: 2

Square Footage: 2,599

Main Level Sq. Ft.: 1,967

Upper Level Sq. Ft.: 632

Bedrooms: 4

Bathrooms: 4

Foundation: Crawl space, slab

Materials List Available: Yes

Price Category: E

Images provided by
designer/architect.

Upper Level Floor Plan

ATTIC

ATTIC

ATTIC

FUTURE ROOM
18' x 21'

HALL 2

BEDROOM 3
14' x 14'
BATH 3
SHELVES
BATH 4
BEDROOM 4
14' x 14'

GARAGE
24' x 24'

Main Level Floor Plan

Copyright by
designer/architect

PORCH 2
24' x 10'

KEEPING ROOM
15' x 10'
14' x 12'

UTILITY
10' x 8'
STORAGE
9' x 8'

CLOSET
7' x 8'
MASTER BATH

KIT.
11' x 16'
LIVING ROOM
18' x 18'
MASTER BEDROOM
15' x 15'

PANTRY
6' x 6'

DINING
17' x 10'
ENTRY
BATH 2
HALL 1
STUDY / BEDROOM
11' x 14'

PORCH 1

48' - 0"

72' - 0"

Plan #181224

Dimensions: 36' W x 39'8" D
Levels: 2
Square Footage: 1,727
Main Level Sq. Ft.: 837
Upper Level Sq. Ft.: 890
Bedrooms: 3
Bathrooms: 2
Foundation: Basement
Material List Available: Yes
Price Category: C

CAD FILE AVAILABLE

This elegant home occupies a small footprint.

Images provided by designer/architect.

Features:

- Living Room: This two-story gathering place features a cozy fireplace and tall windows, which flood the room with natural light.

- Kitchen: This island kitchen has plenty of cabinet and counter space. It is open to the breakfast room.

- Upper Level: On this level you will find a balcony that overlooks the living room. Also, there are three bedrooms and a large bathroom.

- Garage: This one-car garage has room for a car plus some storage area.

Kitchen

Main Level Floor Plan

11'-0" X 13'-8"
3,30 X 4,10

10'-4" X 11'-8"
3,10 X 3,50

12'-0" X 15'-8"
3,60 X 4,70

12'-0" X 24'-0"
3,60 X 7,20

Copyright by designer/architect.

Upper Level Floor Plan

13'-0" X 12'-0"
3,90 X 3,60

12'-4" X 12'-0"
3,70 X 3,60

9'-8" X 9'-4"
2,90 X 2,80

Main Level Floor Plan

48'

NOOK
10'4" X 10'2"
9' CLG.

FAMILY ROOM
15'8" X 18'

MASTER BEDROOM
14'4" X 14'6"
9' CLG.

EATING BAR

VAULTED CEILING
18' CLG.

KITCHEN
10'4" X 11'6"

DESK

REF.

OPTIONAL
BASEMENT STAIRS

MASTER
BATH

BUTLERS
PANTRY

UP

10' CLG.

LIVING ROOM
10'8" X 11'6"
9' CLG.

GARAGE
19'4" X 21'6"

DINING ROOM
10'4" X 11'6"
12' CLG.

VAULTED CEILING

48'

BEDROOM 2
11'8" X 10'8"

OPEN TO BELOW

BEDROOM 3
10'6" X 11'10"

**Upper Level
Floor Plan**

DN

ATTIC

*Copyright by
designer/architect.*

Plan #121172

Dimensions: 48' W x 48' D
Levels: 1.5
Square Footage: 1,897
Main Level Sq. Ft.: 1,448
Upper Level Sq. Ft.: 449
Bedrooms: 3
Bathrooms: 2½
Foundation: Slab; basement for fee
Material List Available: Yes
Price Category: D

*Images provided by
designer/architect.*

*This home, as shown
in the photograph, may
differ from the actual
blueprints. For more
detailed information,
please check the floor
plans carefully.*

Plan #181717

Dimensions: 43'8" W x 40'8" D
Levels: 1
Square Footage: 1,578
Bedrooms: 3
Bathrooms: 1
Foundation: Basement
Material List Available: Yes
Price Category: C

*Images provided by
designer/architect.*

CAD FILE
CAD
AVAILABLE

16'-4" X 14'-8"
4,90 X 4,40

12'-8" X 11'-0"
3,80 X 3,30

13'-4" X 13'-0"
4,00 X 3,90

40'-8"
12,2 m

11'-0" X 9'-0"
3,30 X 2,70

11'-0" X 10'-0"
3,30 X 3,00

12'-0" X 13'-4"
3,60 X 4,00

43'-8"
13,1 m

Copyright by designer/architect.

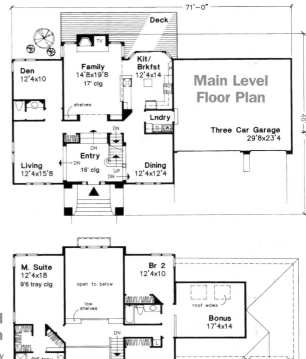

**Main Level
Floor Plan**

Deck

Den
12'4x10

Family
14'8x19'8
17' clg

TV

Kit/
Brkfst
12'4x14

shelves

Lndry
D W

Three Car Garage
29'8x23'4

71'-0"

46'-4"

Living
12'4x15'8

Entry
16' clg

DN
DN
UP
DN

Dining
12'4x12'4

*Images provided by
designer/architect.*

**Upper Level
Floor Plan**

M. Suite
12'4x18
9'6 tray clg

open to below

low
shelves

Br 2
12'4x10

roof wdws

Bonus
17'4x14

9'6 tray
clg

open to below

DN

open to below

Br 3
12'4x10

*Copyright by
designer/architect.*

Plan #271041

Dimensions: 71' W x 47' D
Levels: 2
Square Footage: 2,416
Main Level Sq. Ft.: 1,416
Upper Level Sq. Ft.: 1,000
Bedrooms: 4
Bathrooms: 2½
Foundation: Basement
Materials List Available: No
Price Category: E

Upper Level Floor Plan

Bedroom
14' x 17'9"

Bedroom
13'9" x 13'6"

Balcony

Bath

Bedroom
13'2" x 14'2"

Copyright by designer/architect.

Patio

Informal Dining
15'2" x 18'6"

Kitchen
14'6" x 14'6"

Pub

Great Room
22'3" x 19'

Master
Bedroom
17'6" x 13'2"

Laun.

Three Car
Garage
20'8" x 33'5"

Dining
Room
14'6" x 15'6"

Foyer

Porch

Library
11'6" x 15'7"

65'

**Main Level
Floor Plan**

74'10"

Plan #161036

Dimensions: 74'10" W x 65' D
Levels: 2
Square Footage: 3,664
Main Level Sq. Ft.: 2,497
Upper Level Sq. Ft.: 1,167
Bedrooms: 4
Bathrooms: 2½
Foundation: Basement
Materials List Available: No
Price Category: H

*Images provided by
designer/architect.*

CAD FILE AVAILABLE

Plan #121127

Dimensions: 58' W x 59'4" D
Levels: 1.5
Square Footage: 2,496
Main Level Sq. Ft.: 1,777
Upper Level Sq. Ft.: 719
Bedrooms: 4
Bathrooms: 2½
Foundation: Basement; crawl space for fee
Material List Available: Yes
Price Category: E

Beautiful, unique architecture and classic brick combine to make a breath-taking welcome for friends and family alike.

Features:

- **Great Room:** Through the covered stoop and foyer is this welcoming space for coming home after a hard day of work or for enter-taining guests. Whether in the brightness of the sun or the warm glow of the fireplace, this will be everyone's favorite place to gather.

- **Kitchen:** With utility space on one side and a window-surrounded breakfast room on the other, this kitchen is the height of convenience. With plenty of work and storage space, as well as a large snack bar, the room makes mealtimes simple.

- **Den:** If you're bringing your work home with you or just need a quiet place to use the computer, what you need is just on the other side of French doors in the foyer.

- **Master Bedroom:** Featuring an entry to the backyard to continue relaxing outside, this master bedroom also includes a full master bath with standing shower, his and her sinks, a whirlpool tub, and a walk-in closet. Take some time for yourself.

- **Second Floor:** Bedrooms for three share the second full bathroom between them. If three is one too many, use the larger space for a study or entertainment area.

- **Garage:** A three-bay garage gives you room for every driver or for extra storage or a workshop.

Main Level Floor Plan

Upper Level Floor Plan

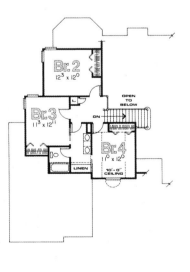

Copyright by designer/architect.

Plan #281016

Dimensions: 46' W x 44' D
Levels: 2
Square Footage: 1,945
Main Level Sq. Ft.: 1,211
Upper Level Sq. Ft.: 734
Bedrooms: 3
Bathrooms: 3
Foundation: Combination basement/slab
Materials List Available: Yes
Price Category: D

Images provided by designer/architect.

The fabulous window shapes on this Tudor-style home give just a hint of the beautiful interior design.

Features:

- **Living Room:** A vaulted ceiling in this raised room adds to its spectacular good looks.

- **Dining Room:** Between the lovely bay window and the convenient door to the covered sundeck, this room is an entertainer's delight.

- **Family Room:** A sunken floor, cozy fireplace, and door to the patio make this room special.

- **Study:** Just off the family room, this quiet spot can be a true retreat away from the crowd.

- **Kitchen:** The family cooks will be delighted by the ample counter and storage space here.

- **Master Suite:** A large walk-in closet, huge picture window, and private bath add luxurious touches to this second-floor retreat.

Main Level Floor Plan

Upper Level Floor Plan

Copyright by designer/architect.

Rear Elevation

Left Side Elevation

Right Side Elevation

Main Level Floor Plan

Master Bedroom 17'2" x 21'6"
Dressing
Hall
Walk in closet
Library 12' x 16'6"
Foyer
Porch
Dining Room 13' x 16'5"
Great Room 15'7" x 20'3"
Kitchen 14'7" x 16'
Breakfast 13' x 14'2"
Hearth Room 15'4" x 18'2"
Laun.
Hall
Porch
Garage 12' x 24'
Two-car Garage 21' x 26'9"

98'6"

Images provided by designer/architect.

Plan #161030

Dimensions: 98'6" W x 61'5" D
Levels: 2
Square Footage: 4,562
Main Level Sq. Ft.: 3,364
Upper Level Sq. Ft.: 1,198
Bedrooms: 4
Bathrooms: 3½
Foundation: Basement
Materials List Available: Yes
Price Category: I

Upper Level Floor Plan

Great Room Below
Bedroom 13' x 16'8"
Balcony
Bath
Bath
Bedroom 15'7" x 17'1"
Bath
Foyer Below
Bedroom 13' x 12'7"

Copyright by designer/architect.

Plan #161060

Dimensions: 113'10" W x 60'6" D
Levels: 2
Square Footage: 5,143
Main Level Sq. Ft.: 3,323
Upper Level Sq. Ft.: 1,820
Bedrooms: 4
Bathrooms: 3½
Foundation: Basement, walkout basement
Materials List Available: No
Price Category: J

Images provided by designer/architect.

Main Level Floor Plan

Master Bedroom 17'8" x 17'
Dressing
Library 14' x 16'4"
Foyer 17'9" x 11'4"
Court Yard
Great Room 17'9" x 29'4"
Dining
Kitchen 16'9" x 19'6"
Dining Room 14' x 16'4"
Deck
Laun.
Pantry
Bath
Mud Room
Three Car Garage 23'6" x 37'2"

113'10"

Upper Level Floor Plan

Bedroom 18'1" x 17'6"
Balcony
Gallery
Bedroom 14' x 17'10"
Bath
Bath
Bedroom 14' x 17'10"
Court Yard Below

Copyright by designer/architect.

Basement Level Floor Plan

Patio
Sitting Room
Exercise Room 13'11" x 17'9"
Media Area 17'9" x 32'
Bath
Wine Storage
Basement
Basement
Unexcavated
Unexcavated
Unexcavated

Plan #271069

Dimensions: 63'5" W x 51'8" D
Levels: 2
Square Footage: 2,376
Main Level Sq. Ft.: 1,248
Upper Level Sq. Ft.: 1,128
Bedrooms: 4
Bathrooms: 2½
Foundation: Crawl space, basement
Materials List Available: No
Price Category: E

Images provided by designer/architect.

This home's Federal-style facade has a simple elegance that is still popular among today's homeowners.

Features:

- Living Room: This formal space is perfect for serious conversation or thoughtful reflection. Optional double doors would open directly into the family room beyond.

- Dining Room: You won't find a more elegant room than this for hosting holiday feasts.

- Kitchen: This room has everything the cook could hope for—a central island, a handy pantry, and a menu desk. Sliding glass doors in the dinette let you step outside for some fresh air with your cup of coffee.

- Family Room: Here's the spot to spend a cold winter evening. Have hot chocolate in front of a crackling fire!

- Master Suite: With an optional vaulted ceiling, the sleeping chamber is bright and spacious. The private bath showcases a splashy whirlpool tub.

Main Level Floor Plan

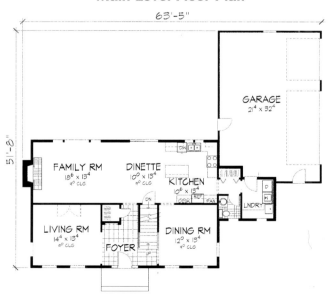

Upper Level Floor Plan

Copyright by designer/architect.

Plan #441024

Dimensions: 90'6" W x 84' D

Levels: 2

Square Footage: 3,517

Main Level Sq. Ft.: 2,698

Upper Level Sq. Ft.: 819

Bedrooms: 3

Bathrooms: 3½

Foundation: Crawl space;
slab or basement available for fee

Materials List Available: No

Price Category: H

You'll feel like royalty every time you pull into the driveway of this European-styled manor house.

CAD FILE AVAILABLE

Features:

- **Kitchen:** This gourmet chef's center hosts an island with a vegetable sink. The arched opening above the primary sink provides a view of the fireplace and entertainment center in the great room. A walk-in food pantry and a butler's pantry are situated between this space and the dining room.

- **Master Suite:** Located on the main level, this private retreat boasts a large sleeping area and a sitting area. The grand master bath features a large walk-in closet, dual vanities, a large tub, and a shower.

- **Bedrooms:** Two secondary bedrooms are located on the upper level, and each has its own bathroom.

- **Laundry Room:** This utility room houses cabinets, a folding counter, and an ironing board.

- **Garage:** This large three-car garage has room for storage. Family members entering the home from this area will find a coat closet and a place to stash briefcases and backpacks.

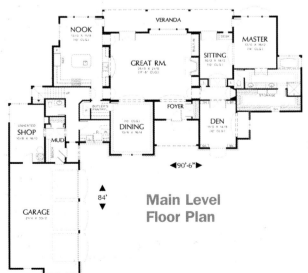

Main Level Floor Plan

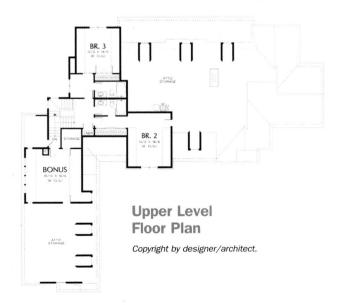

Upper Level Floor Plan

Copyright by designer/architect.

Plan #161104

Dimensions: 130' W x 84'6" D
Levels: 2
Square Footage: 8,088
Main Level Sq. Ft.: 5,418
Upper Level Sq. Ft.: 2,670
Bedrooms: 4
Bathrooms: 4 full, 2 half
Foundation: Basement
Material List Available: No
Price Category: L

Spectacular exterior with solid brick, limestone trim, and custom wood door reflects an authentic European manor.

CAD FILE AVAILABLE

Features:

- **Kitchen:** A 17-ft. high ceiling with arched timber beams, wall oven, island with vegetable sink, and second island with seating all create a true gourmet working space that overlooks the breakfast room and the cozy hearth room.

- **Master Suite:** This palatial suite with curved ceilings, fireplace-side whirlpool tub, large shower, sunken solarium, dressing room with two vanities and dressing table will pamper you. Four closets, including a compartmented double-entry master and secondary laundry area provide unmatched convenience.

- **Bedrooms:** Two sets of stairs lead to the second floor bedrooms—two with private sitting areas. Each bedroom enjoys a private bath and walk-in closet.

- **Additional Space:** A sunken covered porch, enhances the rear-yard enjoyment, while a finished lower level creates additional rooms for fun and entertainment.

Rear View

Copyright by designer/architect.

Upper Level Floor Plan

Main Level Floor Plan

Basement Level Floor Plan

Plan #141033

Dimensions: 38' W x 79' D
Levels: 2
Square Footage: 3,223
Main Level Sq. Ft.: 1,388
Upper Level Sq. Ft.: 1,835
Bedrooms: 4
Bathrooms: 3½
Foundation: Basement
Materials List Available: No
Price Category: G

This brick home with a hint of Craftsman styling adds charm to any neighborhood.

Features:

- **Front Porch:** This covered front porch welcomes guests to your home. It's the perfect spot to sit and sip lemonade while visiting with friends or family.

- **Living Room:** The fireplace, flanked by optional built-in cabinets, is the focal point of this gathering area. On nice days you can expand the area onto the adjacent screened-in porch.

- **Kitchen:** This large island kitchen features a built-in pantry and direct access to the dining room. The bay window in the adjacent breakfast nook will bring in an abundance of natural light.

- **Master Suite:** This upper-level oasis boasts a private sitting area off of the sleeping area. The large master bath pampers you with amenities such as a Jacuzzi tub, dual vanities, and a compartmentalized lavatory.

Main Level Floor Plan

Copyright by designer/architect.

Upper Level Floor Plan

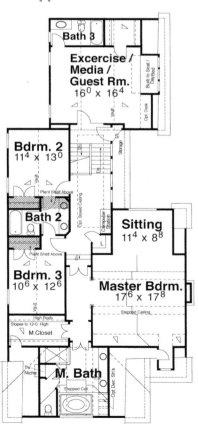

Plan #331005

Dimensions: 85'11" W x 55'7" D
Levels: 2
Square Footage: 3,585
Main Level Sq. Ft.: 2,691
Upper Level Sq. Ft.: 894
Bedrooms: 4
Bathrooms: 3½
Foundation: Crawl space, slab, or basement
Materials List Available: No
Price Category: H

You'll love the stately, traditional exterior design and the contemporary, casual interior layout as they are combined in this elegant home.

Features:

- Foyer: The highlight of this spacious area is the curved stairway to the balcony over head.

- Family Room: The two-story ceiling and second-floor balcony overlooking this room add to its spacious feeling, but you can decorate around the fireplace to create a cozy, intimate area.

- Study: Use this versatile room as a guest room, home office or media room.

- Kitchen: Designed for the modern cook, this kitchen features a step-saving design, an island for added work space, and ample storage space.

- Master Suite: Step out to the rear deck from the bedroom to admire the moonlit scenery or bask in the morning sun. The luxurious bath makes an ideal place to relax in privacy.

Main Level Floor Plan

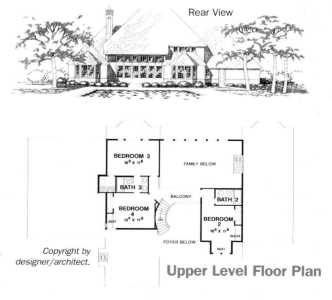

Rear View

Upper Level Floor Plan

Plan #161102

Dimensions: 99'6" W x 84'2" D
Levels: 1
Square Footage: 6,659
Main Level Sq. Ft.: 3,990
Lower Level Sq. Ft: 2,669
Bedrooms: 4
Bathrooms: 4 full, 2 half
Foundation: Walkout; basement for fee
Material List Available: Yes
Price Category: K

Images provided by designer/architect.

A brick-and-stone exterior with limestone trim and arches decorates the exterior, while the interior explodes with design elements and large spaces to dazzle all who enter.

CAD FILE AVAILABLE

Features:

• **Great Room:** The 14-ft. ceiling height in this room is defined with columns and a fireplace wall. Triple French doors with an arched transom create the rear wall, and built-in shelving adds the perfect spot to house your big-screen TV.

• **Kitchen:** This spacious gourmet kitchen opens generously to the great room and allows everyone to enjoy the daily activities. A two-level island with cooktop provides casual seating and additional storage.

• **Breakfast Room:** This room is surrounded by windows, creating a bright and cheery place to start your day. Sliding glass doors to the covered porch in the rear add a rich look for outdoor entertaining, and the built-in fireplace provides a cozy, warm atmosphere.

• **Master Suite:** This master bedroom suite is fit for royalty, with its stepped ceiling treatment, spacious dressing room, and private exercise room.

• **Lower Level:** This lower level is dedicated to fun and entertaining. A large media area, billiards room, and wet bar are central to sharing this spectacular home with your friends.

Front View

Rear Elevation

Right Side Elevation

Left Side Elevation

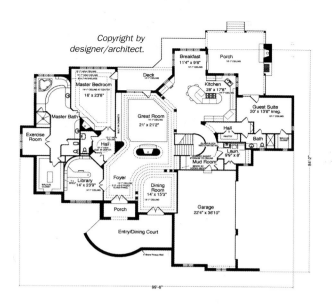

Copyright by designer/architect.

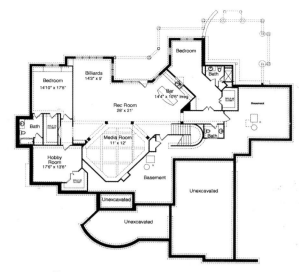

Basement Level Floor Plan

Foyer/Dining Room

Kitchen

Great Room

Porch

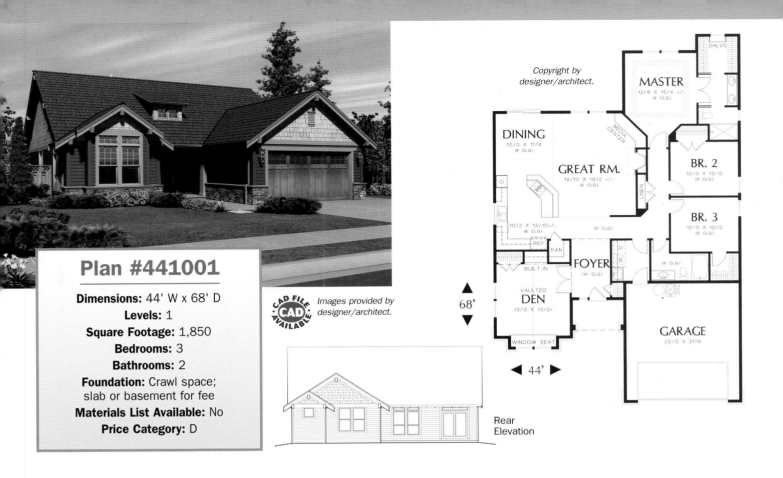

Plan #441001

Dimensions: 44' W x 68' D

Levels: 1

Square Footage: 1,850

Bedrooms: 3

Bathrooms: 2

Foundation: Crawl space; slab or basement for fee

Materials List Available: No

Price Category: D

Images provided by designer/architect.

Rear Elevation

Plan #441005

Dimensions: 50' W x 59' D

Levels: 1

Square Footage: 1,800

Bedrooms: 3

Bathrooms: 2

Foundation: Crawl space; slab or basement for fee

Materials List Available: No

Price Category: D

Images provided by designer/architect.

Rear Elevation

Plan #121125

Dimensions: 54' W x 58'8" D
Levels: 1
Square Footage: 1,978
Bedrooms: 3
Bathrooms: 2½
Foundation: Basement;
crawl space for fee
Material List Available: Yes
Price Category: D

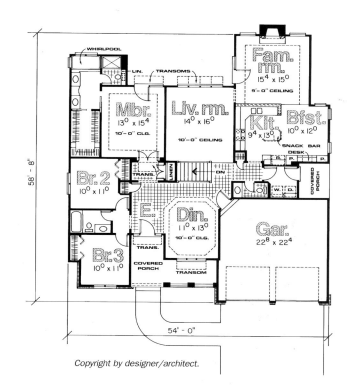

*Images provided by
designer/architect.*

Copyright by designer/architect.

Plan #461124

Dimensions: 37' W x 78' D
Levels: 2
Square Footage: 2,395
Main Level Sq. Ft.: 1,710
Upper Level Sq. Ft.: 685
Bedrooms: 3
Bathrooms: 2½
Foundation: Slab; crawl space
or basement for fee
Material List Available: No
Price Category: E

*Images provided by
designer/architect.*

Main Level Floor Plan

Upper Level Floor Plan

Copyright by designer/architect.

Plan #461074

Dimensions: 40'6" W x 72'6" D
Levels: 2
Square Footage: 2,187
Main Level Sq. Ft.: 1,479
Upper Level Sq. Ft: 708
Bedrooms: 3
Bathrooms: 2½
Foundation: Slab; crawl space or basement for fee
Materials List Available: No
Price Category: D

Images provided by designer/architect.

Upper Level Floor Plan

Main Level Floor Plan

Copyright by designer/architect.

Plan #221076

Dimensions: 56' W x 43' D
Levels: 2
Square Footage: 2,401
Main Level Sq. Ft.: 1,311
Upper Level Sq. Ft: 1,090
Bedrooms: 4
Bathrooms: 3
Foundation: Basement
Materials List Available: No
Price Category: E

Images provided by designer/architect.

Main Level Floor Plan

Upper Level Floor Plan

Copyright by designer/architect.

Plan #141005

Dimensions: 38' W x 66' D
Levels: 1
Square Footage: 1,532
Bedrooms: 3
Bathrooms: 2
Foundation: Slab, basement
Materials List Available: Yes
Price Category: C

Board and batten combine with shake siding to give this cottage an appealing Tudor style.

Features:

- Ceiling Height: 8 ft. unless otherwise noted.

- Entry: This front entry is highlighted by a dormer that opens to the cathedral ceiling of the spacious open great room.

- Open Floor Plan: The living room, dining areas, and kitchen all flow together to create the feeling of a much larger home.

- Kitchen: This kitchen is defined by a curved bar, which can house a bench seat to service a small cafe-style table.

- Master Suite: This private suite is separated from the rest of the bedrooms. It features a volume ceiling and separate sitting area.

- Basement Option: The house is designed primarily for a slab on a narrow lot but can also be built over a basement.

Rear View

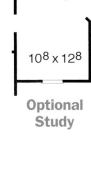

Optional Study

10^8 x 12^8

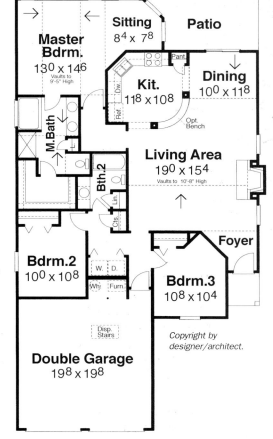

Copyright by designer/architect.

Plan #121124

Dimensions: 55'4" W x 56' D

Levels: 1

Square Footage: 1,806

Bedrooms: 3

Bathrooms: 2

Foundation: Basement; crawl space for fee

Material List Available: Yes

Price Category: D

Images provided by designer/architect.

This brick ranch will be the best-looking home in the neighborhood.

Features:

- **Great Room:** This area is a great place to gather with family and friends. The 10-ft.-high ceiling and arched windows make this room bright and airy. On cold nights, gather by the warmth of the fireplace.

- **Dining Room:** A column off the entry defines this formal dining area. Arched windows and a 10-ft.-high ceiling add to the elegance of the space.

- **Kitchen:** This island kitchen will inspire the chef in the family to create a symphony at every meal. The triple window in the adjoining breakfast area floods this area with natural light.

- **Master Suite:** Located on the opposite side of the home from the secondary bedrooms, this private area features a 10-ft.-high ceiling in the sleeping area. The master bath boasts a compartmentalized lavatory and shower area in addition to dual vanities and a walk-in closet.

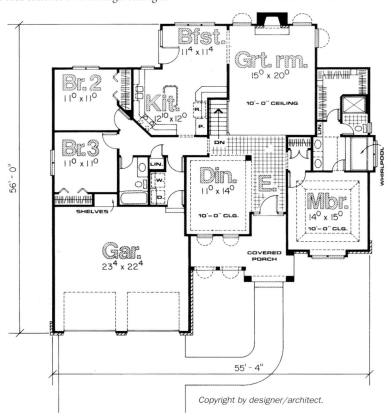

Copyright by designer/architect.

Plan #441006

Dimensions: 48' W x 64' D
Levels: 1
Square Footage: 1,891
Bedrooms: 3
Bathrooms: 2
Foundation: Crawl space; slab or basement for fee
Materials List Available: No
Price Category: D

Images provided by designer/architect.

Rear Elevation

Copyright by designer/architect.

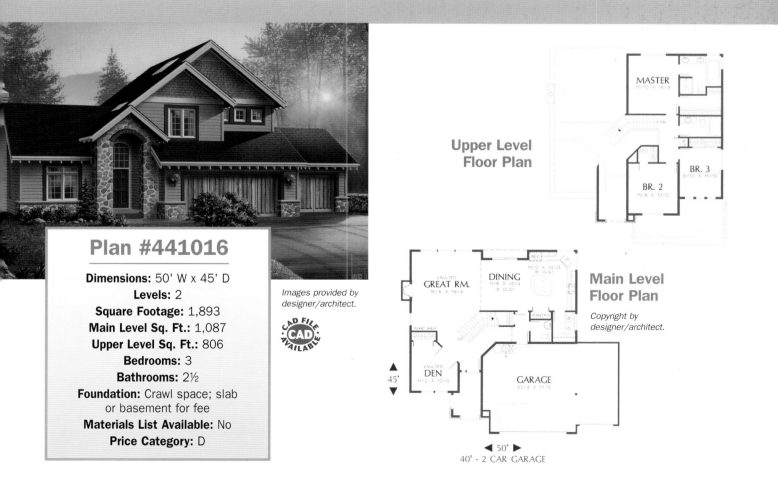

Plan #441016

Dimensions: 50' W x 45' D
Levels: 2
Square Footage: 1,893
Main Level Sq. Ft.: 1,087
Upper Level Sq. Ft.: 806
Bedrooms: 3
Bathrooms: 2½
Foundation: Crawl space; slab or basement for fee
Materials List Available: No
Price Category: D

Images provided by designer/architect.

Upper Level Floor Plan

Main Level Floor Plan

Copyright by designer/architect.

Plan #161033

Dimensions: 78'2" W x 74'6" D
Levels: 2
Square Footage: 5,125
Main Level Sq. Ft.: 2,782
Upper Level Sq. Ft.: 1,027
Optional Basement Level Sq. Ft.:
1,316
Bedrooms: 4
Bathrooms: 3½
Foundation: Basement
Materials List Available: Yes
Price Category: I

The dramatic design of this home, combined with its comfort and luxuries, suit those with discriminating tastes.

Features:

- Great Room: Let the fireplace and 14-ft. ceilings in this room set the stage for all sorts of gatherings, from causal to formal.

- Dining Room: Adjacent to the great room and kitchen fit for a gourmet, the dining room allows you to entertain with ease.

- Music Room: Give your music the space it deserves in this specially-designed room.

- Library: Use this room as an office, or reserve it for quiet reading and studying.

- Master Suite: You'll love the separate dressing area and walk-in closet in the bedroom.

- Lower Level: A bar and recreational area give even more space for entertaining.

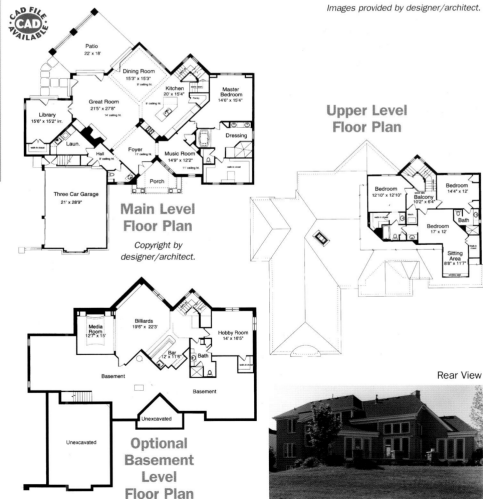

Main Level Floor Plan

Copyright by designer/architect.

Upper Level Floor Plan

Optional Basement Level Floor Plan

Rear View

Plan #151530

Dimensions: 38'10" W x 70'4" D
Levels: 2
Square Footage: 2,146
Main Level Sq. Ft.: 1,654
Upper Level Sq. Ft.: 492
Bedrooms: 3
Bathrooms: 2½
Foundation: Crawl space or slab
CompleteCost List Available: Yes
Price Category: D

Images provided by designer/architect.

Gables, columns, and architectural detailing give this home a warm feeling reminiscent of your grandmother's house.

CAD FILE AVAILABLE

Features:

- **Foyer:** The cozy porch gently welcomes you into this column-lined foyer, which separates the formal dining room from the large great room with fireplace.

- **Kitchen:** This kitchen with breakfast room is centrally located and looks out at the lovely courtyard patio, which is perfect for entertaining.

- **Master Suite:** Your perfect hideaway awaits you in this spacious suite, with its large walk-in closet and master bath packed with amenities.

- **Upper Level:** The upstairs has two bedrooms, each with private access to the full bathroom, as well as future bonus space when desired.

**Main Level
Floor Plan**
*Copyright by
designer/architect.*

**Upper Level
Floor Plan**

Front View

Plan #441015

Dimensions: 130'3" W x 79'3" D
Levels: 1
Square Footage: 4,732
Main Level Sq. Ft.: 2,902
Lower Level Sq. Ft.: 1,830
Bedrooms: 4
Bathrooms: 3 full, 2 half
Foundation: Walkout basement
Materials List Available: No
Price Category: I

An artful use of stone was employed on the exterior of this rustic hillside home to complement other architectural elements, such as the angled, oversize four-car garage and the substantial roofline.

CAD FILE AVAILABLE · CAD

Features:

- Great Room: This massive vaulted room features a large stone fireplace at one end and a formal dining area at the other. A built-in media center and double doors separate the great room from a home office with its own hearth and built-ins.

- Kitchen: This kitchen features a walk-in pantry and snack counter and opens to a skylighted outdoor kitchen. Its appointments include a cooktop and a corner fireplace.

- Home Theatre: This space has a built-in viewing screen, a fireplace, and double terrace access.

- Master Suite: This private space is found at the other side of the home. Look closely for

expansive his and her walk-in closets, a spa tub, a skylighted double vanity area, and a corner fireplace in the salon.

- Bedrooms: Three family bedrooms are on the lower level; bedroom 4 has a private bathroom and walk-in closet.

- Garage: This large garage has room for four cars; don't miss the dog shower and grooming station just off the garage.

Main Level Floor Plan

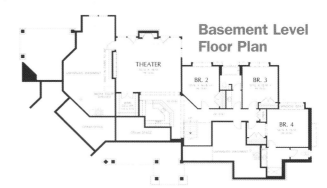

Copyright by designer/architect.

Entry

Basement Level Floor Plan

Plan #121032

Dimensions: 54' W x 45'4" D

Levels: 2

Square Footage: 2,339

Main Level Sq. Ft.: 1,665

Upper Level Sq. Ft.: 674

Bedrooms: 4

Bathrooms: 2½

Foundation: Basement

Materials List Available: Yes

Price Category: E

Images provided by designer/architect.

This home is designed for gracious living and is distinguished by many architectural details.

Features:

• Ceiling Height: 8 ft. unless otherwise noted.

• Foyer: This is truly a grand foyer with a dramatic ceiling that soars to 18 ft.

• Great Room: The foyer's 18-ft. ceiling extends into the great room where an open staircase adds architectural windows. Warm yourself by the fireplace that is framed by windows.

• Kitchen: An island is the centerpiece of this handsome and efficient kitchen that features a breakfast area for informal family meals. The room also includes a handy desk.

• Private Wing: The master suite and study are in a private wing of the house.

• Room to Expand: In addition to the three bedrooms, the second level has an unfinished storage space that can become another bedroom or office.

CAD FILE AVAILABLE — CAD

Main Level Floor Plan

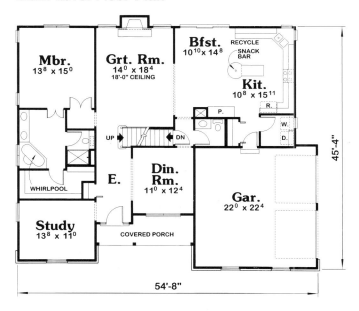

Upper Level Floor Plan

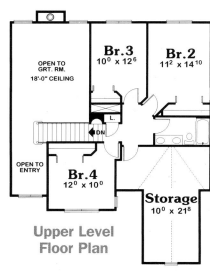

Copyright by designer/architect.

Plan #441014

Dimensions: 119'6" W x 87'6" D
Levels: 1
Square Footage: 3,940
Bedrooms: 3
Bathrooms: 3 full, 2 half
Foundation: Crawl space; slab or basement available for fee
Materials List Available: No
Price Category: H

Though this is but a single-story home, it satisfies and delights on many levels. The exterior has visual appeal, with varied rooflines, a mixture of materials, and graceful traditional lines.

Features:

- **Great Room:** This huge room boasts a sloped, vaulted ceiling, a fireplace, and built-ins. There is also a media room with double-door access.

- **Kitchen:** This kitchen has an island, two sink prep areas, a butler's pantry connecting it to the formal dining room, and a walk-in pantry.

- **Bedrooms:** Family bedrooms sit at the front of the plan and are joined by a Jack-and-Jill bathroom.

- **Master Suite:** This master suite is on the far right side. Its grand salon has an 11-ft.-high ceiling, a fireplace, built-ins, a walk-in closet, and a superb bathroom.

- **Garage:** If you need extra space, there's a bonus room on an upper level above the three-car garage.

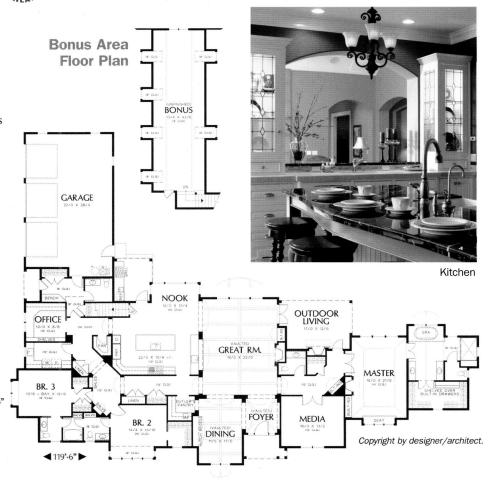

Kitchen

Copyright by designer/architect.

Plan #441033

Dimensions: 67' W x 68' D
Levels: 2
Square Footage: 2,986
Main Level Sq. Ft.: 2,162
Upper Level Sq. Ft.: 824
Bedrooms: 3
Bathrooms: 2½
Foundation: Crawl space;
slab or basement for fee
Materials List Available: No
Price Category: F

This home, as shown in the photograph, may differ from the actual blueprints. For more detailed information, please check the floor plans carefully.

CAD FILE AVAILABLE

Images provided by designer/architect.

Dramatic design coupled with elegant architectural detailing brings this comfortable home a lovely facade.

Features:

- Great Room: This room is two stories tall; the fireplace is flanked by built-ins.

- Dining Room: The interior was specifically created for family lifestyles. This formal room, accented with columns, is also graced by the butler's pantry, which connects it to the kitchen for convenience.

- Master Suite: The left wing is dedicated to this suite. The extensive master bath, with spa tub, separate shower, and walk-in closet, complements the master salon, which features a tray ceiling and large window over looking the rear yard.

- Upper Level: The two family bedrooms are on the second floor; they share the full bathroom with double sinks. The games room opens through double doors just off the loft library.

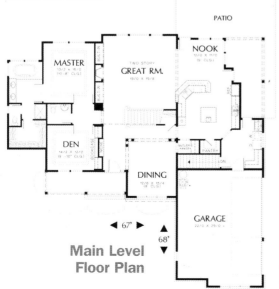

Main Level Floor Plan

Upper Level Floor Plan

Copyright by designer/architect.

Rear Elevation

Front View

Plan #271021

Dimensions: 39' W x 58' D
Levels: 2
Square Footage: 1,551
Main Level Sq. Ft.: 1,099
Upper Level Sq. Ft.: 452
Bedrooms: 3
Bathrooms: 2½
Foundation: Basement
Materials List Available: Yes
Price Category: C

The exterior of this cozy country-style home boasts a charming combination of woodwork and stone that lends an air of England to the facade.

Features:

• Living Room: An arched entryway leads into the living room, with its vaulted ceiling, tall windows, and fireplace.

• Dining Room: This space also features a vaulted ceiling, plus a view of the patio.

• Master Suite: Find a vaulted ceiling here, too, as well as a walk-in closet, and private bath.

Living Room

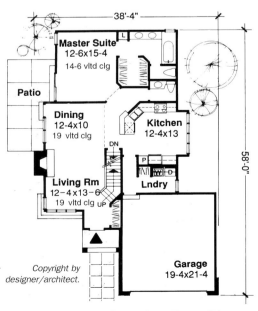

Copyright by designer/architect.

Main Level Floor Plan

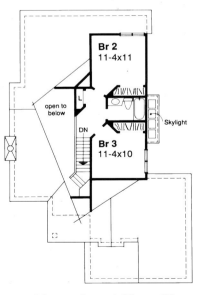

Upper Level Floor Plan

Plan #121203

Dimensions: 67' W x 56' D
Levels: 1.5
Square Footage: 2,690
Main Level Sq. Ft.: 1,792
Upper Level Sq. Ft.: 898
Bedrooms: 4
Bathrooms: 2½
Foundation: Basement; crawl space or slab for fee
Materials List Available: Yes
Price Category: F

Images provided by designer/architect.

This traditional Craftsman-style home has a unique design to accommodate the needs of the growing family.

Features:

• Porch: A long covered porch welcomes guests out of the elements or gives you outdoor living space where you can sit and greet the neighbors while listening to the sounds of the day.

• Great Room: With its cathedral ceiling and glowing fireplace, this room welcomes you home comfortably. Relax with your family or entertain your friends.

• Kitchen: Long counters, a large pantry, a stovetop island and a snack bar make this efficiently designed kitchen ideal for the family cook and expert chef alike. An attached eating area and a nearby formal dining room mean you can cater to any kind of meal.

• Master Bedroom: Unwind in this private space, and enjoy its conveniences. The full master bath includes a standing shower, his and her sinks, a large tub, and a spacious walk-in closet.

• Secondary Bedrooms: Each of the three bedrooms upstairs has ample living space,

large closets, and a desk, and all share access to the second full bathroom, which is compartmentalized.

• Garage: This three-car garage allows for space for both established and budding drivers, or you can use one bay for storage or a workbench.

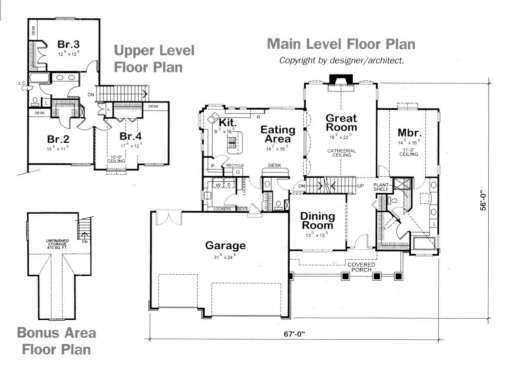

Upper Level Floor Plan

Bonus Area Floor Plan

Main Level Floor Plan
Copyright by designer/architect.

Plan #441050

Dimensions: 50' W x 52'6" D
Levels: 2
Square Footage: 2,296
Main Level Sq. Ft.: 1,464
Upper Level Sq. Ft.: 832
Bedrooms: 3
Bathrooms: 2½
Foundation: Crawl space; slab or basement for fee
Materials List Available: No
Price Category: E

Images provided by designer/architect.

Attention to architectural detail gives this Craftsman style home a unique contemporary appeal.

CAD FILE AVAILABLE

Features:

- Garage: A three-car garage provides plenty of space for the multi-tasking family and all of their hobbies. If two vehicles are enough, use the third bay for workspace or storage.

- Kitchen: This efficient L-shaped kitchen includes a working island with raised bar. The room opens into a sunlit, formal dining room and the fireplace-warmed great room, both vaulted.

- Patio: Through a door in the dining room is a covered patio, perfect for enjoying the breeze and the view while you eat out on warm summer days.

- Master Suite: A vaulted master bedroom opens into a compartmentalized full bath, with his and her sinks, a spa tub and large stall shower.

- Second Floor: Two bedrooms have the upstairs to themselves, a full bathroom with dual sinks just footsteps away. A large bonus space waits for you to mold it to your needs. Create another bedroom, if needed, or an extra entertainment or study space for your family.

Main Level Floor Plan

Copyright by designer/architect.

Upper Level Floor Plan

Rear Elevation

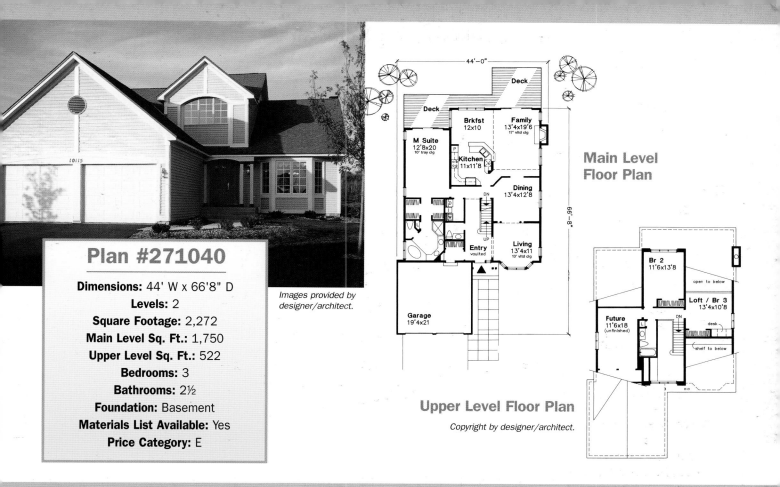

Plan #271040

Dimensions: 44' W x 66'8" D
Levels: 2
Square Footage: 2,272
Main Level Sq. Ft.: 1,750
Upper Level Sq. Ft.: 522
Bedrooms: 3
Bathrooms: 2½
Foundation: Basement
Materials List Available: Yes
Price Category: E

Images provided by designer/architect.

Main Level Floor Plan

Upper Level Floor Plan

Copyright by designer/architect.

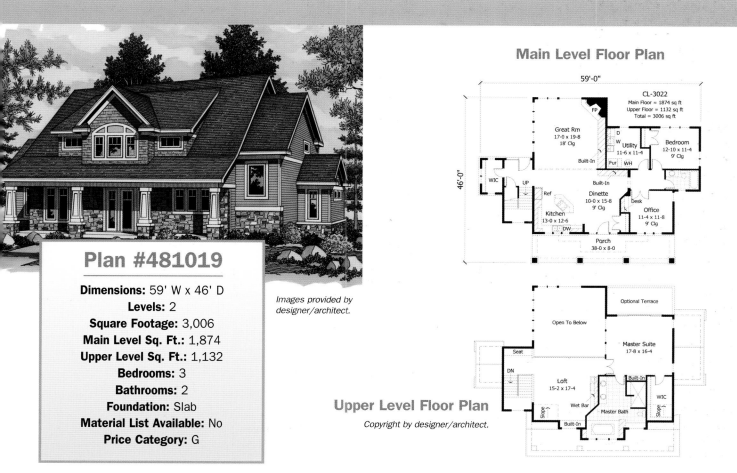

Plan #481019

Dimensions: 59' W x 46' D
Levels: 2
Square Footage: 3,006
Main Level Sq. Ft.: 1,874
Upper Level Sq. Ft.: 1,132
Bedrooms: 3
Bathrooms: 2
Foundation: Slab
Material List Available: No
Price Category: G

Images provided by designer/architect.

Main Level Floor Plan

Upper Level Floor Plan

Copyright by designer/architect.

Plan #271093

Dimensions: 74' W x 52' D
Levels: 2
Square Footage: 2,813
Main Level Sq. Ft.: 1,828
Upper Level Sq. Ft.: 985
Bedrooms: 3
Bathrooms: 3
Foundation: Basement
Materials List Available: No
Price Category: F

This Craftsman-style home will be the envy of your neighbors.

Images provided by designer/architect.

Features:

- Entry: Enter the home through the covered porch and into this entry with a view into the great room.

- Great Room: This large gathering area, with two-sided fireplace, has window looking out to the backyard.

- Kitchen: This peninsula kitchen has plenty of cabinets and counter space. The garage is just a few steps away though the laundry room.

- Hearth Room: Just off the kitchen this hearth room shares the fireplace with the great room and is open into the dining room.

- Master Suite: Located upstairs, with a secondary bedroom, this suite has a sitting area, large closet, and master bath.

Great Room

Kitchen

Main Level Floor Plan

Copyright by designer/architect.

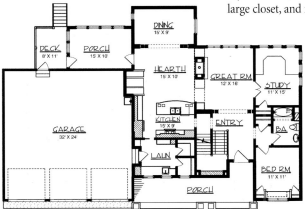

Upper Level Floor Plan

Plan #441046

Dimensions: 50' W x 42' D
Levels: 2
Square Footage: 2,606
Main Level Sq. Ft.: 1,216
Upper Level Sq. Ft.: 1,390
Bedrooms: 4
Bathrooms: 2½
Foundation: Crawl space; slab or basement for fee
Materials List Available: No
Price Category: F

Little things mean a lot, and in this design it's the little details that add up to a marvelous plan.

Features:

- Great Room: If you like, you might include a corner media center in this room to complement the fireplace.

- Den: This vaulted room lies just off the entry and opens through double doors.

- Kitchen: Both formal and casual dining spaces are included and flank this open kitchen, which overlooks the great room.

- Upper Level: Sleeping quarters are upstairs and include three family bedrooms and the master suite. Look for a spa tub, separate shower, dual sinks, and a walk-in closet in the master bath. The family bedrooms share the full bathroom, which has double sinks.

Images provided by designer/architect.

CAD FILE AVAILABLE

Main Level Floor Plan

Rear Elevation

Upper Level Floor Plan

Copyright by designer/architect.

Today's Fireplace Technology

Handsome and romantic, but drafty. Thirty years ago, you might have described a traditional fireplace in this way. But that was before technological advancements finally made fireplaces more efficient. Now, not only can you expect your fireplace to provide ambiance and warmth, you can relax knowing that your energy dollars aren't going up in smoke. Over the centuries, people had tried to improve the efficiency of the fireplace so that it would generate the maximum heat possible from the wood consumed. But real strides didn't come until the energy crisis of the early 1970s. That's when designers of fireplaces and stoves introduced some significant innovations. Today, fireplaces are not only more efficient, but cleaner and easier to use.

The traditional fireplace is an all-masonry construction, consisting of only bricks and mortar. However, new constructions and reconstructions of masonry fireplaces often include either a metal or a ceramic firebox. This type of firebox has double walls. The space between these walls is where cool air heats up after being drawn in through openings near the floor of the room. The warm air exits through openings near the top of the firebox. Although a metal firebox is more efficient than an all-masonry firebox, it doesn't radiate heat very effectively, and the heat from the fireplace is distributed by convection—that is, the circulation of warmed air. This im–provement in heating capacity comes from the warm air emitted by the upper openings. But that doesn't keep your feet toasty

on a cold winter's night—remember, warm air rises.

A more recent development is the ceramic firebox, which is engineered from modern materials such as the type used in kilns. Fires in ceramic fireboxes burn hotter, cleaner, and more efficiently than in all-masonry or metal fireboxes. The main reason is that the back and the walls of a ceramic firebox absorb, retain, and reflect heat effectively. This means that during the time the fire is blazing, more heat radiates into the room than with the other fireboxes. Heat radiation is boosted by the fact that most ceramic units are made with

The warm glow of a realistic-looking modern zero-clearance gas fire, below, can make the hearth the heart of any room in the house.

Zero-Clearance Fireplace

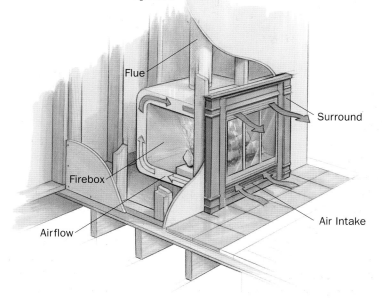

Flue

Surround

Firebox

Airflow

Air Intake

Traditional Masonry Fireplace

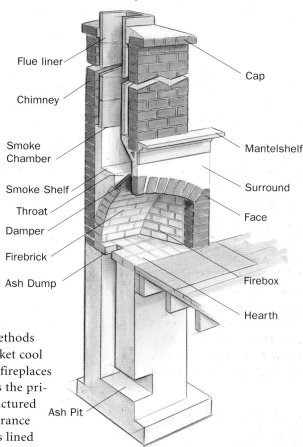

Flue liner

Chimney

Smoke Chamber

Smoke Shelf

Throat

Damper

Firebrick

Ash Dump

Cap

Mantelshelf

Surround

Face

Firebox

Hearth

Ash Pit

thick walls, and so the fire itself is not set as deeply into the hearth as it is with all-masonry or metal fireboxes. As a bonus, because heat is absorbed and retained by the material, the firebox actually radiates a significant amount of heat many hours after the fire has died down. By contrast, a metal firebox cools quickly once the heat source goes out.

In this type of efficient fireplace construction, a metal firebox is usually less expensive than a ceramic one, but the metal does break down over time, in a process professionals refer to as burn-out. In addition, an air-circulating metal firebox can only be installed in masonry constructions that are built with ports for the intake of cool air and the discharge of warmed air, or in masonry fireplaces in which such ports can be added. On the other hand, ceramic fireboxes can be installed in any type of masonry fireplace and are not subject to burnout.

Manufactured Fireplaces

The metal fireplaces that are made today can be zero-clearance or freestanding. The zero-clearance units are so named because they can be installed safely against combustible surfaces such as

wood. Any of a number of methods are used to keep the outer jacket cool enough, but in general, these fireplaces are designed to use cool air as the primary insulator. Many manufactured fireplaces, including zero-clearance units, are made with fireboxes lined with a refractory material. The chimneys are also made of metal, and a variety of designs use noncombustible material or air as insulation to keep the outer surface at a safe temperature.

New-technology and traditional fireplaces are shown above. Woodstove-like inserts, below, make fireplaces more efficient.

The Advantages of a Manufactured Unit

There are some important pluses to choosing a zero-clearance manufactured fireplace. First is the price, which is relatively low, and second is the easy and quick installation. Also, these units are lightweight and can be installed over almost any type of flooring, including wood. This means they do not need elaborate foundations, which is another cost-saver. Manufactured fireplaces are also extremely efficient, and many are designed to provide both radiated heat from the firebox and convection heat from ducting.

Manufactured freestanding fireplaces are, in effect, stoves. They are available in an array of colors, finishes, shapes, and sizes. Like zero-clearance factory-built fireplaces, freestanding models are lightweight, offering the same advantages: no need for heavy masonry or additional reinforcement of flooring. And you have a choice of either a wood-burning or gas-powered unit. Heat efficiency is maximized because, in addition to the firebox, the chimney and all sides of the unit radiate heat into the room. Freestanding units may be the least expensive option because installation requires only a chimney hole and, depending on the type of flooring, a noncombustible pad. A major disadvantage is the space required for placement, because you cannot install most of these units near a combustible wall. Also, a freestanding fireplace is probably not the best choice for families with young children because so much heat is radiated from the exposed surfaces.

Hybrids

If you're looking for a way to get improved efficiency from a masonry fireplace, consider a gas insert (actually a prefabricated firebox equipped with gas logs). You can purchase either a venting insert or one that's nonventing. But be prepared to pay $1,500 to several thousand dollars for the unit in addition to the cost of installation. For a fraction of that amount you can simply replace real wood logs with ceramic logs powered by gas. Like inserts, these logs may or may not require venting. Consult an experienced plumber or heating contractor, and remember that once you convert to gas you cannot burn wood.

Improving a masonry fireplace on the inside by installing a metal firebox might also be an inspiration to think of the fireplace and mantel in a new design way. Pairing two or more finishing materials, such as metal and masonry, can make your fireplace a hybrid in more than one way. For example, combine a stone base with a metal hood and chimney to create a custom-designed fireplace that works as a room divider in a large space. The design options in terms of materials and technology are seemingly endless.

If you have plans for building an innovative custom design, carefully review them with an expert in fireplace construction and maintenance to make sure you're not doing something hazardous. Also, don't forget to check with your local building inspector so that you don't waste time and money on a project that may not comply with codes and regulations set forth where you live.

Enhancing the Basics

You can improve the efficiency of any manufactured fireplace, and of masonry and hybrid constructions as well, with a few extras. In a masonry fireplace, a device commonly referred to as a fresh-air intake accessory or an outside air kit may improve performance. A fresh-air accessory makes use of outside air instead of heated room air for combustion, thus improving the fireplace's efficiency. There is another way to make your fireplace more efficient that isn't high tech at all, however. Simply replace the traditional grate or firebasket with a superior design—one that provides greater air circulation and allows a better placement of logs. Another type, a heat-exchanger grate, works with a fan. The device draws in the room's air, reheats it quickly, and then forces it back into the room.

Capitalizing on Technology

Wood is the traditional fuel for a fireplace, and today's manufactured fireplaces offer designs that make the most of your cord of hardwood. However, wood is not the only fuel option. In fact, in some places, it's not an option at all. There are manufactured units that offer a choice of natural gas or propane as a fuel source, which heats ceramic logs designed to realistically simulate wood. The fire, complete with glowing embers, is often difficult to distinguish from one burning real wood.

In some areas of the country, fireplace emission regulations have become strict—in places such as much of Colorado and parts of Nevada and California so strict that new construction of wood-burning fireplaces has been outlawed. In these areas, manufactured units using alternative fuels allow homeowners all the benefits of a wood-burning fireplace without the adverse impact on air quality.

Most of the units available today also offer a variety of amenities, including built-in thermostatic control and remote-control devices for turning the fire on and off and regulating heat output.

The Importance of a Clean Sweep

Finally, one of the most important factors in the use of a fireplace or stove is the regular inspection and cleaning of the stovepipe, flue, and chimney. To understand why, remember that the burning of wood results in the combustion of solids as well as combustible gases. However, not everything that goes into the firebox is burned, no matter how efficient the appliance. One of the by-products of wood burning is the dark brown or black tar called creosote, a flammable substance that sticks to the linings of chimney flues.

Although the burning temperature of creosote is high, it can ignite and cause a chimney fire. It may be brief and without apparent damage, but a chimney fire may also be prolonged or intense and result in significant fire and smoke damage or, at worst, the loss of your home if the creosote buildup is great enough. Creosote causes other problems, too. It decreases the inside diameter of stovepipes and flues, causing slower burning. This makes burning less efficient and contributes to further deposits of creosote. In addition, because creosote is acidic, it corrodes mortar, metal, and eventually even stainless-steel and ceramic chimney liners.

To prevent costly and dangerous creosote buildup, have your chimney professionally cleaned by a qualified chimney sweep. How often depends on the amount of creosote deposited during the burning season, and this, in turn, depends largely on how and what kind of wood you burn. Professional sweeps usually recommend at least annual cleaning. Depending on where you live, you'll spend about $150, perhaps less, for a cleaning.

You'll enjoy a warm glow at the highest efficiency if you use a glass-front wood-burning or gas-fueled, opposite and right, fireplace insert.

Fireside Arrangements

Creating an attractive, comfortable setting around a fireplace should be easy. Who doesn't like the cozy ambiance of relaxing in front of a fire? But there are times when the presence of a fireplace in a room poses problems with the layout. A fireplace can take up considerable floor and wall space, and like any other permanent feature or built-in piece of furniture, its size or position can limit the design possibilities.

The Fireplace and the Space

What is the room's size and shape—large, small, square, long and narrow, L-shaped? Where is the fireplace located—in the center of a wall, to the side, or in a corner? What other permanent features, such as windows, doors, bookcases, or media units, will you have to work with in your arrangement? How much clearance can you allow around the furniture for easy passage? How close do you want to be to the fire? Think of these questions as you consider the design basics presented below.

Scale and Proportion. Remember the importance of spatial relationships. For example, a fireplace may seem large in a room with a low ceiling; conversely, it may appear small in a room with a vaulted ceiling. Size is relative. Applied to objects on the mantel or the wall above the fireplace, correct scale and proportion happen when the objects are the appropriate size for the wall or the fireplace.

Balance. Sometimes the architectural features of a mantel or surround are so strong, you'll have to match them with furnishings of equal visual weight. Or they may be so ornate or plain that you'll have to play them up or tone them down to make them work with the rest of the decor. That's balance. But balance also refers to arrangements: symmetrical, asymmetrical, and radial.

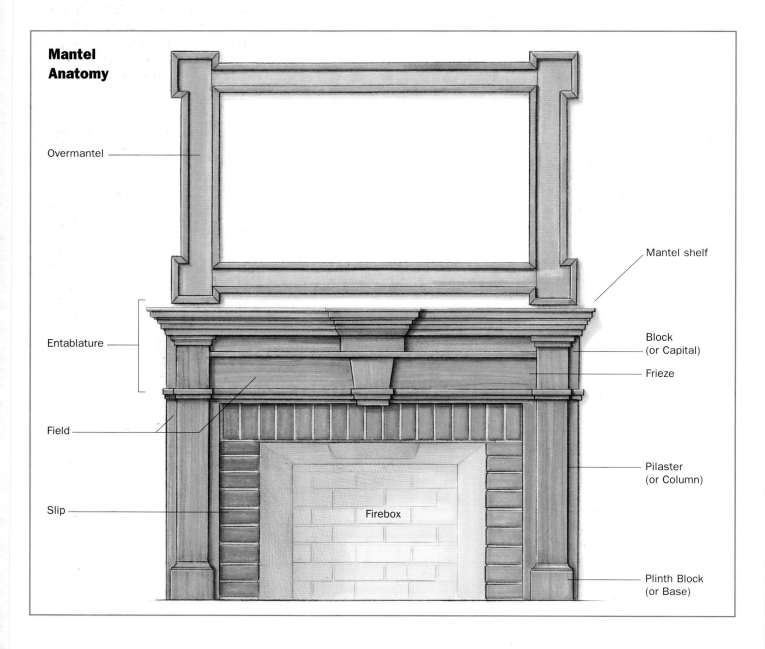

Mantel Anatomy

Overmantel

Mantel shelf

Entablature

Block (or Capital)

Frieze

Field

Pilaster (or Column)

Slip

Firebox

Plinth Block (or Base)

Line. Shape depends on line. Different types of lines suggest various qualities. Pay attention to the lines when you're creating arrangements and relationships among objects. Some lines are inherent in a room or an architectural feature, but you can modify them. For example: vertical lines are stately and dignified, which is just the look you want for your fireplace, but unfortunately, it's rather wide and squat instead. Solution? Create an arrangement above the fireplace that extends high on the wall, or hang a tall mirror or frame over than mantel.

What if the fireplace is too tall? Does it overwhelm the rest of the furniture? Add horizontal lines by moving seating pieces farther apart to the right and left of the hearth. Install wall art on the sides of the fireplace.

If the room is boxy, avoid grouping pieces at right angles to the fireplace and each other. Instead, de-emphasize the boxy shape by placing them on the diagonal to open the square. Use upholstered pieces with rounded arms or curvaceous cushions, legs, or frames. Create a radial arrangement. With the hearth as the central point, create a semicircular hub of furnishings that include seating and a small table or two.

Rhythm. Keep the eye moving at a measured pace by repeating motifs, colors, or shapes. For example, you might pick up the color from a tiled surround to use as an accent color in fabrics on upholstered pieces, curtains, pillows, throws, or other decorative accessories. Or repeat architectural features of the fireplace with other similar elements in the room, such as molding or other woodwork details.

Variety. Don't go overboard trying to match everything exactly. The most interesting rooms and arrangements mix objects of different sizes, shapes, lines, and sometimes even styles (as long as they are compatible).

Harmony. Create harmony among all of the parts of your design by connecting all of the elements either by color or motif. For example, in a display of family photos the frames may all be different shapes, styles, and heights, but because each one is made of brass, the overall appearance looks harmonious. Or you could assemble a wall vignette of frames over the fireplace, all different in finish but tied together by the subject matter of each one—all landscapes, for example, or all pink cabbage roses. Unifying diverse items in this way creates a finished-looking scheme.

How to Make a Hinged Fireboard

You'll need a hinged three-panel wooden fireplace screen, which you can buy or make. If you buy one, you'll have to sand and prime it thoroughly before applying the new finish over the existing one. Ideally, it's best to work on unfinished wood.

The screen used for this project features two 9 x 36-inch side panels and one 26 x 36-inch center panel that were cut from a ¾-inch-thick sheet of plywood. If you aren't handy with a circular saw or table saw, ask your local lumber supplier to cut the panels to your desired dimensions. Attach the side and center panels with two-way (piano) hinges, which are easy to install. Simply mark their location along the inside edges of the panel pieces, drill pilot holes, and then screw the hinges into place. To finish, prime the boards; then paint or stencil a design onto each panel. For Victorian authenticity, decoupage the panels with a motif cut out of a piece of fabric, wallpaper, old greeting cards, or postcards.

Symmetrical versus Asymmetrical Arrangements

If you like the symmetry of classic design, balance your arranged pieces accordingly. For example, position two sofas or love seats of the same size perpendicular to the fireplace and exactly opposite each other. Or place a single sofa parallel with the fireplace, with two chairs opposite one another and equidistant from both the sofa and the hearth. Try out a low coffee table or an oversize ottoman in the center of the arrangement. Leave the peripheral areas outside the main grouping for creating small impromptu conversation areas during parties and gatherings or to accommodate a modest dining area or home-office station.

If your design sense is less formal or contemporary, try an asymmetrical grouping in front of the fire. Turn seating pieces at a 45-degree angle from the hearth.

In a large open space, locate seating not directly in front of the hearth but slightly off to the side. Counterbalance the arrangement with a large table and chairs, a hutch, bookcases, or any element of relatively equal weight. This layout works especially well when the ceiling is vaulted (as most great rooms are) or when the hearth is massive. In many contemporary homes, especially where there is a zero-clearance unit, the fireplace is not on an outside wall, nor is it necessarily in a central location. This means you can put the fireplace almost anywhere.

Comfortable Arrangements

You may want an intimate environment in front of the fire, but the room is so large that it feels and looks impersonal. Large rooms afford lots of leeway for arranging, but people often make the mistake of pushing all of the furniture against the walls. If that's what you're doing, pull the major seating pieces closer together and near the fire, keeping a distance of only 4 to 10 feet between sofas and chairs. For the most comfortable result, create one or more small groupings that can accommodate up to four to six people in different areas of the room.

Modular Seating. Instead of a standard sofa and chairs, consider the convenience of modular seating, too, which comes in any number of armless and single-arm end pieces. The advantage of these separate upholstered units is that you can easily add, take away, or rearrange the modules to suit any of your layout or seating needs. Create an L or a U arrangement in front of the fire; subtract pieces, moving one or two outside of the area for an intimate grouping.

A raised hearth, above, reinforces the idea of a fireplace as a focal point, and it provides seating near the fire. Place other furniture to the sides of the hearth.

Use an area rug to further define the space. Or put the pieces together to make one large arrangement in any configuration. Versatile furnishings such as an ottoman with a hinged top or an antique trunk can double as seating, a low table, or storage.

A Quick Guide to Buying Firewood

How much wood you need to buy in a season depends on a number of factors, but there are three major variables: how often and how long you burn fires; the efficiency of your fireplace or stove; and the type of wood you burn. In general, hard, dense woods are ideal for fuel. As a rule of thumb, the wood from deciduous trees is best. (Deciduous trees are those that shed their leaves annually.) These include oak, maple, walnut, birch, beech, ash, and the wood from fruit trees such as cherry and apple.

Avoid burning wood from evergreens—those cone-bearing (coniferous) trees with needles instead of leaves. The wood of coniferous trees is soft and it will burn faster, so a greater volume of wood will be consumed per hour compared with hardwood. A greater problem with softwoods, however, is the resin content. Resin is the gummy substance that's used in the man-

ufacture of some wood stains and shellacs, and when resin is burned it gives off a byproduct called creosote. Creosote, which is flammable, accumulates in flues and chimneys, and this buildup represents a potential fire hazard.

The wood you purchase should also be seasoned, which means that the tree should have been cut down at least six months or, preferably, a year prior to the burning of the wood. Ideally, the wood should be cut and split soon after the tree is felled, allowing for more effective drying. The moisture in unseasoned (or green) wood tends to have a cooling effect, preventing complete combustion and making it harder to keep a fire blazing. A low-burning fire also increases creosote. (It's okay to burn green wood occasionally, but make sure to use small logs or split sticks and add them to an already hot fire.)

Mantel Vignettes

A grouping of objects on your mantel can be as simple or complex as you like. To make your display lively, choose a variety of shapes and sizes. For dramatic impact, group related objects that you can link in theme or color.

Remember that a symmetrical arrangement has classical overtones and will reinforce the formality of traditional designs. Stick with similar objects: a pair of Chinese ginger jars or antique silver candlesticks arranged in mirror fashion on either side of the mantel equidistant from the center, for example. Or keep the look simple by placing a single but important object in the center; it could be a mantel clock, a floral arrangement, or some other objet d'art.

Asymmetry, on the other hand, brings a different dynamic to a mantel vignette with mismatched pieces. Try placing a large object to one side of the mantel, and then balance that piece by massing several small objects or a different type of object of similar scale on the opposite side. An example might be an arrangement of books of varying heights and sizes at one end of the mantel and a simple large vase at the other end. Or you might oppose tall thin candlesticks with one fat candle.

A simple brick wall, left, serves as a backdrop for a gleaming fireplace insert.

Plan #121031

Dimensions: 52' W x 51'4" D
Levels: 2
Square Footage: 1,772
Main Level Sq. Ft.: 1,314
Upper Level Sq. Ft.: 458
Bedrooms: 3
Bathrooms: 2½
Foundation: Basement
Materials List Available: Yes
Price Category: C

Images provided by designer/architect.

This home features architectural details reminiscent of earlier fine homes.

Features:

- Ceiling Height: 8 ft. unless otherwise noted.
- Foyer: This grand entry soars two-stories high. The U-shaped staircase with window leads to a second-story balcony.
- Great Room: You'll be drawn to the impressive views through the triple-arch windows at the front and rear of this room.
- Kitchen: Designed for maximum efficiency, this kitchen is a pleasure to be in. It features a center island, a full pantry, and a desk for added convenience.
- Breakfast Area: This area adjoins the kitchen. Both rooms are flooded with sunlight streaming from a shared bay window.
- Master Suite: The stylish bedroom includes a walk-in closet. Luxuriate in the whirlpool tub at the end of a long day.

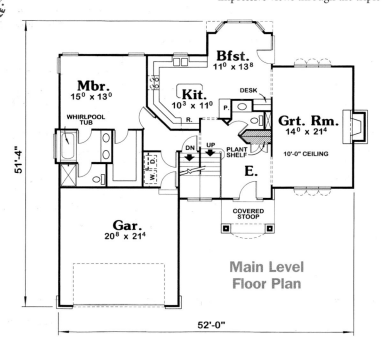

Main Level Floor Plan

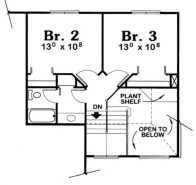

Copyright by designer/architect.

Upper Level Floor Plan

Plan #121029

Dimensions: 58'8" W x 54' D
Levels: 2
Square Footage: 2,576
Main Level Sq. Ft.: 1,735
Upper Level Sq. Ft.: 841
Bedrooms: 4
Bathrooms: 2½
Foundation: Basement
Materials List Available: Yes
Price Category: E

This gracious home is designed with the contemporary lifestyle in mind.

Features:

- Ceiling Height: 8 ft. unless otherwise noted.

- Great Room: This room features a fireplace and entertainment center. It's equally suited for family gatherings and formal entertaining.

- Breakfast Area: The fireplace is two-sided so it shares its warmth with this breakfast area — the perfect spot for informal family meals.

- Master Suite: Halfway up the staircase you'll find double-doors into this truly distinctive suite featuring a barrel-vault ceiling, built-in bookcases, and his and her walk-in closets. Unwind at the end of the day by stretching out in the oval whirlpool tub.

- Computer Loft: This loft overlooks the great room. It is designed as a home office with a built-in desk for your computer.

- Garage: Two bays provide plenty of storage in addition to parking space.

CAD FILE AVAILABLE

Main Level Floor Plan

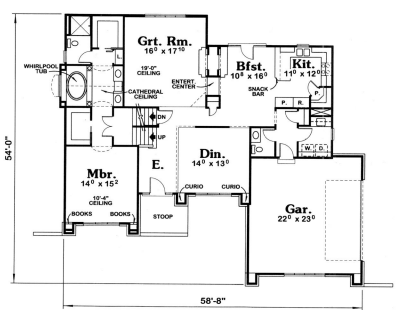

Upper Level Floor Plan

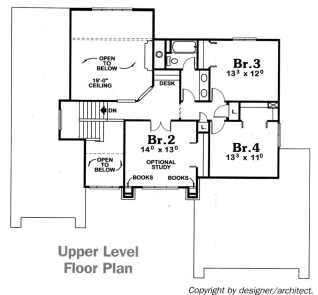

Plan #131033

Dimensions: 84'10" W x 48' D
Levels: 2
Square Footage: 2,813
Main Level Sq. Ft.: 1,890
Upper Level Sq. Ft.: 923
Bedrooms: 5
Bathrooms: 3½
Foundation: Crawl space, slab, or basement
Materials List Available: Yes
Price Category: G

Main Level Floor Plan

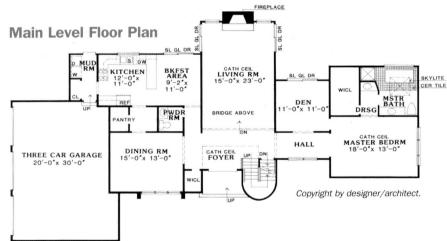

Upper Level Floor Plan

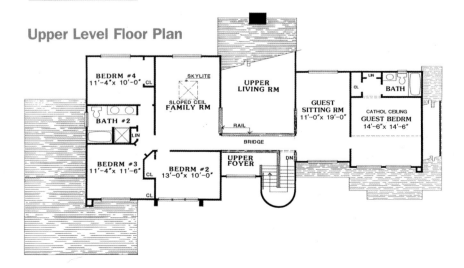

Contemporary styling, luxurious amenities, and the classics that make a house a home are all available here.

Features:

- Family Room: A sloped ceiling with skylight and a railed overlook to make this large space totally up to date.

- Living Room: Sunken for comfort and with a cathedral ceiling for style, this room features a fireplace flanked by windows and sliding glass doors.

- Master Suite: Unwind in this room, with its cathedral ceiling, with a skylight, walk-in closet, and private access to the den.

- Upper Level: A bridge overlooks the living room and foyer and leads through the family room to three bedrooms and a bath.

- Optional Guest Suite: 500 sq. ft. above the master suite and den provides total comfort.

Plan #151021

Dimensions: 75'2" W x 89'6" D
Levels: 2
Square Footage: 3,385
Main Level Sq. Ft.: 2,633
Upper Level Sq. Ft.: 752
Bedrooms: 4
Bathrooms: 4
Foundation: Crawl space, or slab
CompleteCost List Available: Yes
Price Category: G

Images provided by designer/architect.

From the fireplace in the master suite to the well-equipped game room, the amenities in this home will surprise and delight you.

Features:

- Great Room: A bank of windows on the far wall lets sunlight stream into this large room. The fireplace is located across the room and is flanked by the built-in media center and built-in bookshelves. Gracious brick arches create an entry into the breakfast area and kitchen.

- Breakfast Room: Move easily between this room with 10-foot ceiling either into the kitchen or onto the rear covered porch.

- Game Room: An icemaker and refrigerator make entertaining a snap in this room.

- Master Suite: A 10-ft. boxed ceiling, fireplace, and access to the rear porch give romance, while the built-ins in the closet, whirlpool tub with glass blocks, and glass shower give practicality.

Main Level Floor Plan

Upper Level Floor Plan

Copyright by designer/architect.

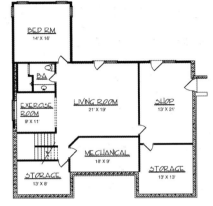

Plan #271078

Dimensions: 83' W x 52' D

Levels: 1

Square Footage: 1,855

Bedrooms: 2

Bathrooms: 1½

Foundation: Daylight basement

Materials List Available: No

Price Category: D

Images provided by designer/architect.

Optional Basement Level Floor Plan

Copyright by designer/architect.

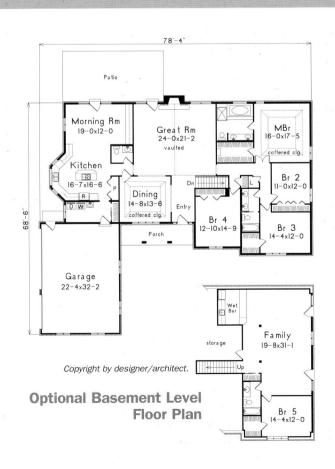

Plan #321036

Dimensions: 78'4" W x 68'6" D

Levels: 1

Square Footage: 2,900

Bedrooms: 4

Bathrooms: 2½

Foundation: Basement

Materials List Available: No

Price Category: F

Images provided by designer/architect.

Copyright by designer/architect.

Optional Basement Level Floor Plan

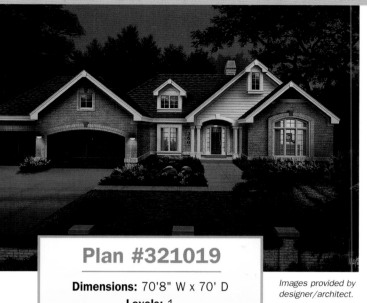

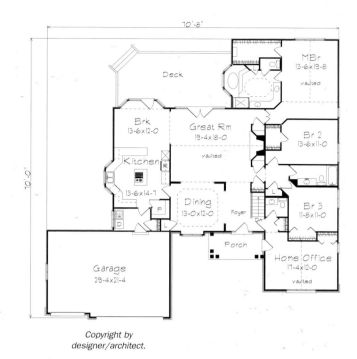

Images provided by designer/architect.

Copyright by designer/architect.

Plan #321019

Dimensions: 70'8" W x 70' D
Levels: 1
Square Footage: 2,452
Bedrooms: 4
Bathrooms: 2½
Foundation: Basement
Materials List Available: Yes
Price Category: E

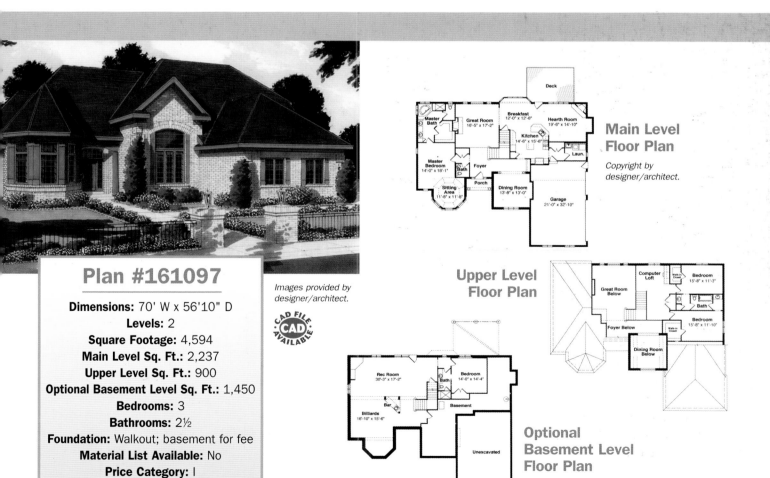

Images provided by designer/architect.

Main Level Floor Plan

Copyright by designer/architect.

Upper Level Floor Plan

Optional Basement Level Floor Plan

Plan #161097

Dimensions: 70' W x 56'10" D
Levels: 2
Square Footage: 4,594
Main Level Sq. Ft.: 2,237
Upper Level Sq. Ft.: 900
Optional Basement Level Sq. Ft.: 1,450
Bedrooms: 3
Bathrooms: 2½
Foundation: Walkout; basement for fee
Material List Available: No
Price Category: I

Plan #121015

Dimensions: 52' W x 47'4" D
Levels: 2
Square Footage: 1,999
Main Level Sq. Ft.: 1,421
Upper Level Sq. Ft.: 578
Bedrooms: 4
Bathrooms: 2½
Foundation: Basement
Materials List Available: Yes
Price Category: D

This home, as shown in the photograph, may differ from the actual blueprints. For more detailed information, please check the floor plans carefully.

Images provided by designer/architect.

Hipped roofs and a trio of gables bring distinction to this plan.

Features:

• Ceiling Height: 8 ft.

• Open Floor Plan: The rooms flow into each other and are flanked by an abundance of windows. The result is a light and airy space that seems much larger than it really is.

• Formal Dining Room: Here is the perfect room for elegant entertaining.

• Breakfast Nook: This bright, bayed nook is the perfect place to start the day. It's also great for intimate get-togethers.

• Great Room: The family will enjoy gathering in this spacious area.

• Bedrooms: This large master bedroom, along with three secondary bedrooms and an extra room, provides plenty of room for a growing family.

• Attached Garage: The garage provides two bays of parking plus plenty of storage space.

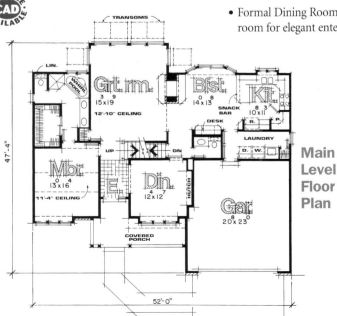

Main Level Floor Plan

Upper Level Floor Plan

Copyright by designer/architect.

Plan #151001

Dimensions: 70' W x 88' D
Levels: 1
Square Footage: 3,124
Bedrooms: 4
Bathrooms: 3½
Foundation: Crawl space, slab
CompleteCost List Available: Yes
Price Category: G

Images provided by designer/architect.

From the double front doors to sleek arches, columns, and a gallery with arched openings to the bedrooms, you'll love this elegant home.

Features:

- Grand Room: With a 13-ft. pan ceiling and column entry, this room opens to the rear covered porch as well as through French doors to the bay-windowed morning room that, in turn, leads to the gathering room.

- Gathering Room: A majestic fireplace, built-in entertainment center, and book shelves give comfort and ease.

- Kitchen: A double oven, built-in desk, and a work island add up to a design for efficiency.

- Master Suite: Enjoy the practicality of walk-in closets, the comfort of a private sitting area, and the convenience of an adjacent study or nursery. The bath features a step-up whirlpool tub and separate shower.

Copyright by designer/architect.

Plan #271018

Dimensions: 67' W x 37' D
Levels: 2
Square Footage: 2,445
Main Level Sq. Ft.: 1,290
Upper Level Sq. Ft.: 1,155
Bedrooms: 4
Bathrooms: 2½
Foundation: Basement
Materials List Available: Yes
Price Category: E

Images provided by designer/architect.

This traditional home re-creates the charm and character of days gone by.

Features:

• **Living Room:** A dramatic skylighted entry preludes this formal, sunken living room, which includes a stunning corner fireplace, a vaulted ceiling, and an adjoining formal dining room.

• **Dining Room:** This quiet space offers a built-in hutch beneath a vaulted ceiling.

• **Kitchen:** A built-in desk and a pantry mark this smartly designed space, which opens to a breakfast room and the family room beyond.

• **Family Room:** Sunken and filled with intrigue, this gathering room features a fireplace flanked by windows, plus French doors that open to a backyard deck.

• **Master Suite:** This luxurious upper-floor retreat boasts a vaulted ceiling, an angled walk-in closet, and a private bath.

Main Level Floor Plan

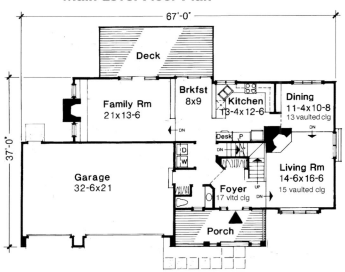

Upper Level Floor Plan

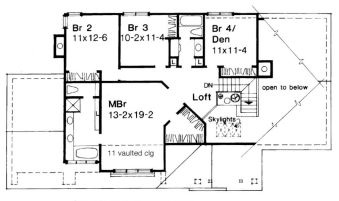

Copyright by designer/architect.

Plan #491003

Dimensions: 46' W x 28' D
Levels: 2
Square Footage: 1,235
Main Level Sq. Ft.: 893
Upper Level Sq. Ft.: 342
Bedrooms: 3
Bathrooms: 2
Foundation: Crawl space
Material List Available: Yes
Price Category: B

Images provided by designer/architect.

The rear-oriented view makes this home perfect for lake-front property.

Features:

- **Living Room:** This gathering area, with its vaulted ceiling and fireplace, has skylights, which flood the space with natural light.

- **Kitchen:** An island kitchen is always a welcome feature. This one is open to the dining and living rooms and makes the home feel spacious.

- **Master Suite:** The upper level is dedicated to this private oasis with vaulted ceiling. The secluded sun deck is the perfect place to watch the sun set.

- **Secondary Bedrooms:** Located on the main level are these two equal-size bedrooms with private closets. Each room also has a view of the backyard.

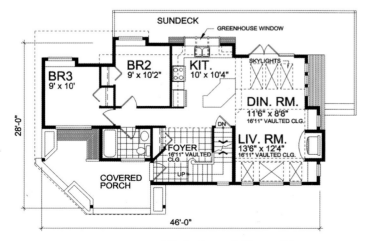

Main Level Floor Plan

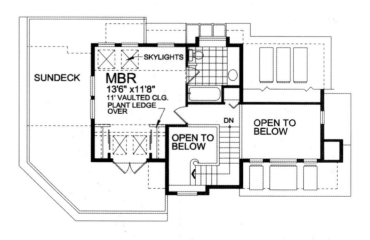

Upper Level Floor Plan

Copyright by designer/architect.

Plan #151027

Dimensions: 37' W x 73' D
Levels: 2
Square Footage: 2,323
Main Level Sq. Ft.: 1,713
Upper Level Sq. Ft.: 619
Bedrooms: 3
Bathrooms: 3
Foundation: Crawl space, slab; optional basement plan available for extra fee
Materials List Available: No
Price Category: E

A traditional design with a covered front porch and high ceilings in many rooms gives this home all the space and comfort you'll ever need.

Features:

- Foyer: A formal foyer with 8-in. wood columns will lead you to an elegant dining area.

- Great Room: This wonderful gathering room has 10-ft. boxed ceilings, a built-in media center, and an atrium door leading to a rear grilling porch.

- Kitchen: Functional yet cozy, this kitchen opens to the breakfast area with built-in computer desk and is open to the great room as well.

- Master Suite: Pamper yourself in this luxurious bedroom with 10-ft. boxed ceilings, large walk-in closets, and a bath area with a whirlpool tub, shower, and double vanity.

- Second Level: A game room and two bedrooms with walk-thru baths make this floor special.

Images provided by designer/architect.

Main Level Floor Plan

Upper Level Floor Plan

Copyright by designer/architect.

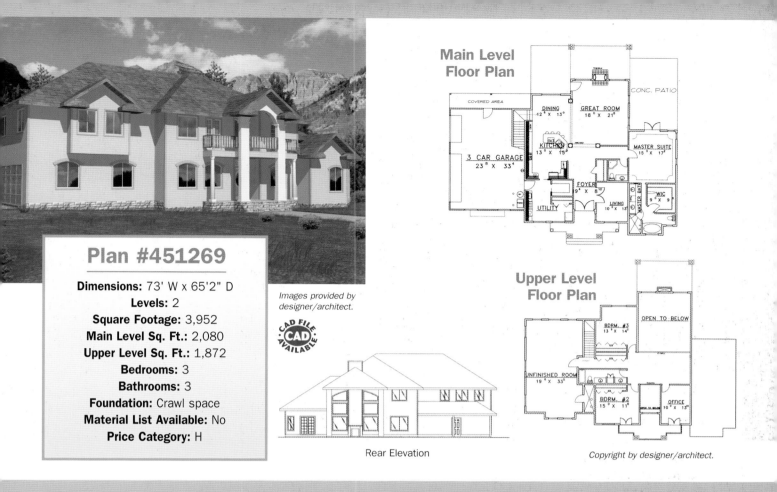

Main Level Floor Plan

COVERED AREA

DINING 12'⁴ X 13'⁸

GREAT ROOM 18'⁰ X 21'⁸

CONC. PATIO

KITCHEN 13'⁰ X 15'⁴

3 CAR GARAGE 23'⁸ X 33'⁴

MASTER SUITE 15'⁵ X 17'²

FOYER 9'⁴ X 8'⁰

LIVING 10'⁵ X 8'⁴

MASTER BATH

WIC 9'⁵ X 7'³

UTILITY

Upper Level Floor Plan

OPEN TO BELOW

BDRM. #3 13'⁵ X 14'⁷

UNFINISHED ROOM 19'⁰ X 33'⁰

BDRM. #2 15'⁵ X 11'⁸

OFFICE 10'⁰ X 13'⁰

OPEN TO BELOW

Images provided by designer/architect.

CAD FILE AVAILABLE

Rear Elevation

Copyright by designer/architect.

Plan #451269

Dimensions: 73' W x 65'2" D
Levels: 2
Square Footage: 3,952
Main Level Sq. Ft.: 2,080
Upper Level Sq. Ft.: 1,872
Bedrooms: 3
Bathrooms: 3
Foundation: Crawl space
Material List Available: No
Price Category: H

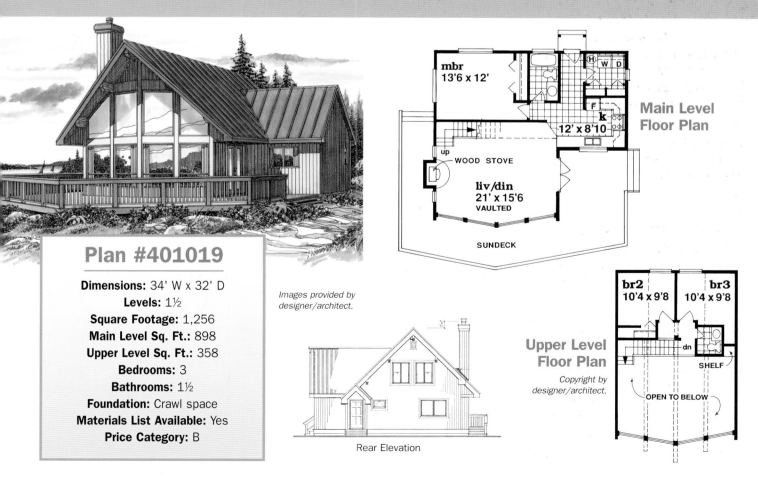

Main Level Floor Plan

mbr 13'6 X 12'

H W D

F

k 12' X 8'10

up

WOOD STOVE

liv/din 21' X 15'6 VAULTED

SUNDECK

Upper Level Floor Plan

br2 10'4 X 9'8

br3 10'4 X 9'8

dn

SHELF

OPEN TO BELOW

Images provided by designer/architect.

Copyright by designer/architect.

Rear Elevation

Plan #401019

Dimensions: 34' W x 32' D
Levels: 1½
Square Footage: 1,256
Main Level Sq. Ft.: 898
Upper Level Sq. Ft.: 358
Bedrooms: 3
Bathrooms: 1½
Foundation: Crawl space
Materials List Available: Yes
Price Category: B

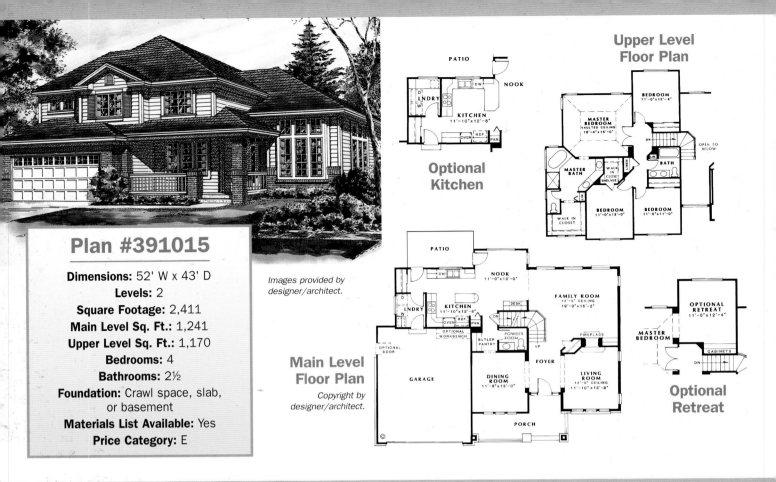

Plan #391015

Dimensions: 52' W x 43' D
Levels: 2
Square Footage: 2,411
Main Level Sq. Ft.: 1,241
Upper Level Sq. Ft.: 1,170
Bedrooms: 4
Bathrooms: 2½
Foundation: Crawl space, slab, or basement
Materials List Available: Yes
Price Category: E

Upper Level Floor Plan

Optional Kitchen

Images provided by designer/architect.

Main Level Floor Plan

Copyright by designer/architect.

Optional Retreat

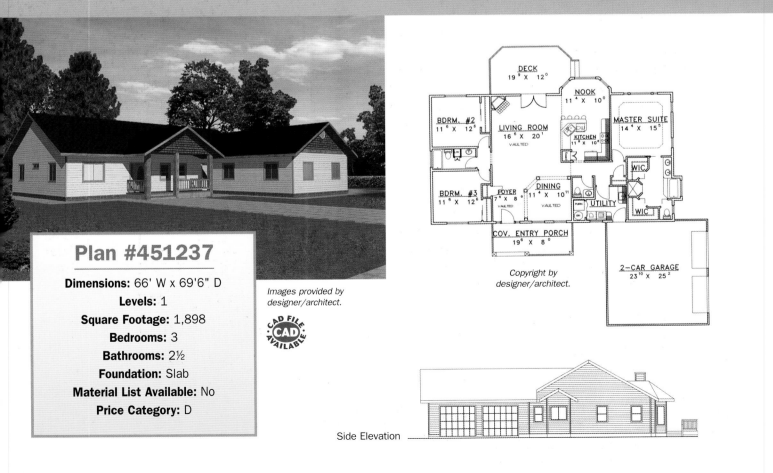

Plan #451237

Dimensions: 66' W x 69'6" D
Levels: 1
Square Footage: 1,898
Bedrooms: 3
Bathrooms: 2½
Foundation: Slab
Material List Available: No
Price Category: D

Images provided by designer/architect.

CAD FILE AVAILABLE

Copyright by designer/architect.

Side Elevation

Plan #121025

Dimensions: 60' W x 59'4" D
Levels: 2
Square Footage: 2,562
Main Level Sq. Ft.: 1,875
Upper Level Square Footage: 687
Bedrooms: 4
Bathrooms: 2½
Foundation: Basement
Materials List Available: Yes
Price Category: E

Images provided by designer/architect.

Dramatic arches are the reoccurring architectural theme in this distinctive home.

Features:

- Ceiling Height: 8 ft. unless otherwise noted.
- Foyer: This is a grand two-story entrance. Plants will thrive on the plant shelf thanks to light streaming through the arched window.
- Great Room: The foyer flows into the great room through dramatic 15-ft.-high arched openings.

- Kitchen: An island is the centerpiece of this highly functional kitchen that includes a separate breakfast area.
- Office: French doors open into this versatile office that features a 10-ft. ceiling and transom-topped windows.
- Master Suite: The master suite features a volume ceiling, built-in dresser, and two closets. You'll unwind in the beautiful corner whirlpool bath with its elegant window treatment.

Main Level Floor Plan

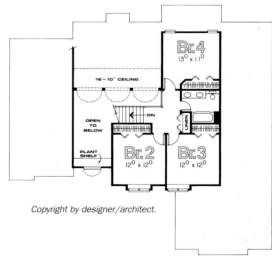

Upper Level Floor Plan

Copyright by designer/architect.

Plan #161113

Dimensions: 120'2" W x 60'4" D
Levels: 2
Square Footage: 6,126
Main Level Sq. Ft.: 3,298
Upper Level Sq. Ft.: 1,067
Lower Level Sq. Ft.: 1,761
Bedrooms: 5
Bathrooms: 3½
Foundation: Basement
Materials List Available: No
Price Category: K

Images provided by designer/architect.

A covered porch welcomes friends and family to this elegant home.

Features:

• **Library:** Just off the foyer is this library, which can be used as a home office. Notice the connecting door to the master bathroom.

• **Kitchen:** Release the chef inside of you into this gourmet kitchen, complete with seating at the island and open to the breakfast area. Step through the triple sliding door, and arrive on the rear porch.

• **Master Suite:** This luxurious master suite features a stepped ceiling in the sleeping area and private access to the rear patio. The master bath boasts an oversized stall shower, a whirlpool bath, dual vanities, and an enormous walk-in closet.

• **Lower Level:** For family fun times, this lower level is finished to provide a wet bar, billiard room, and media room. The area also includes two additional bedrooms and an exercise room.

• **Garage:** You'll have storage galore in this four-car garage, complete with an additional set of stairs to the unfinished part of the basement.

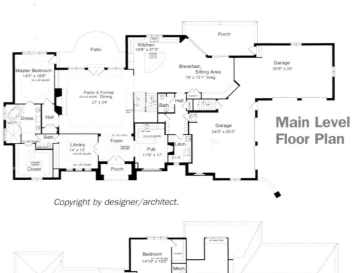

Main Level Floor Plan

Copyright by designer/architect.

Upper Level Floor Plan

Dining Room/Great Room

Great Room

Dining Room

Kitchen

Rear Elevation

Basement Level Floor Plan

Exercise Room
14' x 19'

Media Area
15'9" x 14'

Unexcavated

Basement

Unexcavated

Bedroom
13'10" x 14'

Hall

Billiard Room
20'6" x 14'7"

Unexcavated

Bedroom
13'1" x 13'

Bar

Unex.

Game Room

Plan #121009

Dimensions: 50' W x 58' D
Levels: 1
Square Footage: 1,422
Bedrooms: 3
Bathrooms: 2
Foundation: Basement
Materials List Available: Yes
Price Category: B

This amenity-filled home is perfect for the growing family or as a retirement retreat.

Features:

- Ceiling Height: 8 ft. unless otherwise noted.

- Great Room: This inviting space is the perfect place for gatherings of all sizes. It shares 12-ft. ceilings with the dining room and kitchen.

- Dining Room: In addition to the 12-ft. ceiling, arched openings, and built-in book cases make this an elegant place to dine.

- Private Porch: After dinner, step through a door in the dining room to enjoy a summer breeze in this inviting porch.

- Master Suite: The boxed ceiling lends drama to this suite and a walk-in closet adds convenience. Luxury comes from the whirlpool bath.

- Garage: You won't be short of parking and storage space in this two-bay garage. As a bonus there is space for a workbench.

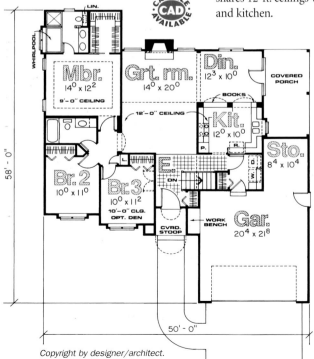

Copyright by designer/architect.

SMARTtip

Window Cornices

You can transform plain rooms by making jogs in cornice molding that will hold shades, blinds, and other window treatments. You can create individual pockets over each window or continue the molding past narrow wall sections between windows to form a more expansive detail. Housings below the cornice can be painted or papered.

Plan #451092

Dimensions: 100' W x 68'5" D

Levels: 1

Square Footage: 2,521

Bedrooms: 2

Bathrooms: 2½

Foundation: Walkout basement

Material List Available: No

Price Category: E

Images provided by designer/architect.

Main Level Floor Plan

Rear Elevation

Optional Basement Level Floor Plan

Copyright by designer/architect.

Plan #361493

Images provided by designer/architect.

Dimensions: 73' W x 60'8" D

Levels: 1

Square Footage: 2,350

Bedrooms: 2

Bathrooms: 2½

Foundation: Crawl space

Material List Available: No

Price Category: E

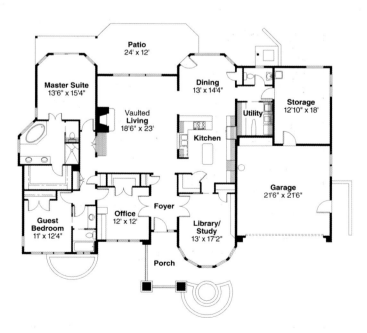

Copyright by designer/architect.

Plan #321079

Dimensions: 69'8" W x 46' D
Levels: 2
Square Footage: 2,624
Main Level Sq. Ft.: 1,774
Upper Level Sq. Ft.: 850
Bedrooms: 4
Bathrooms: 2½
Foundation: Basement
Materials List Available: Yes
Price Category: F

Images provided by designer/architect.

The dramatic exterior design allows natural light to flow into the spacious living area of this home.

Features:

- **Entry:** This two-story area opens into the dining room through a classic colonnade.

- **Dining Room:** A large bay window, stately columns, and doorway to the kitchen make this room both beautiful and convenient.

- **Great Room:** Enjoy light from the fireplace or the three Palladian windows in the 18-ft. ceiling.

- **Kitchen:** The step-saving design features a walk-in pantry as well as good counter space.

- **Breakfast Room:** You'll love the light that flows through the windows flanking the back door.

- **Master Suite:** The vaulted ceiling and bayed areas in both the bed and bath add elegance. You'll love the two walk-in closets and bath with a sunken tub, two vanities, and separate shower.

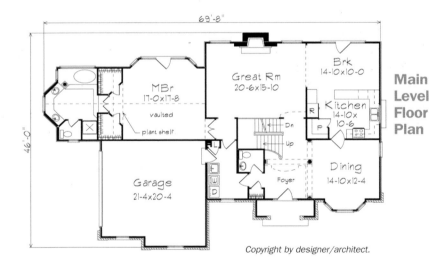

Main Level Floor Plan

Copyright by designer/architect.

Great Room

Upper Level Floor Plan

Plan #271061

Dimensions: 68' W x 52' D
Levels: 1
Square Footage: 1,750
Bedrooms: 1
Bathrooms: 1½
Foundation: Walkout basement
Material List Available: No
Price Category: C

Stucco and a contemporary design give this home a simplistically elegant look.

CAD FILE AVAILABLE

Features:

- Entry: A small porch area welcomes guests out of the weather and into the warmth. Inside, this entryway provides an inviting introduction to the rest of the home.

- Kitchen: Opening to both the full dining room and a bayed dinette, this kitchen is both beautifully and efficiently designed. The space includes a walk-in pantry and plenty of workspace for the budding gourmet.

- Master Suite: This space is fit for the king (or queen) of the castle. Separated from the rest

of the house by a small entry, the suite includes its own full bath with dual sinks, bathtub, shower stall, and water closet.

- Basement: This area can be finished to include two bedrooms with wide closets, a full bathroom, a family room, and storage space.

- Garage: Whether you actually have three cars you need kept from the climate, you are a collector of things, or you prefer a hobby area, this three-bay garage has plenty of space to fit your needs.

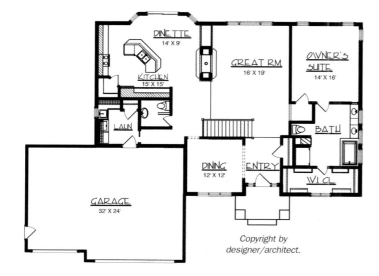

Copyright by designer/architect.

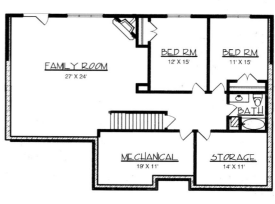

Optional Basement Level Floor Plan

Plan #271034

Dimensions: 45' W x 43' D
Levels: 2
Square Footage: 1,531
Main Level Sq. Ft.: 1,062
Upper Level Sq. Ft.: 469
Bedrooms: 4
Bathrooms: 2
Foundation: Basement
Materials List Available: Yes
Price Category: C

This versatile home design adapts to today's constantly changing and nontraditional families.

Features:

- Great Room: Both old and young are sure to enjoy this great room's warm and charming fireplace. The vaulted ceiling and high fixed windows add volume and light to the room.

- Family/Kitchen: This joined space is perfect for weekend get-togethers. On warm evenings, step through the sliding glass doors to the backyard deck.

- Den/Bedroom: The flexible den can serve as a nursery or as a guestroom for visiting family members of any age.

- Master Bedroom: When the golden years near, you'll appreciate its main-floor locale.

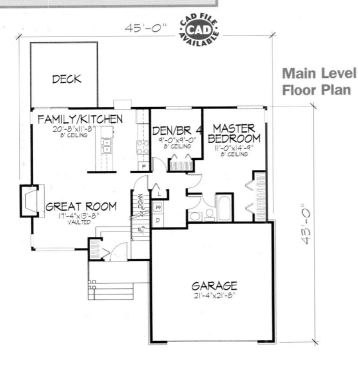

Main Level Floor Plan

Upper Level Floor Plan

Copyright by designer/architect.

Plan #121017

Dimensions: 54' W x 50' D
Levels: 2
Square Footage: 2,353
Main Level Sq. Ft.: 1,653
Upper Level Sq. Ft.: 700
Bedrooms: 4
Bathrooms: 2½
Foundation: Basement
Materials List Available: Yes
Price Category: E

The dramatic two-story entry with bent staircase is the first sign that this is a gracious home.

Features:

• Ceiling Height: 8 ft. except as noted.

• Great Room: A row of transom-topped windows and a tall, beamed ceiling add a sense of spaciousness to this family gathering area.

• Formal Dining Room: The bayed window helps make this an inviting place to entertain.

• See-through Fireplace: This feature spreads warmth and coziness throughout the informal areas of the home.

• Breakfast Area: This sunny area shares a see-through fireplace with the great room. It's the perfect place to start the day.

• Master Suite: Here are all the features you expect to find in large luxury homes. Wake up to tall, sloped ceilings, and enjoy the corner whirlpool, separate shower, and vanity. A large walk-in closet provides plenty of wardrobe storage.

Main Level Floor Plan

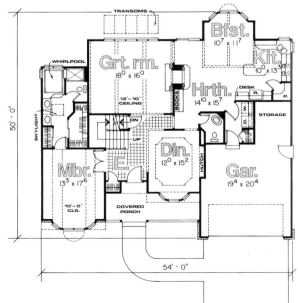

Upper Level Floor Plan

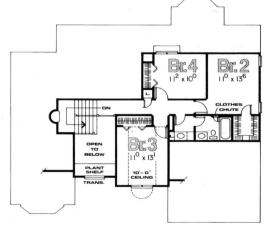

Copyright by designer/architect.

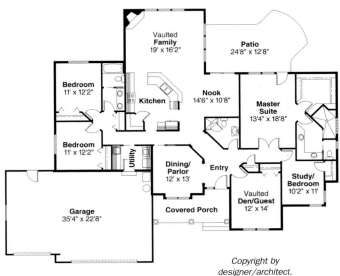

Plan #361435

Dimensions: 81' W x 64' D

Levels: 1

Square Footage: 2,507

Bedrooms: 5

Bathrooms: 3

Foundation: Crawl space or basement

Materials List Available: No

Price Category: E

Images provided by designer/architect.

CAD FILE AVAILABLE

Copyright by designer/architect.

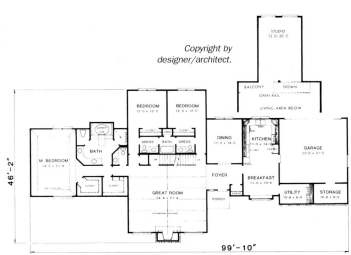

Plan #301001

Dimensions: 99'10" W x 46'2" D

Levels: 1

Square Footage: 2,720

Bedrooms: 3

Bathrooms: 2

Foundation: Crawl space, slab

Materials List Available: Yes

Price Category: F

Images provided by designer/architect.

Copyright by designer/architect.

Plan #121024

Dimensions: 60' W x 58' D
Levels: 2
Square Footage: 3,057
Main Level Sq. Ft.: 1,631
Second Level Sq. Ft.: 1,426
Bedrooms: 4
Bathrooms: 2½
Foundation: Basement
Materials List Available: Yes
Price Category: G

Images provided by designer/architect.

This distinctive home offers plenty of space and is designed for gracious and convenient living.

Features:

- Ceiling Height: 8 ft. unless otherwise noted.
- Foyer: A curved staircase in this elegant entry will greet your guests.
- Living Room: This room invites you with a volume ceiling flanked by transom-topped windows that flood the room with sunlight.
- Screened Veranda: On warm summer nights, throw open the French doors in the living room and enjoy a breeze on the huge screened veranda.
- Dining Room: This distinctive room is overlooked by the veranda.
- Family Room: At the back of the home is this comfortable family retreat with its soaring cathedral ceiling and handsome fireplace flanked by bookcases.
- Master Bedroom: This bayed bedroom features a 10-ft. vaulted ceiling.

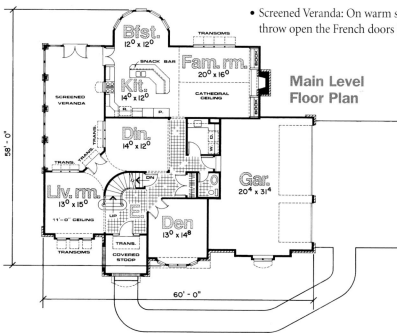

Main Level Floor Plan

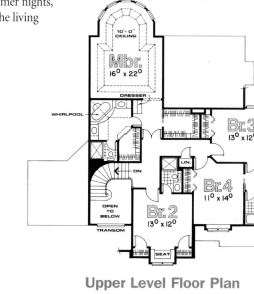

Upper Level Floor Plan

Copyright by designer/architect.

Plan #271036

Dimensions: 43'4" W x 50' D
Levels: 2
Square Footage: 1,602
Main Level Sq. Ft.: 1,112
Upper Level Sq. Ft.: 490
Bedrooms: 3
Bathrooms: 2½
Foundation: Basement
Materials List Available: No
Price Category: C

A country-styled home, like this one, is a perfect fit for any neighborhood.

Images provided by designer/architect.

Features:

- Living Room: Just off the entry you will find this large gathering area with a cozy fireplace. The front wall of windows will allow the area to be flooded with natural light.

- Kitchen: The chef in the family will love the layout of this efficiently designed kitchen. On nice days step out the glass doors onto the rear patio, and dine in the sunshine.

- Master Bedroom: This main-level retreat features an elegant double-door entry. The master bath offers efficiency in a compact design.

- Secondary Bedrooms: Located on the upper level, these two bedrooms offer adequate space for furniture and toys. The second full bathroom is located close by.

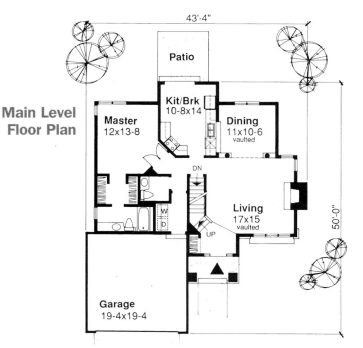

Main Level Floor Plan

Patio

Kit/Brk 10-8x14

Master 12x13-8

Dining 11x10-6 vaulted

DN

Living 17x15 vaulted

UP

Garage 19-4x19-4

43'-4"

50'-0"

Upper Level Floor Plan

Br 2 10-6x13-8

Br 3 10x10

DN

open to below

unfinished storage

Plant Shelf

Copyright by designer/architect.

Plan #271016

Dimensions: 45'4" W x 49'6" D
Levels: 2
Square Footage: 2,170
Main Level Sq. Ft.: 1,169
Upper Level Sq. Ft.: 1,001
Bedrooms: 3
Bathrooms: 2½
Foundation: Basement
Materials List Available: Yes
Price Category: D

Images provided by designer/architect.

With plenty of living space, this attractive design is just right for a growing family.

Features:

- **Entry:** This two-story reception area welcomes guests with sincerity and style. A coat closet stands ready to take winter wraps.

- **Great Room:** This sunken and vaulted space hosts gatherings and formal meals of any size, and a handsome fireplace adds warmth and ambiance.

- **Kitchen:** A U-shaped counter keeps the family cook organized. A bayed breakfast nook overlooks a backyard deck.

- **Family Room:** The home's second fireplace adds a cozy touch to this casual area. Relax here with the family after playing in the snow!

- **Master Suite:** A vaulted ceiling presides over the master bedroom. The private bath hosts a separate tub and shower, a dual-sink vanity, and two walk-in closets.

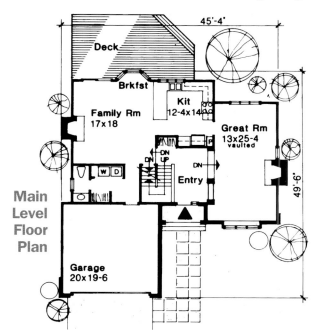

Main Level Floor Plan

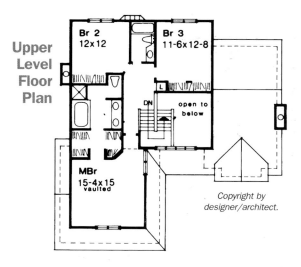

Upper Level Floor Plan

Copyright by designer/architect.

Plan #151384

Dimensions: 76'8" W x 77'7" D
Levels: 1.5
Square Footage: 2,742
Bedrooms: 3
Bathrooms: 2½
Foundation: Crawl space or slab
CompleteCost List Available: Yes
Price Category: F

Images provided by designer/architect.

With its fine detailing, this is a home created for the ages.

Features:

• Great Room: A fireplace nicely settled between built-ins punctuates this enormous room.

• Hobby Room: This oversized room offers space galore for those do-it-yourself home projects.

• Master Suite: This elaborate suite presents an entire wall of built-ins, along with an angled private entrance to the porch.

• Bedrooms: The two secondary bedrooms are located on the opposite side of the home from the master suite and share the full bathroom adjacent to Bedroom 2.

Copyright by designer/architect.

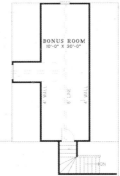

Bonus Area Floor Plan

Front View

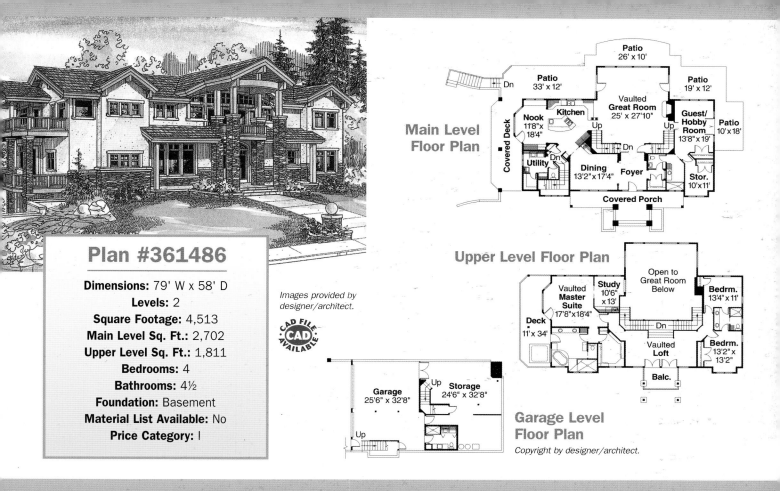

Plan #361486

Dimensions: 79' W x 58' D
Levels: 2
Square Footage: 4,513
Main Level Sq. Ft.: 2,702
Upper Level Sq. Ft.: 1,811
Bedrooms: 4
Bathrooms: 4½
Foundation: Basement
Material List Available: No
Price Category: I

Images provided by designer/architect.

CAD FILE AVAILABLE

Main Level Floor Plan

Patio 26' x 10'
Patio 33' x 12'
Patio 19' x 12'
Patio 10' x 18'
Covered Deck
Nook 11'8" x 18'4"
Kitchen
Vaulted Great Room 25' x 27'10"
Guest/Hobby Room 13'8" x 19'
Up
Utility
Dn
Dining 13'2" x 17'4"
Foyer
Stor. 10' x 11'
Dn
Covered Porch

Upper Level Floor Plan

Open to Great Room Below
Vaulted Master Suite 17'8" x 18'4"
Study 10'6" x 13'
Bedrm. 13'4" x 11'
Deck 11' x 34'
Dn
Vaulted Loft
Bedrm. 13'2" x 13'2"
Balc.

Garage Level Floor Plan

Garage 25'6" x 32'8"
Up
Storage 24'6" x 32'8"
Up

Copyright by designer/architect.

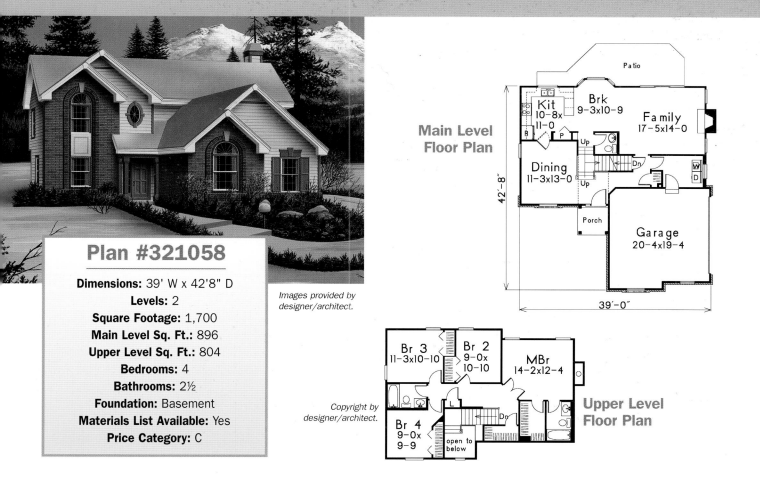

Plan #321058

Dimensions: 39' W x 42'8" D
Levels: 2
Square Footage: 1,700
Main Level Sq. Ft.: 896
Upper Level Sq. Ft.: 804
Bedrooms: 4
Bathrooms: 2½
Foundation: Basement
Materials List Available: Yes
Price Category: C

Images provided by designer/architect.

Main Level Floor Plan

Patio
Kit 10-8x11-0
Brk 9-3x10-9
Family 17-5x14-0
Dining 11-3x13-0
Up
Dn
Up
Porch
Garage 20-4x19-4
42'-8"
39'-0"

Copyright by designer/architect.

Upper Level Floor Plan

Br 3 11-3x10-10
Br 2 9-0x10-10
MBr 14-2x12-4
Br 4 9-0x9-9
Dn
open to below

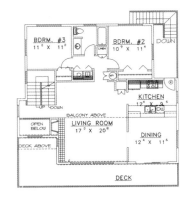

Main Level Floor Plan

Copyright by designer/architect.

Images provided by designer/architect.

CAD FILE AVAILABLE

Lower Level Floor Plan

Upper Level Floor Plan

Plan #451200

Dimensions: 40' W x 45' D
Levels: 2
Square Footage: 2,142
Main Level Sq. Ft.: 1,303
Upper Level Sq. Ft.: 839
Bedrooms: 3
Bathrooms: 3
Foundation: Crawl space
Materials List Available: No
Price Category: D

Images provided by designer/architect.

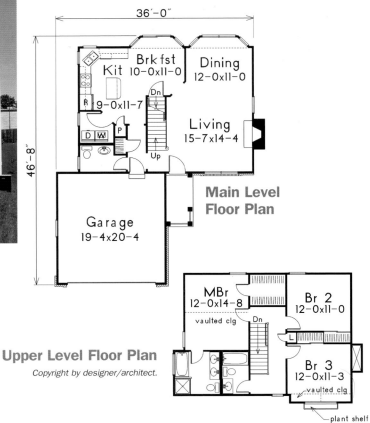

Main Level Floor Plan

Upper Level Floor Plan

Copyright by designer/architect.

Plan #321060

Dimensions: 36' W x 46'8" D
Levels: 2
Square Footage: 1,575
Main Level Sq. Ft.: 802
Upper Level Sq. Ft.: 773
Bedrooms: 3
Bathrooms: 2½
Foundation: Basement
Materials List Available: Yes
Price Category: C

Main Level Floor Plan

38'-0"

39'-4"

Patio

Living 17-8x12-0

MBr 12-4x15-4

Kit 10-6x 10-6

Dn

Garage 19-4x20-4

Dining 10-6x9-10

Up

Porch

Images provided by designer/architect.

Plan #321057

Dimensions: 38' W x 39'4" D
Levels: 2
Square Footage: 1,524
Main Level Sq. Ft.: 951
Upper Level Sq. Ft.: 573
Bedrooms: 3
Bathrooms: 2½
Foundation: Basement
Materials List Available: Yes
Price Category: C

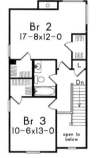

Br 2 17-8x12-0

Br 3 10-6x13-0

Dn

open to below

Upper Level Floor Plan

Copyright by designer/architect.

Plan #361231

Dimensions: 77' W x 83' D
Levels: 1
Square Footage: 3,026
Bedrooms: 3
Bathrooms: 3
Foundation: Crawl space
Material List Available: No
Price Category: G

Images provided by designer/architect.

CAD FILE AVAILABLE

Patio

Covered Patio

Nook

Vaulted Family 27' x 23'

Kitchen

Patio 13' x 10'

Bedroom 12'10" x 12'

Bedroom 12'2" x 18'6"

Master Suite 20'8" x 18'6"

Sitting

Utility

Dining 12'2" x 14'2"

Entry

Vaulted Living 15' x 18'

Covered Porch

Garage 25' x 31'6"

Copyright by designer/architect.

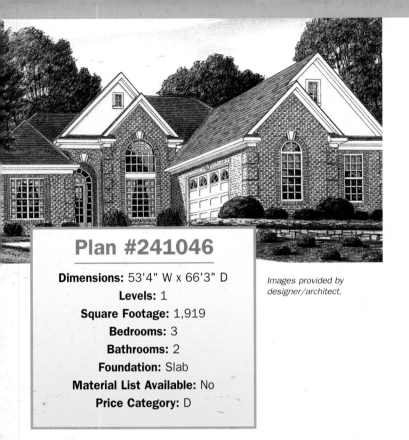

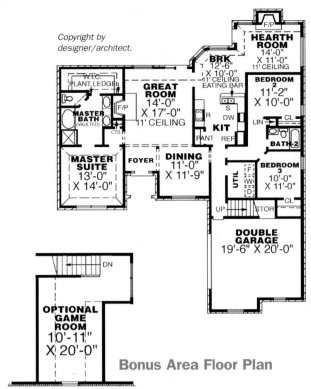

Copyright by designer/architect.

W.I.C.
PLANT LEDGE

MASTER
BATH
(VAULTED)

GREAT
ROOM
14'-0"
X 17'-0"
11' CEILING

BRK
12'-6"
X 10'-0"
11' CEILING
EATING BAR

HEARTH
ROOM
14'-0"
X 11'-0"
11' CEILING

BEDROOM
2
11'-2"
X 10'-0"

KIT

BATH-2

MASTER
SUITE
13'-0"
X 14'-0"

FOYER

DINING
11'-0"
X 11'-9"

UTIL

BEDROOM
3
10'-0"
X 11'-0"

UP

STOR

DOUBLE
GARAGE
19'-6" X 20'-0"

Plan #241046

Dimensions: 53'4" W x 66'3" D
Levels: 1
Square Footage: 1,919
Bedrooms: 3
Bathrooms: 2
Foundation: Slab
Material List Available: No
Price Category: D

Images provided by designer/architect.

DN

OPTIONAL
GAME
ROOM
10'-11"
X 20'-0"

Bonus Area Floor Plan

Plan #181412

Dimensions: 28' W x 34' D
Levels: 1
Square Footage: 947
Bedrooms: 2
Bathrooms: 1
Foundation: Basement
Material List Available: Yes
Price Category: A

Images provided by designer/architect.

CAD FILE AVAILABLE

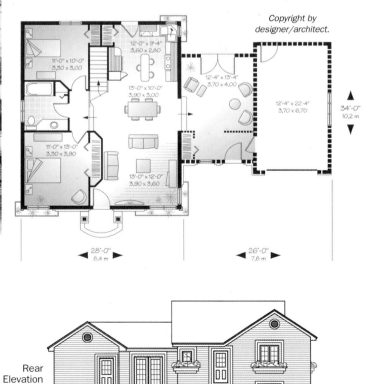

Copyright by designer/architect.

12'-0" x 9'-4"
3,60 x 2,80

11'-0" x 10'-0"
3,30 x 3,00

13'-0" x 10'-0"
3,90 x 3,00

12'-4" x 13'-4"
3,70 x 4,00

12'-4" x 22'-4"
3,70 x 6,70

11'-0" x 13'-0"
3,30 x 3,90

13'-0" x 12'-4"
3,90 x 3,60

34'-0"
10,2 m

28'-0"
8,4 m

26'-0"
7,8 m

Rear
Elevation

Plan #121120

Dimensions: 55'4" W x 37'8" D
Levels: 2
Square Footage: 2,131
Main Level Sq. Ft.: 1,093
Upper Level Sq. Ft.: 1,038
Bedrooms: 4
Bathrooms: 2½
Foundation: Basement;
crawl space for fee
Materials List Available: Yes
Price Category: D

A gorgeous contemporary exterior design and an extravagant interior will combine to make this home your favorite place to be.

Images provided by designer/architect.

Features:

- Family Room: This spacious family area gives you room to entertain friends and family alike. Through French doors is the living room, which can add to that space or become your home office, made even more ideal by the glow from the bay windows.

- Kitchen-Dining Areas: This L-shape kitchen, with ample storage and workspace and an island range, is open to the breakfast area to create a space that simplifies the morning chaos. The kitchen also moves into a formal dining area, complete with hutch and curio, which looks out onto the covered porch for peaceful dinners.

- Master Bedroom: Located far from the daily hubbub, this master bedroom is your private hideaway. Attached is a full bathroom with stall shower, his and her sinks, a whirlpool tub, and a unique walk-in closet that gives both of you plenty of space.

- Secondary Bedrooms: Three bedrooms sit down the hall from the master, sharing the second full bathroom (with dual sinks to simplify the mornings). If three is one too many for you, use the versatile last bedroom as a study or entertainment space.

Main Level Floor Plan

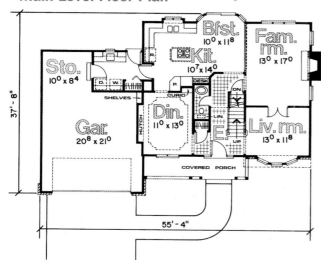

Upper Level Floor Plan

Copyright by designer/architect.

Plan #271025

Dimensions: 61'4" W x 56'4" D
Levels: 2
Square Footage: 2,223
Main Level Sq. Ft.: 1,689
Upper Level Sq. Ft.: 534
Bedrooms: 3
Bathrooms: 2½
Foundation: Basement
Materials List Available: Yes
Price Category: E

Images provided by designer/architect.

This traditional home's unique design combines a dynamic, exciting exterior with a fantastic floor plan.

Features:

• Living Room: To the left of the column-lined, barrel-vaulted entry, this inviting space features a curved wall and corner windows.

• Dining Room: A tray ceiling enhances this formal meal room.

• Kitchen: This island-equipped kitchen includes a corner pantry and a built-in desk. Nearby, the sunny breakfast room opens onto a backyard deck via sliding glass doors.

• Family Room: A corner bank of windows provides a glassy backdrop for this room's handsome fireplace. Munchies may be served on the snack bar from the breakfast nook.

• Master Suite: This main-floor retreat is simply stunning, and includes a vaulted ceiling, access to a private courtyard, and of course, a sumptuous bath with every creature comfort.

Main Level Floor Plan

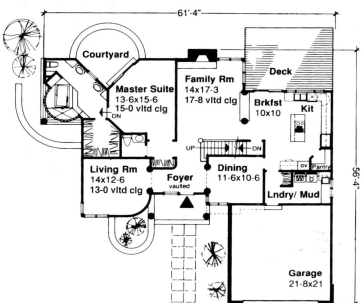

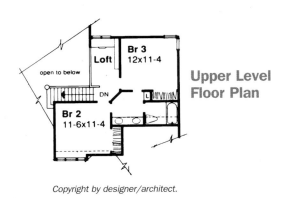

Upper Level Floor Plan

Copyright by designer/architect.

Plan #151383

Dimensions: 70'4" W x 57'2" D
Levels: 1
Square Footage: 2,534
Bedrooms: 3
Bathrooms: 2
Foundation: Crawl space or slab
CompleteCost List Available: Yes
Price Category: E

The arched entry of the covered porch welcomes you to this magnificent home.

Features:

• Foyer: Welcome your guests in this warm foyer before leading them into the impressive dining room with magnificent columns framing the entry.

• Great Room: After dinner, your guests will enjoy conversation in this spacious room, complete with fireplace and built-ins.

• Study: Beautiful French doors open into this quiet space, where you'll be able to concentrate on that work away from the office.

• Rear Porch: This relaxing spot may be reached from the breakfast room or your secluded master suite.

Images provided by designer/architect.

CAD FILE AVAILABLE

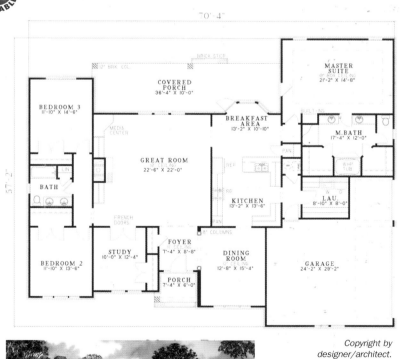

Copyright by designer/architect.

Front View

Plan #361096

Dimensions: 82' W x 55' D

Levels: 1

Square Footage: 2,950

Bedrooms: 3

Bathrooms: 3

Foundation: Crawl space

Material List Available: No

Price Category: F

Images provided by designer/architect.

CAD FILE AVAILABLE

Patio 34' x 12'

Nook 10' x 7'

Kitchen

Vaulted Family 18'8" x 17'10"

Master Suite 17'4" x 15'6"

Garage 21'8" x 30'2"

Utility

Bedroom 11'6" x 11'

Up

Entry

Bedroom 15'4" x 11'6"

Porch

Office 18' x 17'6"

Dining 13'2" x 12'2"

Living 14' x 16'10"

Porch

Bonus Room 24'6" x 14'8"   Dn

Bonus Area Floor Plan

Copyright by designer/architect.

Plan #181407

Dimensions: 34' W x 32' D

Levels: 2

Square Footage: 1,369

Main Level Sq. Ft.: 716

Upper Level Sq. Ft.: 653

Bedrooms: 3

Bathrooms: 1½

Foundation: Basement

Material List Available: Yes

Price Category: B

Images provided by designer/architect.

CAD FILE AVAILABLE

13'-0" X 11'-4"
3,90 X 3,40

9'-0" X 11'-4"
2,70 X 3,40

12'-0" X 10'-0"
3,60 X 3,00

Upper Level Floor Plan

10'-0" X 12'-0"
3,00 X 3,60

5'-0" X 8'-8"
1,50 X 2,60

10'-0" X 12'-0"
3,00 X 3,60

12'-0" X 21'-0"
3,60 X 6,30

12'-0" X 14'-0"
3,60 X 4,20

32'-0"
9,6 m

Main Level Floor Plan

Copyright by designer/architect.

34'-0"
10,2 m

Plan #121111

Dimensions: 52' W x 45'4" D
Levels: 1.5
Square Footage: 1,685
Main Level Sq. Ft.: 1,297
Upper Level Sq. Ft.: 388
Bedrooms: 3
Bathrooms: 2½
Foundation: Basement;
crawl space for fee
Materials List Available: Yes
Price Category: C

Images provided by designer/architect.

Beauty meets practicality in this charming home. Lovely architectural details and an interior designed with daily living in mind create an ideal environment for the growing family.

Features:

- Great Room: When the day is done and its time to relax, this is the place where the family will gather. The fireplace is a great start to creating an atmosphere tailored to your family's lifestyle.

- Kitchen: Great for the busy family, the kitchen has all the workspace and storage that the family chef needs, as well as a snack bar that acts as a transition to the large breakfast room.

- Dining Room: A triplet of windows projecting onto the covered front porch creates a warm

atmosphere for formal dining.

- Master Bedroom: A romantic space, this master bedroom features a window seat facing the front elevation and a compartmentalized full master bath that includes his and her sinks, a walk-in closet, and a whirlpool tub with a skylight.

- Second Floor: In a quiet space of their own, the two secondary bedrooms both include ample closet space and access to the second full bathroom.

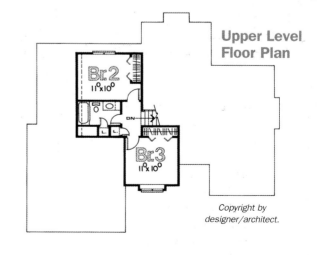

Copyright by designer/architect.

Plan #271019

Dimensions: 41' W x 4' D
Levels: 2
Square Footage: 1,556
Main Level Sq. Ft.: 834
Upper Level Sq. Ft.: 722
Bedrooms: 3
Bathrooms: 2½
Foundation: Basement
Materials List Available: Yes
Price Category: C

Images provided by designer/architect.

This traditional home features a combination of stone and wood, lending it a distinctive old-world flavor.

Features:

• Kitchen: The centerpiece of the home, this country kitchen features ample work surfaces, a nice-sized eating area with built-in bookshelves, and access to a large backyard deck.

• Dining Room: This formal eating space is highlighted by a dramatic three-sided fireplace that is shared with the adjoining living room.

• Living Room: Enhanced by a dramatic vaulted ceiling, this living room also boasts corner windows that flood the area with natural light.

• Master Suite: Residing on the upper floor along with two other bedrooms, the master bedroom features a vaulted ceiling and a plant shelf that tops the entry to a private bath and walk-in closet.

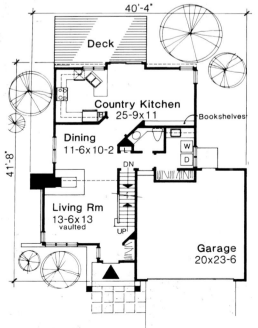

Main Level Floor Plan

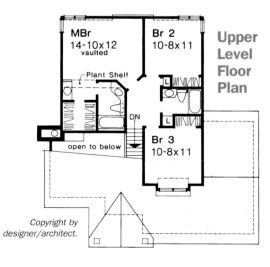

Upper Level Floor Plan

Copyright by designer/architect.

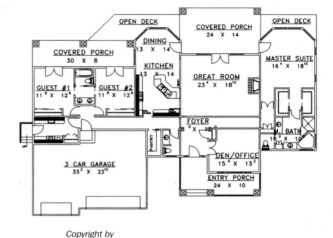

Plan #451194

Dimensions: 87'8" W x 58' D

Levels: 1

Square Footage: 2,618

Bedrooms: 3

Bathrooms: 2½

Foundation: Crawl space

Materials List Available: No

Price Category: F

Images provided by designer/architect.

Copyright by designer/architect.

Plan #181403

Dimensions: 34' W x 32' D

Levels: 1

Square Footage: 1,917

Main Level Sq. Ft.: 1,014

Lower Level Sq. Ft.: 903

Bedrooms: 3

Bathrooms: 2

Foundation: Basement

Material List Available: Yes

Price Category: D

Images provided by designer/architect.

Basement Level Floor Plan

Copyright by designer/architect.

Images provided by designer/architect.

Copyright by designer/architect.

Plan #241039

Dimensions: 48'10" W x 40'4" D
Levels: 1
Square Footage: 1,379
Bedrooms: 3
Bathrooms: 2
Foundation: Slab
Material List Available: No
Price Category: B

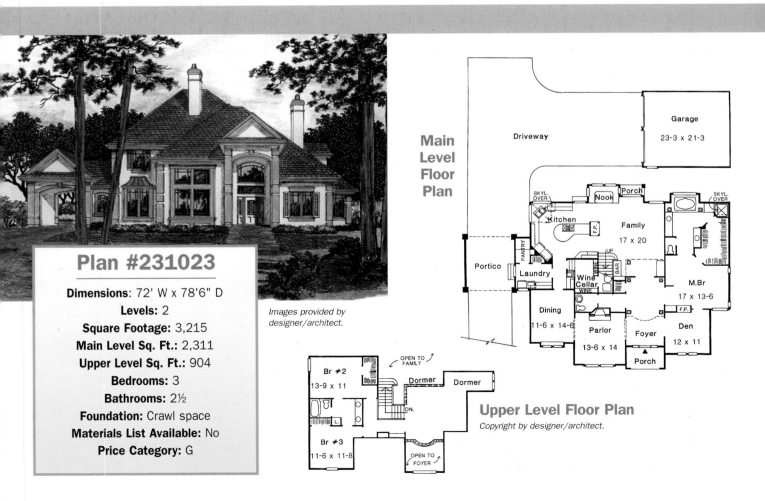

Images provided by designer/architect.

Plan #231023

Dimensions: 72' W x 78'6" D
Levels: 2
Square Footage: 3,215
Main Level Sq. Ft.: 2,311
Upper Level Sq. Ft.: 904
Bedrooms: 3
Bathrooms: 2½
Foundation: Crawl space
Materials List Available: No
Price Category: G

Plan #151711

Dimensions: 64' W x 60'2" D
Levels: 1
Square Footage: 2,554
Bedrooms: 4
Bathrooms: 2½
Foundation: Crawl space or slab
CompleteCost List Available: Yes
Price Category: E

An alluring arched entry welcomes guests into your home, giving them a taste of the lavishness they'll find once inside.

Features:

- **Kitchen:** Counter space on all sides and a center island provide ample space for the budding chef. This kitchen is located across the hall from the dining room and opens into the hearth room, providing easy transitions between preparing and serving. A snack bar acts as a shift between the kitchen and hearth room.

- **Hearth Room:** This spacious area is lined with windows on one side, shares a gas fire place with the great room, and opens onto the grilling porch, which makes it ideal for gatherings of all kinds and sizes.

- **Master Suite:** Larger than any space in the house, this room will truly make you feel like the master. The bedroom is a blank canvas waiting for your personal touch and has a door opening to the backyard. The compartmentalized master bath includes his and her walk-in closets and sinks, a glass shower stall, and a whirlpool bathtub.

- **Secondary Bedrooms:** If three bedrooms is one too many, the second bedroom can easily be used as a study with optional French doors opening from the foyer. Every additional bedroom has a large closet and access to the central full bathroom.

Images provided by designer/architect.

Copyright by designer/architect.

Front View

This home, as shown in the photograph, may differ from the actual blueprints. For more detailed information, please check the floor plans carefully.

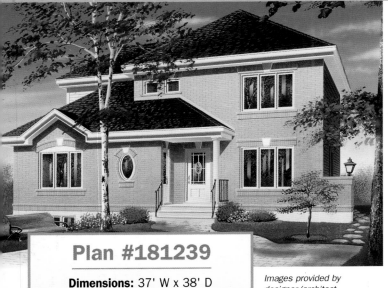

Upper Level Floor Plan

Images provided by designer/architect.

Plan #181239

Dimensions: 37' W x 38' D

Levels: 2

Square Footage: 2,181

Main Level Sq. Ft.: 1,307

Upper Level Sq. Ft.: 874

Bedrooms: 4

Bathrooms: 2½

Foundation: Basement

Materials List Available: Yes

Price Category: D

Main Level Floor Plan

Copyright by designer/architect.

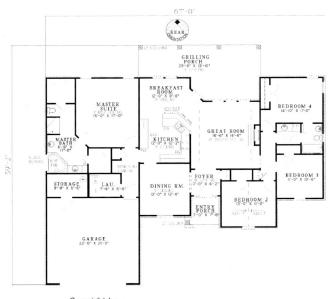

Images provided by designer/architect.

Plan #151240

Dimensions: 67' W x 59'2" D

Levels: 1

Square Footage: 2,007

Bedrooms: 4

Bathrooms: 2

Foundation: Crawl space or slab

CompleteCost List Available: Yes

Price Category: E

Copyright by designer/architect.

Plan #121114

Dimensions: 64' W x 52' D
Levels: 1.5
Square Footage: 2,115
Main Level Sq. Ft.: 1,505
Upper Level Sq. Ft.: 610
Bedrooms: 4
Bathrooms: 2½
Foundation: Basement;
crawl space for fee
Materials List Available: Yes
Price Category: D

This contemporary home is not only beautifully designed on the outside; it has everything you need on the inside. It will be the envy of the neighborhood.

CAD FILE AVAILABLE

Images provided by designer/architect.

Features:

- **Great Room:** The cathedral ceiling and cozy fireplace strike a balance that creates the perfect gathering place for family and friends. An abundance of space allows you to tailor this room to your needs.

- **Kitchen/Breakfast Room:** This combined area features a flood of natural light, workspace to spare, an island with a snack bar, and a door that opens to the backyard, creating an ideal space for outdoor meals and gatherings.

- **Dining Room:** A triplet of windows projecting onto the covered front porch creates a warm atmosphere for formal dining.

- **Master Bedroom:** Away from the busy areas of the home, this master suite is ideal for shedding your daily cares and relaxing in a romantic atmosphere. It includes a full master bath with skylight, his and her sinks, a stall shower, a whirlpool tub, and a walk-in closet.

- **Second Floor:** Three more bedrooms and the second full bathroom upstairs give you plenty of room for a large family. Or if you only need two extra rooms, use the fourth bedroom as a study or entertainment area for the kids.

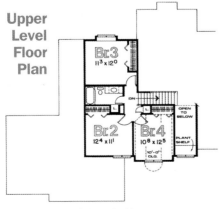

Upper Level Floor Plan

Copyright by designer/architect.

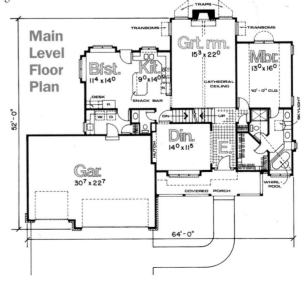

Main Level Floor Plan

Plan #211009

Dimensions: 72' W x 60' D
Levels: 1
Square Footage: 2,396
Bedrooms: 4
Bathrooms: 2
Foundation: Slab
Materials List Available: Yes
Price Category: E

Beautiful arched windows lend a luxurious feeling to the exterior of this one-story home.

Features:

- Ceiling Height: 9 ft. unless otherwise noted.

- Entry: Guests will be greeted by a dramatic 12-ft. ceiling in this elegant foyer.

- Living Room: The 12-ft. ceiling continues through the foyer into this inviting living room. Everyone will feel welcomed by the crackling fire in the handsome fireplace.

- Covered Porch: When the weather is warm, invite guests to step out of the living room directly into this covered porch.

- Kitchen: This bright and cheery kitchen is designed for the way we live today. It includes a pantry and an angled eating bar that will see plenty of impromptu family meals.

- Energy-Efficient Walls: All the outside walls are framed with 2x6 lumber instead of 2x4. The extra thickness makes room for more insulation to lower your heating and cooling bills.

Images provided by designer/architect.

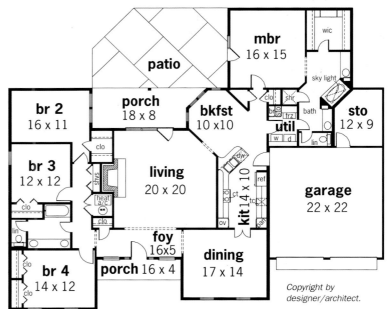

Copyright by designer/architect.

SMARTtip

Ornaments in a Garden

Placement is everything with ornaments in a garden. Some elements are best sitting by themselves. Others are better when they are part of a cohesive whole, perhaps placed in the greenery at a corner or flanking a structure.

Plan #271015

Dimensions: 48' W x 28' D
Levels: 2
Square Footage: 1,359
Main Level Sq. Ft.: 668
Upper Level Sq. Ft.: 691
Bedrooms: 3
Bathrooms: 2½
Foundation: Basement
Materials List Available: Yes
Price Category: B

Images provided by designer/architect.

Strong vertical lines and pairs of narrow windows give this compact home an airy feel. Its clever floor plan makes good use of every square foot of space.

Features:

• Living Room: Beyond the sidelighted front door, the living room enjoys a vaulted ceiling and a flood of light from a striking corner window arrangement.

• Kitchen/Dining: A central fireplace separates the living room from this kitchen/dining room, where a French door opens to a rear deck.

• Master Suite: Sacrifice no luxuries in this sweet, upper-floor retreat, where a boxed-out window catches morning rays or evening stars. Next to the roomy walk-in closet, the private split bath enjoys a window of its own.

• Secondary Bedrooms: A balcony overlooks the living room and leads to one bedroom and the flexible loft.

Main Level Floor Plan

Upper Level Floor Plan

Copyright by designer/architect.

Main Level Floor Plan

Copyright by designer/architect.

Upper Level Floor Plan

Images provided by designer/architect.

Basement Level Floor Plan

Plan #451259

Dimensions: 75'2" W x 55'6" D
Levels: 2
Square Footage: 3,798
Main Level Sq. Ft.: 2,485
Upper Level Sq. Ft.: 1,313
Bedrooms: 6
Bathrooms: 6½
Foundation: Walk-out basement
Materials List Available: No
Price Category: H

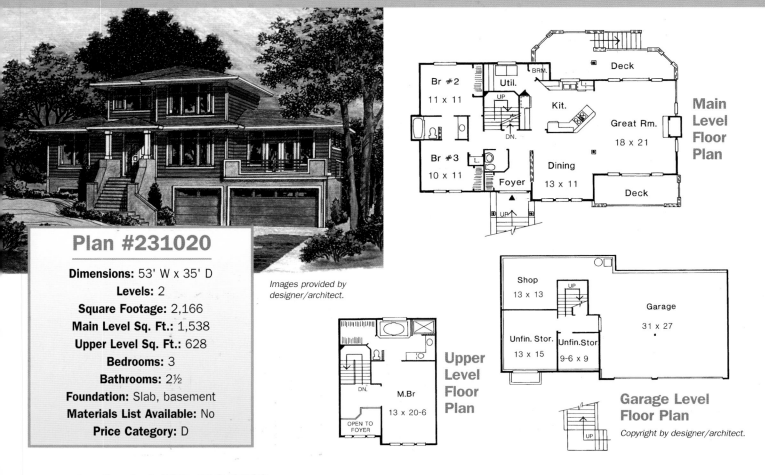

Main Level Floor Plan

Images provided by designer/architect.

Upper Level Floor Plan

Garage Level Floor Plan

Copyright by designer/architect.

Plan #231020

Dimensions: 53' W x 35' D
Levels: 2
Square Footage: 2,166
Main Level Sq. Ft.: 1,538
Upper Level Sq. Ft.: 628
Bedrooms: 3
Bathrooms: 2½
Foundation: Slab, basement
Materials List Available: No
Price Category: D

Plan #321042

Dimensions: 71' W x 54'7" D
Levels: 2
Square Footage: 3,368
Main Level Sq. Ft.: 2,150
Upper Level Sq. Ft.: 1,218
Bedrooms: 4
Full Bathrooms: 3
Half Bathrooms: 2
Foundation: Basement
Materials List Available: Yes
Price Category: G

Inside this traditional exterior lies a home filled with contemporary amenities and design features that are sure to charm the whole family.

Features:

- Great Room: Relax in this sunken room with a cathedral ceiling, wooden beams, skylights, and a masonry fireplace.

- Breakfast Room: Octagon-shaped with a domed ceiling, this room leads to the outdoor patio.

- Library: Situated for privacy and quiet, this room opens from the master bedroom and the foyer.

- Kitchen: The central island here adds to the ample work and storage space.

- Dining Room: Just off the foyer, this room is ideal for formal dinners and quiet times.

- Master Suite: Enjoy the large bedroom and bath with a luxurious corner tub, separate shower, two vanities, walk-in closet, and dressing area.

Images provided by designer/architect.

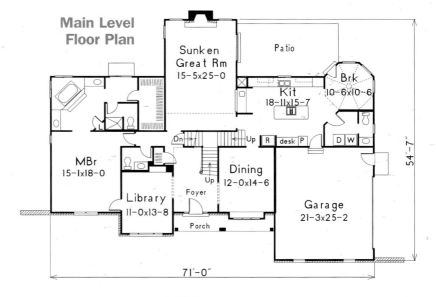

Main Level Floor Plan

Sunken Great Rm 15-5x25-0
Patio
Brk 10-6x10-6
Kit 18-11x15-7
MBr 15-1x18-0
Dining 12-0x14-6
Library 11-0x13-8
Foyer
Garage 21-3x25-2
Porch
54'-7"
71'-0"

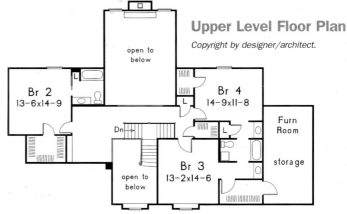

Upper Level Floor Plan

Copyright by designer/architect.

open to below
Br 2 13-6x14-9
Br 4 14-9x11-8
Furn Room
storage
Br 3 13-2x14-6
open to below

Images provided by designer/architect.

Plan #151203

Dimensions: 46' W x 38'10" D

Levels: 1

Square Footage: 1,214

Bedrooms: 3

Bathrooms: 2

Foundation: Crawl space, slab; basement or walkout basement option for fee

CompleteCost List Available: Yes

Price Category: B

Copyright by designer/architect.

Images provided by designer/architect.

Plan #151277

Dimensions: 67'8" W x 58' D

Levels: 1

Square Footage: 2,216

Bedrooms: 3

Bathrooms: 2½

Foundation: Crawl space or slab

CompleteCost List Available: Yes

Price Category: E

Copyright by designer/architect.

Images provided by
designer/architect.

Plan #141021

Dimensions: 70'10" W x 78'9" D

Levels: 1

Square Footage: 2,614

Bedrooms: 3

Bathrooms: 2½

Foundation: Basement

Materials List Available: Yes

Price Category: F

Living Room

Dining Room

Copyright by
designer/architect.

Rear View

Plan #151202

Dimensions: 55'10" W x 65'8" D

Levels: 2

Square Footage: 2,651

Main Level Sq. Ft.: 1,793

Upper Level Sq. Ft.: 858

Opt. Bonus Sq. Ft.: 418

Bedrooms: 4

Bathrooms: 2

Foundation: Crawl space, slab;
basement or walkout basement
option for fee

CompleteCost List Available: Yes

Price Category: F

Images
provided by
designer/
architect.

CAD FILE AVAILABLE

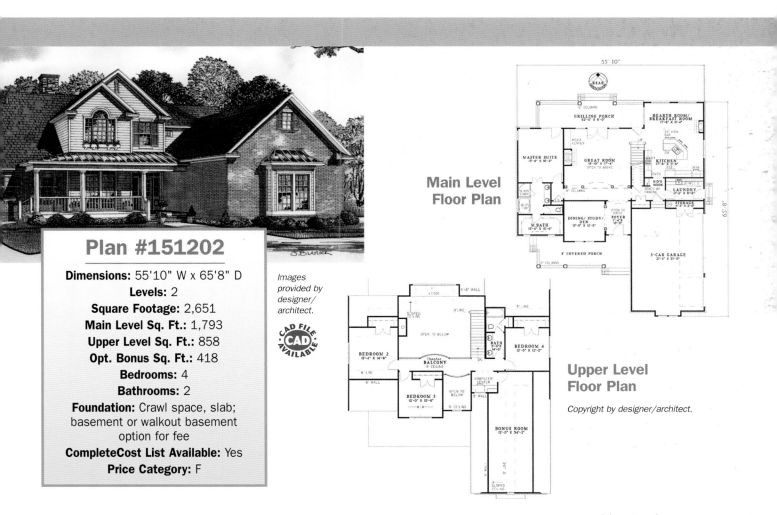

**Main Level
Floor Plan**

**Upper Level
Floor Plan**

Copyright by designer/architect.

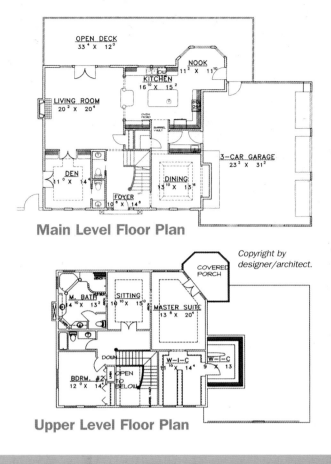

Main Level Floor Plan

Copyright by designer/architect.

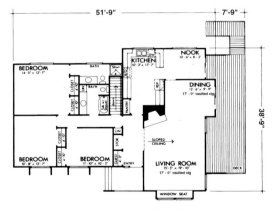

Upper Level Floor Plan

Plan #451201

Dimensions: 64'4" W x 52' D
Levels: 2
Square Footage: 2,800
Main Level Sq. Ft.: 1,466
Upper Level Sq. Ft.: 1,334
Bedrooms: 2
Bathrooms: 2 full, 2 half
Foundation: Crawl space
Material List Available: No
Price Category: F

Images provided by designer/architect.

Optional Basement Level Floor Plan

Copyright by designer/architect.

Plan #271084

Dimensions: 51'9" W x 38'9" D
Levels: 1
Square Footage: 1,602
Bedrooms: 3
Bathrooms: 1½
Foundation: Daylight
Materials List Available: Yes
Price Category: C

Images provided by designer/architect.

Upper Level Floor Plan

Bedroom
10'4" x 13'4"

Bedroom
10'4" x 13'4"

Open to Entry Below

Loft

Dn

Bonus Room
12' x 20'6"

Main Level Floor Plan

Master Suite
14' x 16'

Great Room
17' x 18'

Dining
11'6" x 14'8"

Kitchen

Up

Entry

Utility

Covered Porch

Garage
24' x 24'

Covered Porch

Copyright by designer/architect.

Plan #361073

Dimensions: 54' W x 57' D
Levels: 2
Square Footage: 2,093
Main Level Sq. Ft.: 1,488
Upper Level Sq. Ft.: 605
Bedrooms: 3
Bathrooms: 2½
Foundation: Crawl space
Material List Available: No
Price Category: F

Images provided by designer/architect.

CAD FILE AVAILABLE

Main Level Floor Plan

11'-4" x 13'-2"
3.40 x 3.95

11'-0" x 13'-2"
3.30 x 3.95

11'-8" x 21'-4"
3.50 x 6.40

11'-10" x 15'-0"
3.55 x 4.50

34'-0"
10.2 m

36'-0"
10.8 m

Upper Level Floor Plan

12'-0" x 13'-2"
3.60 x 3.95

11'-8" x 11'-0"
3.50 x 3.30

10'-0" x 9'-6"
3.00 x 2.85

Copyright by designer/architect.

Plan #181304

Dimensions: 36' W x 34' D
Levels: 2
Square Footage: 1,721
Main Level Sq. Ft.: 774
Upper Level Sq. Ft.: 947
Bedrooms: 3
Bathrooms: 1½
Foundation: Basement
Materials List Available: Yes
Price Category: C

Images provided by designer/architect.

CAD FILE AVAILABLE

Images provided by
designer/architect.

Copyright by designer/architect.

Plan #341024

Dimensions: 49'6" W x 39'8" D

Levels: 1

Square Footage: 1,310

Bedrooms: 3

Bathrooms: 2

Foundation: Crawl space, slab, or basement

Materials List Available: Yes

Price Category: B

Main Level Floor Plan

Upper Level Floor Plan

Copyright by designer/architect.

Plan #391057

Dimensions: 62'8" W x 50' D

Levels: 2

Square Footage: 2,851

Main Level Sq. Ft.: 1,933

Upper Level Sq. Ft.: 918

Bedrooms: 4

Bathrooms: 2½

Foundation: Crawl space or basement

Material List Available: Yes

Price Category: F

Images provided by
designer/architect.

Plan #271011

Dimensions: 36' W x 40'8" D
Levels: 2
Square Footage: 1,296
Main Level Sq. Ft.: 891
Upper Level Sq. Ft.: 405
Bedrooms: 3
Bathrooms: 2
Foundation: Basement
Materials List Available: Yes
Price Category: B

Images provided by designer/architect.

Perfectly sized for a narrow lot, this charming modern cottage boasts space efficiency and affordability.

Features:

• Living Room: The inviting raised foyer steps down into this vaulted living room, with its bright windows and eye-catching fireplace.

• Dining Room: This vaulted formal eating space includes sliding-glass-door access to a backyard deck.

• Kitchen: Everything is here: U-shaped efficiency, handy pantry—even bright windows.

• Master Suite: Main-floor location ensures accessibility in later years, plus there's a walk-in closet and full bathroom.

• Secondary Bedrooms: On the upper floor, a bedroom and a loft reside near a full bath. The loft can be converted easily to a third bedroom, or use it as a study or play space.

CAD FILE AVAILABLE

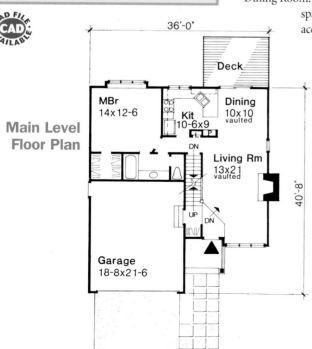

Main Level Floor Plan

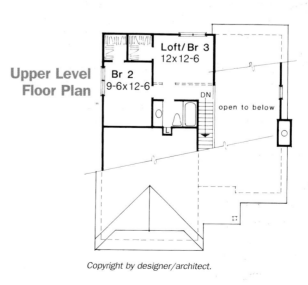

Upper Level Floor Plan

Copyright by designer/architect.

Plan #151026

Dimensions: 34' W x 66'8" D
Levels: 2
Square Footage: 1,574
Main Level Sq. Ft.: 1,131
Upper Level Sq. Ft.: 443
Bedrooms: 3
Bathrooms: 2½
Foundation: Crawl space, slab; optional full basement plan available for extra fee
CompleteCost List Available: Yes
Price Category: C

This French Country home gives space for entertaining and offers privacy.

Features:

- **Great Room:** Move through the gracious foyer framed by wooden columns into the great room with its lofty 10-ft. ceilings and gas fireplace.

- **Dining Room:** Set off by 8-in. columns, the dining room opens to the kitchen, both with 9-foot ceilings.

- **Master Suite:** Enjoy relaxing in the bedroom with its 10-ft. boxed ceiling and well-placed windows. Atrium doors open to the backyard, where you can make a secluded garden. A glass-bricked corner whirlpool tub, corner shower, and double vanity make the master bath luxurious.

- **Bedrooms:** Upstairs, two large bedrooms with a walk-through bath provide plenty of room as well as privacy for kids or guests.

Images provided by designer/architect.

Main Level Floor Plan

Upper Level Floor Plan

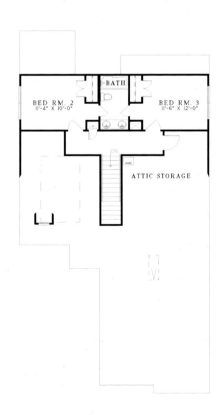

Copyright by designer/architect.

Plan #121011

Dimensions: 50' W x 50' D
Levels: 1
Square Footage: 1,724
Bedrooms: 3
Bathrooms: 2
Foundation: Slab, basement
Materials List Available: Yes
Price Category: C

This home, as shown in the photograph, may differ from the actual blueprints. For more detailed information, please check the floor plans carefully.

CAD FILE AVAILABLE CAD

This one-level home is perfect for retirement or for convenient living for the growing family.

Features:

- Ceiling Height: 8 ft.

- Master Suite: For privacy and quiet, the master suite is segregated from the other bedrooms.

- Family Room: Sit by the fire and read as light streams through the windows flanking the fireplace. Or enjoy the built-in entertainment center.

- Breakfast Area: Located just off the family room, the sunny breakfast area will lure you to linger over impromptu family meals. Here you will find a built-in desk for compiling shopping lists and menus.

- Private Porch: Step out of the breakfast area to enjoy a breeze on this porch.

- Kitchen: Efficient and attractive, this kitchen offers an angled pantry and an island that doubles as a snack bar.

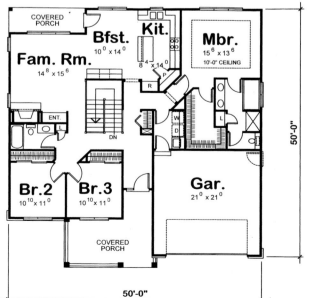

Copyright by designer/architect.

SMARTtip

Measuring for Kitchen Countertops

Custom cabinetmakers will sometimes come to your house to measure for a countertop, but home centers and kitchen stores may require that you come to them with the dimensions already in hand. Be sure to double-check measurements carefully. Being off by only ½ in. can be quite upsetting.

To ensure accuracy, sketch out the countertop on a sheet of graph paper. Include all the essential dimensions. To be on the safe side, have someone else double-check your numbers.

Plan #161096

Dimensions: 67'6" W x 75'6" D
Levels: 2
Square Footage: 3,435
Main Level Sq. Ft.: 2,479
Upper Level Sq. Ft.: 956
Bedrooms: 4
Bathrooms: 3½
Foundation: Walkout basement; basement for fee
Material List Available: No
Price Category: G

A stone-and-brick exterior is excellently coordinated to create a warm and charming showplace.

Features:

- Great Room: The spacious foyer leads directly into this room, which visually opens to the rear yard, providing natural light and outdoor charm.

- Kitchen: This fully equipped kitchen is located to provide the utmost convenience in serving the formal dining room and the breakfast area, which is surrounded by windows and has a double-soffit ceiling treatment. The combination of breakfast room, hearth room, and kitchen creatively forms a comfortable family gathering place.

- Master Suite: A tray ceiling tops this suite and its luxurious dressing area, which will pamper you after a hard day.

- Balcony: Wood rails decorate the stairs leading to this balcony, which offers a dramatic view of the great room and foyer below.

- Bedrooms: A secondary private bedroom suite with personal bath, plus two bedrooms that share a Jack-and-Jill bathroom, complete the exciting home.

Great Room

Main Level Floor Plan

Copyright by designer/architect.

Deck

Hearth Room
15'11" X 17'3"
Irregular

Breakfast
12'5" X 12'10"
Irregular

Kitchen
13'6" X 16'11"
Irregular

Laun.

Garage
21'2" X 33'10"
Irregular

Dining Room
12'4" X 13'10"
Double Soffit Ceiling

Porch

Foyer

Great Room
18'6" X 22'3"

Dressing

WALK-IN CLOSET

Master Bedroom
13'8" X 17'0"
Tray Ceiling

Hall

Bath

Library
12'4" X 12'3"
Irregular

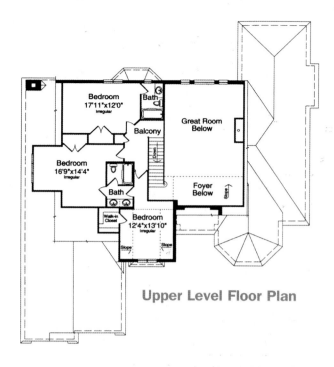

Upper Level Floor Plan

Bedroom
17'11"x12'0"
Irregular

Bath

Balcony

Great Room Below

Bedroom
16'9"x14'4"
Irregular

Closet

Bath

Walk-in Closet

Bedroom
12'4"x13'10"
Irregular

Slope

Slope

Foyer Below

Slope

Hearth Room

Front View

Left Side Elevation

Rear Elevation

Right Side Elevation

Plan #271002

Dimensions: 44'8" W x 50'8" D

Levels: 1

Square Footage: 1,252

Bedrooms: 3

Bathrooms: 2

Foundation: Basement

Materials List Available: Yes

Price Category: B

Images provided by designer/architect.

This traditional home combines a modest square footage with stylish extras.

Features:

- Living Room: Spacious and inviting, this gathering spot is brightened by a Palladian window arrangement, warmed by a fireplace, and topped by a vaulted ceiling.

- Dining Room: The vaulted ceiling also crowns this room, which shares the living room's fireplace. Sliding doors lead to a backyard deck.

- Kitchen: Smart design ensures a place for everything.

- Master Suite: The master bedroom boasts a vaulted ceiling, cheery windows, and a private bath.

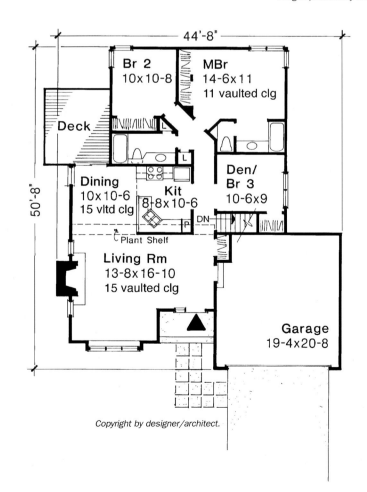

Copyright by designer/architect.

Plan #361440

Dimensions: 34' W x 56' D
Levels: 2
Square Footage: 1,528
Main Level Sq. Ft.: 1,095
Upper Level Sq. Ft.: 433
Bedrooms: 3
Bathrooms: 2½
Foundation: Crawl space
Materials List Available: No
Price Category: C

Brick accents add a stylish flair to this home.

Features:

- **Foyer:** Step into the home from the covered porch, and this foyer with a vaulted ceiling greets you. A half-bath is close to the entry for convenience.

- **Living Room:** The vaulted ceiling in this gathering area creates an open and airy feeling. The fireplace flanked by windows adds a touch of cozy comfort.

- **Master Suite:** Located on the main level for convenience and privacy, this retreat offers a large sleeping area. The master bath boasts dual vanities and a stall shower.

- **Upper Level:** This level is dedicated to two secondary bedrooms and the second full bathroom. A walk-in linen closet is always a welcome feature.

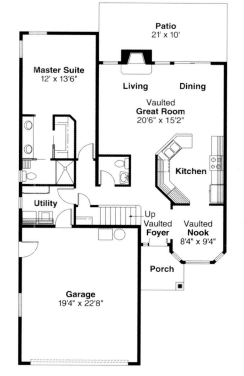

**Main Level
Floor Plan**

**Upper Level
Floor Plan**

*Copyright by
designer/architect.*

Plan #151242

Dimensions: 74'4" W x 77' D
Levels: 2
Square Footage: 2,710
Main Level Sq. Ft.: 1,819
Upper Level Sq. Ft.: 891
Bedrooms: 4
Bathrooms: 2½
Foundation: Crawl space or slab; basement or walkout for fee
CompleteCost List Available: Yes
Price Category: F

Images provided by designer/architect.

- Dining Room: The 8-in.-dia. round columns at the entry add elegance to this formal eating area. The kitchen is close by, making serving guests convenient.

- Kitchen: This efficient kitchen features a raised bar to handle the overflow from the breakfast room. The pantry cabinet is always a welcome bonus.

- Master Suite: Located on the lower level for privacy, this retreat boasts a large sleeping area allowing for many different furniture layouts. Pamper yourself in the elegant master bath, complete with glass shower, whirlpool tub, and dual vanities.

Multiple rooflines give this home an elegant and unique look.

Features:

- Great Room: This large entertaining area features a gas fireplace flanked by built-in cabinets. The atrium doors, which lead to the rear covered porch, will allow plenty of natural light to fill this room.

Upper Level Floor Plan

Copyright by designer/architect.

Main Level Floor Plan

Plan #181063

Dimensions: 55' W x 41' D
Levels: 2
Square Footage: 2,037
Main Level Sq. Ft.: 1,347
Upper Level Sq. Ft.: 690
Bedrooms: 4
Bathrooms: 2
Foundation: Full basement
Materials List Available: Yes
Price Category: D

Quaint brick and stone, plus deeply pitched rooflines, create the storybook aura folks fall for when they see this home, but it's the serenely versatile interior layout that captures their hearts.

CAD FILE AVAILABLE

Features:

- Family Room: The floor plan is configured to bring a panoramic view to nearly every room, beginning with this room, with its fireplace and towering cathedral ceiling.

- Kitchen: This kitchen, with its crowd-pleasing island, has an eye on the outdoors. It also has all the counter and storage space a cook would want, plus a lunch counter with comfy seats and multiple windows to bring in the breeze.

- Bedrooms: Downstairs, you'll find the master bedroom, with its adjoining master bath. Upstairs, three uniquely shaped bedrooms, styled with clever nooks and windows to dream by, easily share a large bathroom.

- Mezzanine: This sweeping mezzanine overlooks the open living and dining rooms.

Images provided by designer/architect.

This home, as shown in the photograph, may differ from the actual blueprints. For more detailed information, please check the floor plans carefully.

Front View

Living Room

Master Bath

Upper Level Floor Plan

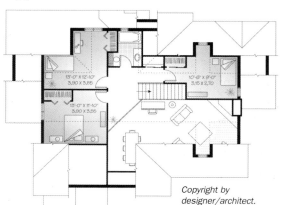

Copyright by designer/architect.

Main Level Floor Plan

Plan #161027

Dimensions: 59'10" W x 37'4" D

Levels: 2

Square Footage: 2,388

Main Level Sq. Ft.: 1,207

Upper Level Sq. Ft.: 1,181

Bedrooms: 4

Bathrooms: 2½

Foundation: Basement

Materials List Available: No

Price Category: E

Double gables, wood trim, an arched window, and sidelights at the entry give elegance to this family-friendly home.

Features:

- Foyer: Friends and family will see the angled stairs, formal dining room, living room, and library from this foyer.

- Family Room: A fireplace makes this room cozy in the evenings on those chilly days, and multiple windows let natural light stream into it.

- Kitchen: You'll love the island and the ample counter space here as well as the butler's pantry. A breakfast nook makes a comfortable place to snack or just curl up and talk to the cook.

- Master Suite: Tucked away on the upper level, this master suite provides both privacy and luxury.

- Additional Bedrooms: These three additional bedrooms make this home ideal for any family.

Images provided by designer/architect.

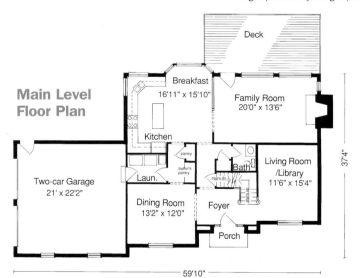

Copyright by designer/architect.

Plan #121020

Dimensions: 64' W x 46' D
Levels: 2
Square Footage: 2,480
Main Level Sq. Ft.: 1,369
Upper Level Sq. Ft.: 1,111
Bedrooms: 4
Bathrooms: 3
Foundation: Basement
Materials List Available: Yes
Price Category: E

Tapered columns and an angled stairway give this home a classical style.

Features:

• Ceiling Height: 8 ft.

• Living Room: Just off the dramatic two-story entry is this distinctive living room, with its tapered columns, transom-topped windows, and boxed ceiling.

• Formal Dining Room: The tapered columns, transom-topped windows, and boxed ceiling found in the living room continue into this gracious dining space.

• Family Room: Located on the opposite side of the house from the living room and dining room, the family room features a beamed ceiling and fireplace framed by windows.

• Kitchen: An island is the centerpiece of this convenient kitchen.

• Master Suite: Upstairs, a tiered ceiling and corner windows enhance the master bedroom, which is served by a pampering bath.

Main Level Floor Plan

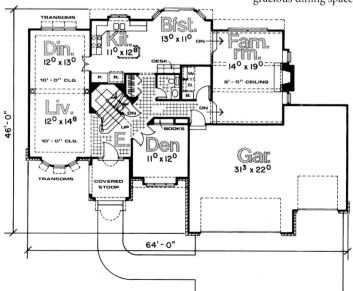

Upper Level Floor Plan

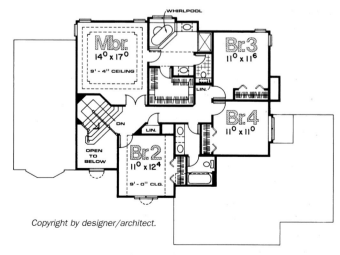

Copyright by designer/architect.

Plan #271005

Dimensions: 48'4" W x 48'4" D
Levels: 1
Square Footage: 1,368
Bedrooms: 3
Bathrooms: 2
Foundation: Basement
Materials List Available: Yes
Price Category: B

This traditional home boasts an open floor plan that is further expanded by soaring vaulted ceilings.

Features:

- Great Room: Front and center, this large multipurpose room features a gorgeous corner fireplace, an eye-catching boxed out window, and dedicated space for casual dining—all beneath a vaulted ceiling.

- Kitchen: A vaulted ceiling crowns this galley kitchen and its adjoining breakfast nook.

- Master Suite: This spacious master bedroom, brightened by a boxed-out window, features a vaulted ceiling in the sleeping chamber and the private bath.

Images provided by designer/architect.

48'-4"

Mas. Suite
14x12-6
12 vaulted clg

Br 2
12x10

Patio

Den/
Br 3
11x9

DN

Kit/Brkfst
19x10-8
12 vltd
clg

Dining

DN

Garage
21-4x19-4

48'-4"

Great Room
19x18
12 vaulted clg

Copyright by designer/architect.

SMARTtip

Design with Computers

Consider using a computer-aided design (CAD) program to plan your deck. Some programs let you see three-dimensional views of your design complete with railings, stairs, planters, hot tubs, and the surrounding landscaping.

Plan #281030

Dimensions: 50' W x 48'6" D
Levels: 2
Square Footage: 2,517
Main Level Sq. Ft.: 1,384
Upper Level Sq. Ft.: 1,133
Bedrooms: 4
Bathrooms: 3
Foundation: Basement
Materials List Available: Yes
Price Category: E

Images provided by designer/architect.

A tall covered entry welcomes you home.

Features:

- Entry: This spacious entry, accented by a regal curved stairway and a full two-story-high ceiling, sets the theme for this unique home.

- Living Room: This formal gathering area is just off of the foyer and is open into the formal dining room. The gas fireplace will add an elegant feel.

- Family Room: This large casual gathering area is open to the kitchen and the breakfast nook.

French doors open to the rear covered patio.

- Master Suite: Located on the upper level, this retreat features a private sitting area. The master bath boasts dual vanities, a whirlpool tub, and a stand-up shower.

- Garage: This side-loading two-car garage gives the front of the home a nice, clean look.

Main Level Floor Plan

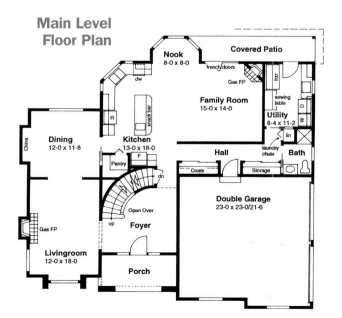

Upper Level Floor Plan

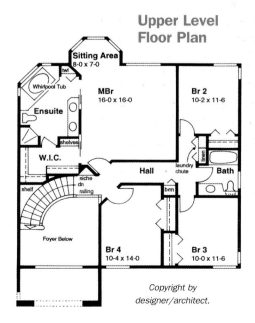

Copyright by designer/architect.

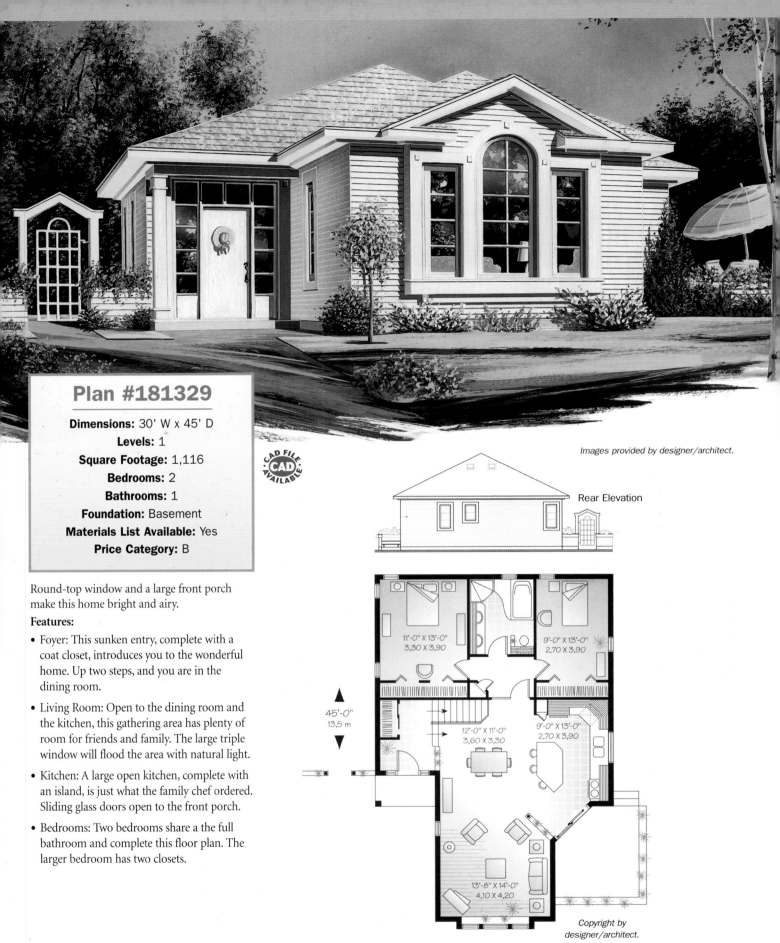

Plan #181329

Dimensions: 30' W x 45' D

Levels: 1

Square Footage: 1,116

Bedrooms: 2

Bathrooms: 1

Foundation: Basement

Materials List Available: Yes

Price Category: B

Round-top window and a large front porch make this home bright and airy.

Features:

- **Foyer:** This sunken entry, complete with a coat closet, introduces you to the wonderful home. Up two steps, and you are in the dining room.

- **Living Room:** Open to the dining room and the kitchen, this gathering area has plenty of room for friends and family. The large triple window will flood the area with natural light.

- **Kitchen:** A large open kitchen, complete with an island, is just what the family chef ordered. Sliding glass doors open to the front porch.

- **Bedrooms:** Two bedrooms share a the full bathroom and complete this floor plan. The larger bedroom has two closets.

Images provided by designer/architect.

Rear Elevation

45'-0"
13,5 m

11'-0" X 13'-0"
3,30 X 3,90

9'-0" X 13'-0"
2,70 X 3,90

12'-0" X 11'-0"
3,60 X 3,30

9'-0" X 13'-0"
2,70 X 3,90

13'-8" X 14'-0"
4,10 X 4,20

Copyright by designer/architect.

30'-0"
9,0 m

Plan #441007

Dimensions: 70' W x 64' D
Levels: 1
Square Footage: 2,197
Bedrooms: 4
Bathrooms: 2½
Foundation: Crawl space
Materials List Available: No
Price Category: D

Welcome to this roomy ranch, embellished with a brick facade, intriguing roof peaks, and decorative quoins on all the front corners.

CAD FILE AVAILABLE

Features:

- **Great Room:** There's a direct sightline from the front door through the trio of windows in this room. The rooms are defined by columns and changes in ceiling height rather than by walls, so light bounces from dining room to breakfast nook to kitchen.

- **Kitchen:** The primary workstation in this kitchen is a peninsula, which faces the fireplace. The peninsula is equipped with a sink, dishwasher, downdraft cooktop, and snack counter.

- **Den/Home Office:** Conveniently located off the foyer, this room would work well as a home office.

- **Master Suite:** The double doors provide an air of seclusion for this suite. The vaulted bedroom features sliding patio doors to the backyard and an arch-top window. The adjoining bath is equipped with a whirlpool tub, shower, double vanity, and walk-in closet.

- **Secondary Bedrooms:** The two additional bedrooms, each with direct access to the shared bathroom, occupy the left wing of the ranch.

Rear Elevation

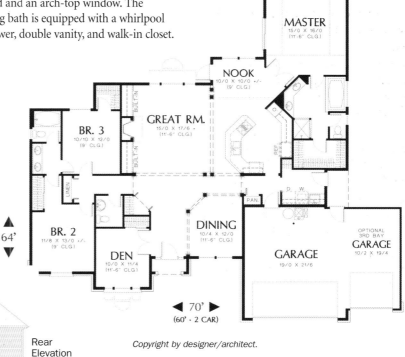

Copyright by designer/architect.

Plan #131040

Dimensions: 50' W x 37' D
Levels: 1
Square Footage: 1,630
Bedrooms: 3
Bathrooms: 2
Foundation: Crawl space, slab, or basement
Materials List Available: Yes
Price Category: D

The raised main level of this home makes this plan ideal for any site that has an expansive view, and you can finish the lower level as an office, library, or space for the kids to play.

Features:

- **Living Room:** This sunken living room with a prow-shaped front is sure to be a focal point where both guests and family gather in this lovely ranch home. A see-through fireplace separates this room from the dining room.

- **Dining Room:** A dramatic vaulted ceiling covers both this room and the adjacent living room, creating a spacious feeling.

- **Kitchen:** Designed for efficiency, you'll love the features and location of this convenient kitchen.

- **Master Suite:** Luxuriate in the privacy this suite affords and enjoy the two large closets, sumptuous private bath, and sliding glass doors that can open to the optional rear deck.

Rear Elevation

Main Level Floor Plan

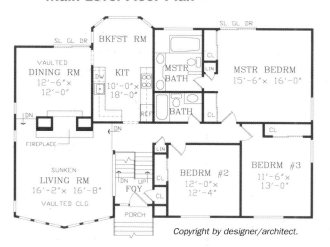

Copyright by designer/architect.

Lower Level Floor Plan

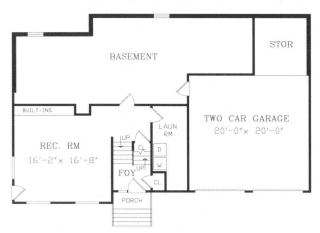

Plan #161031

Dimensions: 99'8" W x 68'8" D
Levels: 2
Square Footage: 5,381
Main Level Sq. Ft.: 3,793
Upper Level Sq. Ft.: 1,588
Bedrooms: 4
Bathrooms: 3½
Foundation: Basement
Materials List Available: Yes
Price Category: I

If you're looking for a compatible mixture of formal and informal areas in a home, look no further!

Features:

- Great Room: Columns at the entry to this room and the formal dining room set a gracious tone that is easy around which to decorate.

- Library: Set up an office or just a cozy reading area in this quiet room.

- Hearth Room: Spacious and inviting, this hearth room is positioned so that friends and family can flow from here to the breakfast area and kitchen.

- Master Suite: The luxury of this area is capped by the access it gives to the rear yard.

- Lower Level: Enjoy the 9-ft.-tall ceilings as you walk out to the rear yard from this area.

Images provided by designer/architect.

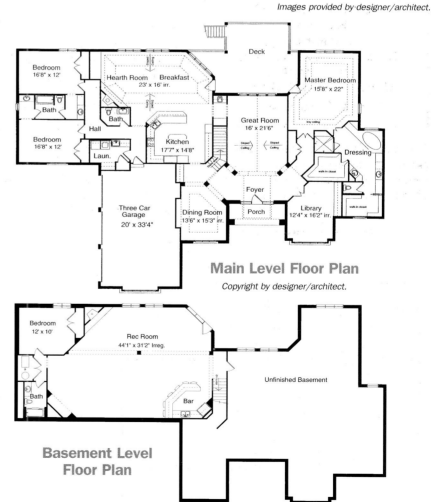

Main Level Floor Plan

Copyright by designer/architect.

Basement Level Floor Plan

Plan #181228

Dimensions: 68' W x 36' D
Levels: 2
Square Footage: 2,393
Main Level Sq. Ft.: 1,279
Upper Level Sq. Ft.: 1,114
Bedrooms: 4
Bathrooms: 2
Foundation: Slab
Materials List Available: Yes
Price Category: E

Come home to this fine home, and relax on the front or rear porch.

Features:

- **Living Room:** This large, open entertaining area has a cozy fireplace and is flooded with natural light.

- **Kitchen:** This fully equipped kitchen has an abundance of cabinets and counter space. Access the rear porch is through a glass door.

- **Laundry Room:** Located on the main level, this laundry area also has space for storage.

- **Upper Level:** Climb the U-shaped staircase, and you'll find four large bedrooms that share a common bathroom.

Main Level Floor Plan

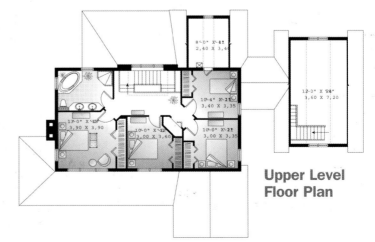

Upper Level Floor Plan

Rear View

Dining Room

Living Room

Living Room

Kitchen

Master Bath

Plan #371092

Dimensions: 71'6" W x 70'8" D
Levels: 2
Square Footage: 3,836
Main Level Sq. Ft.: 2,981
Upper Level Sq. Ft.: 855
Bedrooms: 5
Bathrooms: 4
Foundation: Slab
Materials List Available: No
Price Category: H

This grand home has an arched covered entry and great styling that would make this home a focal point of the neighborhood.

Features:

- **Family Room:** This large gathering area boasts a fireplace flanked by a built-in media center. Large windows flood the room with natural light, and there is access to the rear porch.

- **Kitchen:** This large island kitchen has a raised bar and is open to the family room. Its walk-in pantry has plenty of room for supplies.

- **Master Suite:** This retreat features a stepped ceiling and a see-through fireplace to the master bath, which has a large walk-in closet, dual vanities, a glass shower, and a marble tub.

- **Secondary Bedrooms:** Bedrooms 2 and 3 are located on the main level and share a common bathroom. Bedrooms 4 and 5 are located on the upper level and share a Jack-and-Jill bathroom.

Upper Level Floor Plan

Main Level Floor Plan

Copyright by designer/architect.

Let Us Help You
Plan Your
Dream Home

Whether you've always dreamed of building your own home or you can't find the right house from among the dozens you've toured, our collection of two-story plans can help you achieve the home of your dreams. You could have an architect create a one-of-a-kind home for you, but the design services alone could end up costing up to 15 percent of the cost of construction—a hefty premium for any building project. Isn't it a better idea to select from among the hundreds of unique designs shown in our collection for a fraction of the cost?

What does Creative Homeowner Offer?

In this book, Creative Homeowner provides hundreds of home plans from the country's best architects and designers. Our designs are among the most popular available. Whether your taste runs from traditional to contemporary, Victorian to early American, you are sure to find the best house design for you and your family. Our plans packages include detailed drawings to help you or your builder construct your dream house. **(See page 278.)**

Can I Make Changes to the Plans?

Creative Homeowner offers three ways to help you achieve a truly unique home design. Our customizing service allows for extensive changes to our designs. **(See page 279.)** We also provide reverse images of our plans, or we can give you and your builder the tools for making minor changes on your own. **(See page 282.)**

Can You Help Me Stay on Budget?

Building a house is a large financial investment. To help you stay within your budget, Creative Homeowner can provide you with general construction costs based on your zip code. **(See page 282.)** Also, many of our plans come with the option of buying detailed materials lists to help you price out construction costs.

How Can I Get Started with the Building Process?

We've teamed up with the leading estimating company to provide one of the most accurate, complete, and reliable building material take-offs in the industry. **(See page 280.)** If you plan on doing all or part of the work yourself, or want to keep tabs on your builder, we offer best-selling building and design books at attractive prices. See our Web site at www.creativehomeowner.com.

Our Plans Packages Offer:

All of our home plans are the result of many hours of work by leading architects and professional designers. Most of our home plans include each of the following.

Frontal Sheet

This artist's rendering of the front of the house gives you an idea of how the house will look once it is completed and the property landscaped.

Detailed Floor Plans

These plans show the size and layout of the rooms. They also provide the locations of doors, windows, fireplaces, closets, stairs, and electrical outlets and switches.

Foundation Plan

A foundation plan gives the dimensions of basements, walk-out basements, crawl spaces, pier foundations, and slab construction. Each house design lists the type of foundation included. If the plan you choose does not have the foundation type you require, our customer service department can help you customize the plan to meet your needs.

Roof Plan

In addition to providing the pitch of the roof, these plans also show the locations of dormers, skylights, and other elements.

Exterior Elevations

These drawings show the front, rear, and sides of the house as if you were looking at it head on. Elevations also provide information about architectural features and finish materials.

Interior Elevations and Details

Interior elevations show specific details of such elements as fireplaces, kitchen and bathroom cabinets, built-ins, and other unique features of the design.

Cross Sections

These show the structure as if it were sliced to reveal construction requirements, such as insulation, flooring, and roofing details.

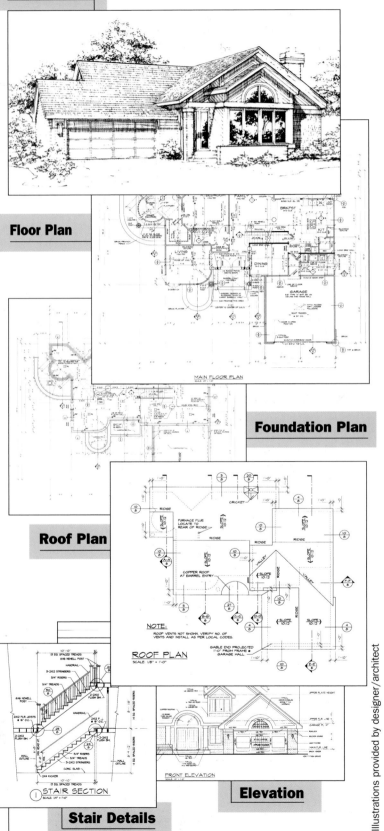

Frontal Sheet

Floor Plan

Foundation Plan

Roof Plan

Cross Sections

Stair Details

Elevation

Illustrations provided by designer/architect

Customize Your Plans in 4 Easy Steps

1 **Select the home plan** that most closely meets your needs. Purchase of a reproducible master is necessary in order to make changes to a plan.

2 **Call 1-800-523-6789 to place your order.** Tell our sales representative you are interested in customizing your plan. To receive your customization cost estimate, we will send you a checklist (via fax or email) for you to complete indicating the changes you would like to make to your plan. There is a $50 nonrefundable consultation fee for this service. If you decide to continue with the custom changes, the $50 fee is credited to the total amount charged.

3 **Fax the completed checklist** to 1-201-760-2431 or email it to us at customize@creativehomeowner.com. Within three business days of receipt of your checklist, a detailed cost estimate will be provided to you.

4 **Once you approve the estimate,** a 75% retainer fee is collected and customization work begins. Preliminary drawings typically take 10 to 15 business days. After approval, we will collect the balance of your customization order cost before shipping the completed plans. You will receive five sets of blueprints or a reproducible master, plus a customized materials list if desired.

Modification Pricing Guide

Categories	Average Cost For Modification
Add or remove living space	Quote required
Bathroom layout redesign	Starting at $120
Kitchen layout redesign	Starting at $120
Garage: add or remove	Starting at $400
Garage: front entry to side load or vice versa	Starting at $300
Foundation changes	Starting at $220
Exterior building materials change	Starting at $200
Exterior openings: add, move, or remove	$65 per opening
Roof line changes	Starting at $360
Ceiling height adjustments	Starting at $280
Fireplace: add or remove	Starting at $90
Screened porch: add	Starting at $280
Wall framing change from 2x4 to 2x6	Starting at $200
Bearing and/or exterior walls changes	Quote required
Non-bearing wall or room changes	$65 per room
Metric conversion of home plan	Starting at $400
Adjust plan for handicapped accessibility	Quote required
Adapt plans for local building code requirements	Quote required
Engineering stamping only	Quote required
Any other engineering services	Quote required
Interactive illustrations (choices of exterior materials)	Quote required

Note: *Any home plan can be customized to accommodate your desired changes. The average prices above are provided only as examples of the most commonly requested changes, and are subject to change without notice. Prices for changes will vary according to the number of modifications requested, plan size, style, and method of design used by the original designer. To obtain a detailed cost estimate, please contact us.*

Before Customization

After

Turn your **dream home** into **reality** with

Ultimate**Estimate**

When purchasing a home plan with Creative Homeowner, we recommend
you order one of the most complete materials lists in the industry.

1 | ## What comes with an Ultimate Estimate?

Quote

- Basis of the entire estimate.

- Detailed list of all the framing materials needed to build your project, listed from the bottom up, in the order that each one will actually be used.

Comments

- Details pertinent information beyond the cost of materials.

- Includes any notes from our estimator.

Express List

- A version of the Quote with space for SKU numbers listed for purchasing the items at your local lumberyard.

- Your local lumberyard can then price out the materials list.

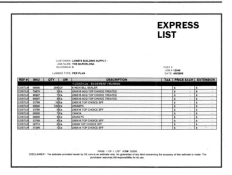

Construction-Ready Framing Diagrams

- Your "map" to exact roof and floor framing.

Millwork Report

- A complete count of the windows, doors, molding, and trim.

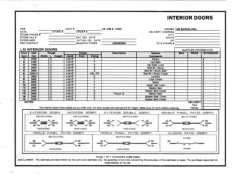

Man-Hour Report

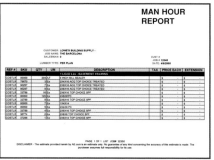

- Calculates labor on a line-by-line basis for all items quoted and presented in man-hours.

2 Why an Ultimate Estimate?

Accurate. Professional estimators break down each individual item from the blueprints using advanced software, techniques, and equipment.

Timely. You will be able to start your home-building project quickly—knowing the exact framing materials you need to order from your local lumberyard.

Detailed. Work with your local lumberyard associate to complete your quote with the remaining products needed for your new home.

3 So how much does it cost?

Pricing is determined by the total square feet of the home plan—including living area, garages, decks, porches, finished basements, and finished attics.

Square Feet Range	UE Tier*	Price
Up to 2,000 total square feet	XA	$249.00
2,001 to 5,000 total square feet	XB	$339.00
5,001 to 10,000 total square feet	XC	$499.00

*Please see the Plan Index to determine your plan's Material Take-off Tier (MT Tier).
Note: All prices subject to change.

Call our toll-free number (800-523-6789), or visit ultimateplans.com to order your Material Take-off.

4 What else do I need to know?

Call our toll-free number (800-523-6789), or visit **ultimateplans.com** to order your Ultimate Estimate.

Turn your dream home into reality.

Decide What Type of Plan Package You Need

How many Plans Should You Order?

Standard 8-Set Package. We've found that our 8-set package is the best value for someone who is ready to start building. Once the process begins, a number of people will require their own set of blueprints. The 8-set package provides plans for you, your builder, the subcontractors, mortgage lender, and the building department.

Minimum 5-Set Package. If you are in the bidding process, you may want to order only five sets for the bidding round and reorder additional sets as needed.

1-Set Study Package. The 1-set package allows you to review your home plan in detail. The plan will be marked as a study print, and it is illegal to build a house from a study print alone. It is a violation of copyright law to reproduce a blueprint without permission.

Buying Additional Sets

If you require additional copies of blueprints for your home construction, you can order additional sets within 60 days of the original order date at a reduced price. The cost is $45.00 for each additional set. For more information, contact customer service.

Reproducible Masters

If you plan to make minor changes to one of our home plans, you can purchase reproducible masters. Printed on vellum paper, an erasable paper that you can reproduce in a copying machine, reproducible masters allow an architect, designer, or builder to alter our plans to give you a customized home design. This package also allows you to print as many copies of the modified plans as you need for construction.

CAD Files

CAD files are the complete set of home plans in an electronic file format. Choose this option if there are multiple changes you wish made to the home plans and you have a local design professional able to make the changes. Not available for all plans. Please contact our order department or visit our website to check the availability of CAD files for your plan.

Mirror-Reverse Sets/Right-Reading Reverse

Plans can be printed in mirror-reverse—we can "flip" plans to create a mirror image of the design. This is useful when the house would fit your site or personal preferences if all the rooms were on the opposite side than shown. As the image is reversed, the lettering and dimensions will also be reversed, meaning they will read backwards. Therefore, when ordering mirror-reverse drawings, you must order at least one set of right-reading plans. A $50.00 fee per plan order will be charged for mirror-reverse (regardless of the number of mirror-reverse sets ordered). Some plans are available in right-reading reverse, this feature will show the plan in reverse, but the writing on the plan will be readable. A $150.00 fee per plan order will be charged for right-reading reverse (regardless of the number of right-reading reverse sets ordered). Please contact our order department or visit our website to check the availibility of this feature for your chosen plan.

EZ Quote: Home Cost Estimator

EZ Quote is our response to one of the most frequently asked questions we hear from customers: "How much will the house cost me to build?" EZ Quote: Home Cost Estimator will enable you to obtain a calculated building cost to construct your home, based on labor rates and building material costs within your zip code area. This summary is useful for those who want to get an idea of the total construction costs before purchasing sets of home plans. It will also provide a level of comfort when you begin soliciting bids. The cost is $29.95 for the first EZ Quote and $14.95 for each additional one. Available only in the U.S. and Canada.

Materials List

Available for most of our plans, the Materials List provides you an invaluable resource in planning and estimating the cost of your home. Each Materials List outlines the quantity, dimensions, and type of materials needed to build your home (with the exception of mechanical systems). You will get faster, more-accurate bids from your contractors and building suppliers. A Materials List may only be ordered with the purchase of at least five sets of home plans.

CompleteCost Estimator

CompleteCost Estimator is a valuable tool for use in planning and constructing your new home. It provides more detail than a materials list and will act as a checklist for all items you will need to select or coordinate during your building process. CompleteCost Estimator is only available for certain plans (please see Plan Index) and may only be ordered with the purchase of at least five sets of home plans. The cost is $125.00 for CompleteCost Estimator.

Order Toll Free by Phone
1-800-523-6789
By Fax: 201-760-2431

Regular office hours are
8:30AM–7:30PM ET, Mon–Fri
Orders received 3PM ET, will be processed and shipped within two business days.

Order Online
www.ultimateplans.com

Mail Your Order
Creative Homeowner
Attn: Home Plans
24 Park Way
Upper Saddle River, NJ 07458

Canadian Customers
Order Toll Free 1-800-393-1883

Mail Your Order (Canada)
Creative Homeowner Canada
Attn: Home Plans
113-437 Martin St., Ste. 215
Penticton, BC V2A 5L1

Before You Order

Our Exchange Policy

Blueprints are nonrefundable. However, should you find that the plan you have purchased does not fit your needs, you may exchange that plan for another plan in our collection within 60 days from the date of your original order. The entire content of your original order must be returned before an exchange will be processed. You will be charged a processing fee of 20% of the amount of the original order, the cost difference between the new plan set and the original plan set (if applicable), and all related shipping costs for the new plans. Contact our order department for more information. Please note: reproducible masters may only be exchanged if the package is unopened and CAD files cannot be exchanged and are nonrefundable.

Building Codes and Requirements

At the time of creation, our plans meet the buliding code requirements published by the Building Officials and Code Administrators International, the Southern Building Code Congress International, the International Conference of Building Officials, or the Council of American Building Officials. Because building codes vary from area to area, some drawing modifications and/or the assistance of a professional designer or architect may be necessary to comply with your local codes or to accommodate specific building site conditions. We strongly advise you to consult with your local building official for information regarding codes governing your area.

Blueprint Price Schedule

Price Code	1 Set	5 Sets	8 Sets	Reproducible Masters	CAD	Materials List
A	$300	$345	$395	$530	$950	$85
B	$375	$435	$480	$600	$1,100	$85
C	$435	$500	$550	$650	$1,200	$85
D	$490	$560	$610	$710	$1,300	$95
E	$550	$620	$660	$770	$1,400	$95
F	$610	$680	$720	$830	$1,500	$95
G	$670	$740	$780	$890	$1,600	$95
H	$760	$830	$870	$980	$1,700	$95
I	$860	$930	$970	$1,080	$1,800	$105
J	$960	$1,030	$1,070	$1,190	$1,900	$105
K	$1,070	$1,150	$1,190	$1,320	$2,030	$105
L	$1,180	$1,270	$1,310	$1,460	$2,170	$105

Note: All prices subject to change

Ultimate Estimate Tier (UE Tier)

MT Tier*	Price
XA	$249
XB	$339
XC	$499

* Please see the Plan Index to determine your plan's Ultimate Estimate Tier (UE Tier).

Shipping & Handling

	1-4 Sets	5-7 Sets	8+ Sets or Reproducibles	CAD
US Regular (7–10 business days)	$18	$20	$25	$25
US Priority (3–5 business days)	$25	$30	$35	$35
US Express (1–2 business days)	$40	$45	$50	$50
Canada Express (1–2 business days)	$60	$70	$80	$80
Worldwide Express (3–5 business days)	$80	$80	$80	$80

Note: All delivery times are from date the blueprint package is shipped (typically within 1-2 days of placing order).

Order Form Please send me the following:

Plan Number: _____ **Price Code:** _____ (See Plan Index.)

Indicate Foundation Type: (Select ONE. See plan page for availability.)

❑ Slab   ❑ Crawl space   ❑ Basement   ❑ Walk-out basement

❑ Optional Foundation for Fee _____ $_____
(Please enter foundation here)

*Please call all our order department or visit our website for optional foundation fee

Basic Blueprint Package   Cost

❑ Reproducible Masters $_____
❑ 8-Set Plan Package $_____
❑ 5-Set Plan Package $_____
❑ 1-Set Study Package $_____
❑ Additional plan sets:
  __ sets at $45.00 per set $_____
❑ Print in mirror-reverse: $50.00 per order $_____
  *Please call all our order department
  or visit our website for availibility
❑ Print in right-reading reverse: $150.00 per order $_____
  *Please call all our order department
  or visit our website for availibility

Important Extras

❑ Materials List $_____
❑ CompleteCost Materials Report at $125.00 $_____
  Zip Code of Home/Building Site _____
❑ EZ Quote for Plan #_____at $29.95 $_____
❑ Additional EZ Quotes for Plan #s_____ $_____
  at $14.95 each
❑ Ultimate Estimate (See Price Tier above.) $_____
Shipping (see chart above) $_____
SUBTOTAL $_____
Sales Tax (NJ residents only, add 6%) $_____
TOTAL $_____

Order Toll Free: 1-800-523-6789   By Fax: 201-760-2431
Creative Homeowner
24 Park Way
Upper Saddle River, NJ 07458

Name _____
      (Please print or type)

Street _____
      (Please do not use a P.O. Box)

City _____ State _____

Country _____ Zip _____

Daytime telephone ( )_____

Fax ( )_____
      (Required for reproducible orders)

E-Mail _____

Payment   ❑ Check/money order *Make checks payable to Creative Homeowner*

❑ VISA   ❑ MasterCard   ❑ American Express Cards   ❑ DISCOVER

Credit card number _____

Expiration date (mm/yy) _____

Signature _____

Please check the appropriate box:
❑ Licensed builder/contractor   ❑ Homeowner   ❑ Renter

SOURCE CODE CA352   www.ultimateplans.com   283

Copyright Notice

Index
For pricing, see page 379.

Plan #	Price Code	Page	Total Finished Area Square Feet	Materials List Available	Complete Cost	UE Tier
101004	C	19	1,787	Y	N	XA
101005	D	123	1,992	Y	N	XA
101009	D	43	2,097	N	N	XB
101010	D	135	2,187	Y	N	XB
101011	D	19	2,184	Y	N	XB
101013	F	22	2,564	Y	N	XB
101014	C	66	1,598	N	N	XA
101019	F	131	2,954	N	N	XB
101022	D	120	1,992	Y	N	XA
111004	F	12	2,968	N	N	XB
111006	E	158	2,241	N	N	XB
111009	E	81	2,514	N	N	XB
111010	D	96	1,804	N	N	XA
111015	E	117	2,208	N	N	XB
111017	E	136	2,323	N	N	XB
111024	E	121	2,356	N	N	XB
111026	E	128	2,406	N	N	XB
111047	D	100	1,863	N	N	XA
121001	D	25	1,911	Y	N	XA
121006	C	75	1,762	Y	N	XA
121009	B	222	1,422	Y	N	XA
121011	C	259	1,724	Y	N	XA
121013	B	92	1,375	Y	N	XA
121014	D	74	1,869	Y	N	XA
121015	D	212	1,999	Y	N	XA
121017	E	227	2,353	Y	N	XB
121018	H	145	3,950	Y	N	XB
121019	H	134	3,775	Y	N	XB
121020	E	267	2,480	Y	N	XB
121023	H	143	3,904	Y	N	XB
121024	G	229	3,057	Y	N	XB
121025	E	219	2,562	Y	N	XB
121028	F	41	2,644	Y	N	XB
121029	E	207	2,576	Y	N	XB
121030	F	44	2,613	Y	N	XB
121031	C	206	1,772	Y	N	XA
121032	E	189	2,339	Y	N	XB
121036	B	78	1,297	Y	N	XA
121037	E	80	2,292	Y	N	XB
121045	C	96	1,575	Y	N	XA
121047	G	64	3,072	Y	N	XB
121049	G	37	3,335	Y	N	XB
121050	D	129	1,996	Y	N	XA
121062	G	14	3,448	Y	N	XB
121063	G	114	3,473	Y	N	XB
121064	D	13	1,846	Y	N	XA
121065	G	138	3,407	Y	N	XB
121073	E	139	2,579	Y	N	XB
121074	E	130	2,486	Y	N	XB
121082	F	140	2,932	Y	N	XB
121083	F	69	2,695	Y	N	XB
121090	F	46	2,645	Y	N	XB
121111	C	241	1,685	Y	N	XA
121114	D	247	2,115	Y	N	XB
121120	D	237	2,131	Y	N	XB
121124	D	184	1,806	Y	N	XA
121125	D	181	1,978	Y	N	XA
121127	E	170	2,496	Y	N	XB
121172	D	168	1,897	Y	N	XA
121203	F	193	2,690	Y	N	XB
131001	D	70	1,615	Y	N	XA
131002	C	65	1,709	Y	N	XA
131003	C	24	1,466	Y	N	XA
131004	B	84	1,097	Y	N	XA
131005	C	15	1,595	Y	N	XA
131007	D	40	1,595	Y	N	XA
131008	C	91	1,299	Y	N	XA
131014	C	23	1,380	Y	N	XA
131019	F	42	2,243	Y	N	XB
131021	H	79	3,110	Y	N	XB
131022	E	18	2,092	Y	N	XB
131023	F	35	2,460	Y	N	XB
131027	F	118	2,567	Y	N	XB
131028	G	29	2,696	Y	N	XB
131030	F	63	2,470	Y	N	XB
131031	I	10	4,027	Y	N	XB
131032	F	156	2,455	Y	N	XB
131033	G	208	2,813	Y	N	XB
131035	D	67	1,892	Y	N	XA
131040	D	272	1,630	Y	N	XA
131041	D	76	1,679	Y	N	XA
131043	D	67	1,945	Y	N	XA
131046	F	127	2,245	Y	N	XB
131047	D	62	1,793	Y	N	XA
131050	F	30	2,874	Y	N	XB
131051	F	72	2,431	Y	N	XB
131056	C	87	1,396	Y	N	XA
141005	C	183	1,532	Y	N	XA
141011	D	31	1,869	Y	N	XA
141021	F	253	2,614	Y	N	XB
141022	F	126	2,911	N	N	XB
141033	G	176	3,223	N	N	XB
141034	H	165	3,588	Y	N	XB
151001	G	213	3,124	N	Y	XB
151002	E	132	2,444	N	Y	XB
151004	D	142	2,107	N	Y	XB
151006	C	73	1,783	N	Y	XA
151007	C	139	1,787	N	Y	XA
151009	C	49	1,601	N	Y	XA
151011	G	144	3,437	N	Y	XB
151014	F	28	2,698	N	Y	XB
151018	F	115	2,755	N	Y	XB

Index

Plan #	Price Code	Page	Total Finished Area Square Feet	Materials List Available	Complete Cost	UE Tier
151020	I	11	4,532	N	Y	XB
151021	G	209	3,385	N	Y	XB
151026	C	258	1,574	N	Y	XA
151027	E	216	2,323	N	Y	XB
151031	G	16	3,130	N	Y	XB
151034	D	34	2,133	N	Y	XB
151089	D	22	1,921	N	Y	XA
151101	F	124	2,804	N	Y	XB
151115	H	121	3,859	N	Y	XB
151117	D	42	1,957	N	Y	XA
151202	F	253	2,651	N	Y	XB
151203	B	252	1,214	N	Y	XA
151240	D	246	2,007	N	Y	XB
151242	F	264	2,710	N	Y	XB
151253	I	155	4,882	N	Y	XB
151277	E	252	2,216	N	Y	XB
151383	E	239	2,534	N	Y	XB
151384	F	232	2,742	N	Y	XB
151432	C	128	1,672	N	Y	XA
151529	B	88	1,474	N	Y	XA
151530	D	187	2,146	N	Y	XB
151711	E	245	2,554	N	Y	XB
151791	F	101	2,660	N	Y	XB
161001	C	141	1,782	Y	N	XA
161002	D	17	1,860	Y	N	XA
161007	C	36	1,611	Y	N	XA
161016	D	133	2,101	Y	N	XB
161017	F	27	2,653	Y	N	XB
161018	F	32	2,816	Y	N	XB
161019	E	158	2,428	N	N	XB
161025	F	33	2,738	Y	N	XB
161027	E	266	2,388	N	N	XB
161029	I	154	4,589	Y	N	XB
161030	I	172	4,562	Y	N	XB
161031	J	273	5,381	Y	N	XC
161033	J	186	5,125	Y	N	XC
161034	D	50	2,156	N	N	XB
161035	H	8	3,688	N	N	XB
161035	H	9	3,688	N	N	XB
161036	H	169	3,664	N	N	XB
161037	E	94	2,469	Y	N	XB
161041	F	166	2,738	Y	N	XB
161060	J	172	5,143	N	N	XC
161096	G	260	3,435	N	N	XB
161096	G	261	3,435	N	N	XB
161097	I	211	4,594	N	N	XB
161100	J	157	5,377	N	N	XC
161102	K	178	6,659	Y	N	XC
161102	K	179	6,659	Y	N	XC
161103	J	164	5,633	N	N	XC
161104	L	175	8,088	N	N	XC
161105	K	163	6,806	N	N	XC
161113	K	220	6,126	N	N	XC
161113	K	221	6,126	N	N	XC
161114	E	116	2,253	Y	N	XB
171004	E	137	2,256	Y	N	XB
171018	E	166	2,599	Y	N	XB
181013	B	95	1,147	Y	N	XA
181034	F	66	2,687	Y	N	XB
181063	D	265	2,037	Y	N	XB
181078	E	81	2,292	Y	N	XB
181079	G	162	3,016	Y	N	XB
181081	E	85	2,350	Y	N	XB
181085	D	62	2,183	Y	N	XB
181094	D	78	2,099	Y	N	XB
181111	B	102	1,304	Y	N	XA
181117	B	101	1,325	Y	N	XA
181120	B	85	1,480	Y	N	XA
181145	A	89	840	Y	N	XA
181151	E	68	2,283	Y	N	XB
181224	C	167	1,727	Y	N	XA
181228	E	274	2,393	Y	N	XB
181228	E	275	2,393	Y	N	XB
181239	D	246	2,181	Y	N	XB
181304	B	255	1,285	Y	N	XA
181329	B	270	1,116	Y	N	XA
181403	D	243	1,917	Y	N	XA
181407	B	240	1,369	Y	N	XA
181412	A	236	947	Y	N	XA
181717	C	168	1,578	Y	N	XA
191013	E	117	2,293	N	N	XB
191014	E	122	2,435	N	N	XB
191016	E	120	2,421	N	N	XB
191027	E	71	2,354	N	N	XB
191030	A	84	864	N	N	XA
201025	D	71	1,379	Y	N	XA
211002	C	144	1,792	Y	N	XA
211003	D	47	1,865	Y	N	XA
211009	E	248	2,396	Y	N	XB
211011	F	138	2,791	Y	N	XB
211069	C	77	1,600	Y	N	XA
211077	J	45	5,560	Y	N	XC
211127	J	82	5,474	N	N	XC
211127	J	83	5,474	N	N	XC
221022	G	137	3,382	N	N	XB
221050	F	119	2,683	N	N	XB
221076	E	182	2,401	N	N	XB
231020	D	250	2,166	N	N	XB
231023	G	244	3,215	N	N	XB
241005	C	53	1,670	N	N	XA
241008	E	18	2,526	N	N	XB
241013	F	26	2,779	N	N	XB
241014	G	77	3,046	N	N	XB
241039	B	244	1,379	N	N	XA

Index

Plan #	Price Code	Page	Total Finished Area Square Feet	Materials List Available	Complete Cost	UE Tier
241046	D	236	1,919	N	N	XA
251004	C	76	1,550	Y	N	XA
271002	B	262	1,252	Y	N	XA
271005	B	268	1,368	Y	N	XA
271011	B	257	1,296	Y	N	XA
271013	B	103	1,498	Y	N	XA
271015	B	249	1,359	Y	N	XA
271016	D	231	2,170	Y	N	XB
271018	E	214	2,445	Y	N	XB
271019	C	242	1,556	Y	N	XA
271021	C	192	1,551	Y	N	XA
271025	E	238	2,223	Y	N	XB
271034	C	226	1,516	Y	N	XA
271036	C	230	1,602	N	N	XA
271040	E	195	2,272	Y	N	XB
271041	E	169	2,416	N	N	XB
271052	C	104	1,779	Y	N	XA
271053	E	90	2,458	N	N	XB
271061	C	225	1,750	N	N	XA
271069	E	173	2,376	N	N	XB
271077	C	52	1,786	N	N	XA
271078	H	210	3,620	N	N	XB
271079	E	145	2,228	N	N	XB
271081	E	51	2,539	N	N	XB
271084	C	254	1,602	Y	N	XA
271086	D	98	1,910	Y	N	XA
271093	F	196	2,813	N	N	XB
271096	G	125	3,190	N	N	XB
281004	B	86	1,426	Y	N	XA
281016	D	171	1,945	Y	N	XA
281030	E	269	2,517	Y	N	XB
291015	F	97	2,901	N	N	XB
301001	F	228	2,720	Y	N	XB
311001	D	48	2,085	N	N	XB
311003	E	123	2,428	Y	N	XB
311043	D	165	2,062	N	N	XB
321001	C	39	1,721	Y	N	XA
321003	C	23	1,791	Y	N	XA
321005	E	48	2,483	Y	N	XB
321006	D	39	1,977	Y	N	XA
321007	F	30	2,695	Y	N	XB
321008	C	36	1,761	Y	N	XA
321009	E	86	2,295	Y	N	XB
321019	E	211	2,452	Y	N	XB
321022	B	122	1,140	Y	N	XA
321030	D	53	2,029	Y	N	XB
321036	F	210	2,900	Y	N	XB
321037	E	136	2,397	Y	N	XB
321038	B	105	1,452	Y	N	XA
321040	B	89	1,084	Y	N	XA
321042	G	251	3,368	Y	N	XB
321057	C	235	1,524	Y	N	XA
321058	C	233	1,700	Y	N	XA
321060	C	234	1,575	Y	N	XA
321079	F	224	2,624	Y	N	XB
331005	H	177	3,585	N	N	XB
341024	B	256	1,310	Y	N	XA
351008	E	38	2,002	Y	N	XB
361035	B	95	1,384	N	N	XA
361073	D	255	2,093	N	N	XB
361096	F	240	2,950	N	N	XB
361231	G	235	3,026	N	N	XB
361267	D	157	2,051	N	N	XB
361435	E	228	2,507	N	N	XB
361440	C	263	1,528	N	N	XA
361486	I	233	4,513	N	N	XB
361493	E	223	2,350	N	N	XB
371092	H	276	3,836	N	N	XB
391001	D	102	2,015	Y	N	XB
391015	E	218	2,411	Y	N	XB
391018	H	162	3,746	Y	N	XB
391050	F	161	2,674	Y	N	XB
391057	F	256	2,851	Y	N	XB
401001	D	135	2,071	Y	N	XB
401019	B	217	1,256	Y	N	XA
401050	K	160	6,841	Y	N	XC
441001	D	180	1,850	N	N	XA
441005	D	180	1,800	N	N	XA
441006	D	185	1,891	N	N	XA
441007	D	271	2,197	N	N	XB
441014	D	190	2,196	N	N	XB
441015	I	188	4,732	N	N	XB
441016	D	185	1,893	N	N	XA
441024	H	174	3,517	N	N	XB
441028	G	99	3,165	N	N	XB
441031	I	20	4,150	N	N	XB
441031	I	21	4,150	N	N	XB
441033	F	191	2,986	N	N	XB
441046	F	197	2,606	N	N	XB
441050	E	194	2,296	N	N	XB
451035	F	105	2,883	N	N	XB
451092	E	223	2,521	N	N	XB
451194	F	243	2,618	N	N	XB
451200	D	234	2,142	N	N	XB
451201	F	254	2,800	N	N	XB
451223	H	93	3,650	N	N	XB
451237	D	218	1,898	N	N	XA
451259	H	250	3,798	N	N	XB
451269	H	217	3,952	N	N	XB
461074	D	182	2,187	N	N	XB
461124	E	181	2,395	N	N	XB
481019	G	195	3,006	N	N	XB
481034	F	159	2,830	N	N	XB
491003	B	215	1,235	Y	N	XA